THE BONANNO FAMILY

A History of New York's Bonanno Mafia Family

ANDY PETEPIECE

Tellwell Talent

www.tellwell.ca

ISBN

978-0-2288-5291-9 (Paperback)

978-0-2288-5292-6 (eBook)

Acknowledgments

To Patti
My best friend

To Our Best Friends
Dook, Boomer, Tanner, and Digger

To our wonderful family for sharing your best friends with us.

Sam, Ike, Norman, Cindy, Sheba, Wolf 1, Alex, Max, Wolf 2 and Ajax

Sparky and Oscar

Belle

Piper, Casey, Zephyr and Masey

Piper, Buffy, and Drummer

CAUTION ONE:

At the beginning of each of my books, I warn potential purchasers/readers that I am not a great writer. Also, my editing skills are less than perfect. If these weaknesses bother you, please save yourself some aggravation by not buying or reading this book. On the other hand, if you would like to learn a ton of details about the Bonanno Family history, you are in the right place.

CAUTION TWO:

I have a bias against Joe Bonanno and his son Bill. That developed after observing years of attempts by them to rewrite their histories in La Cosa Nostra. Please make your own decisions as to their characters as you read this book.

HOLLYWOOD

Last summer, a respected Hollywood producer contacted me about my Commission book. He optioned the material in hopes of developing a TV series around it. Omar is a great guy, and I had a lot of fun assisting in creating "the pitch" for the proposed series. It's probably a long shot that this project ever appears on TV, but one never knows.

OTHER BOOKS BY ANDY PETEPIECE

The Commission
The Colombo Family

Introduction

This book attempts to summarize the more than 100-year history of the Bonanno Family. It is impossible to include every event during this period. Hopefully, I have captured the major points and characters.

The writings of Joe Bonanno and Nicola Gentile provide much of the information from the early years. Other insights came from government agencies, court documents, a few informers, and newspaper accounts.

Much more detail began to emerge after the famous 1957 debacle when New York State Troopers and other agents came upon a National Meeting of La Cosa Nostra in Apalachin, New York. The endless hearings and inquiries produced much information about the Bonannos and others. As the decades passed, the floodgates opened on the once-secret society. Informers, the Freedom of Information Act, electronic surveillance, and new laws were the main reasons for this change.

Unfortunately, there are many pitfalls with material on La Cosa Nostra. FBI files contain errors due to lies or exaggerations from informers. Also, there have been instances when agents deliberately entered falsehoods to deceive a variety of people. Even electronic surveillance transcripts may contain untruths. Just because the good guys captured specific conversations does not make the contents truthful. The bad guys often lied to each other.

The trick is to compare the material to other intelligence to see if they match up. It's an inexact science, and I have been fooled many times over the decades. Revisiting these errors is embarrassing but a necessary exercise if the intent is to seek the truth.

At the time of this writing (2021), this book is my best understanding of the Bonanno Family history. Hopefully, you will enjoy it.

Notes

NOTE ONE:

The proper name of the Italian American Mafia is Cosa Nostra. I use La Cosa Nostra since that is the practice of the FBI.

NOTE TWO:

I will use the names of the five New York Mafia Families that came into public use in the 1960s to indicate their previous histories. This decision is not technically correct, but hopefully, it will make following the accounts easier.

Table of Contents

Appendix C:
Joe Bonanno and Lino Saputo

Appendix D:
The State of New Jersey Commission of Investigation 1989 Report

Appendix E:
The FBI's Bonanno Leadership 1968

Appendix F:
The FBI's List of Bonanno Members in 1963

CHAPTER ONE

Early Bonanno Leaders

SEBASTIANO DI GAETANO

First Boss?

Salvatore, "The Dude" Clemente, was a notorious counterfeiter in the early 1900s. Not surprisingly, the Secret Service took a strong interest in the hood and eventually converted him to an informer. It's from Clemente that we learn of the identity of the possible first Bonanno Family Boss.

According to Clemente, Sebastiano Di Gaetano led the fledgling Bonanno group. He was born in Castellammare del Golfo in Sicily in 1864 and arrived in the USA aboard the Neustria on October 24, 1898. On January 9, 1908, Di Gaetano filled out a Declaration of Intention, a step to gaining citizenship. According to the document, he had brown eyes, grey hair, stood 5' 4" tall, and weighed 200 pounds. He listed his occupation as a barber and his address as 232 North 5th Street in Brooklyn.

Di Gaetano came to the public's attention in December of 1910. The police arrested Di Gaetano, seven other men, and two women in association with two young boys' kidnappings for ransom. The authorities labeled him as an accessory and indicated the abductions of two other children connected to Di Gaetano.

Newspaper accounts said that Di Gaetano was either "the suspected ringleader" or a "go-between." However, the authorities were not able to bring charges that stood up. Nevertheless, Di Gaetano's name was in the news connected to a sordid business. According to Clemente, this close call spooked the gang leader, and he gave up his leadership position. A reasonable estimate of the date would be 1912. Next up was Nicolo Shiro.

Note:
Researchers Warner, Santino, and Van't Reit make a strong argument that Di Gaetano was a Bonanno Boss. They also state he was the interim Boss of Bosses after the authorities incarcerated Giuseppe Morello in 1910. The trio adds that Paolo Orlando was likely the first Boss of this group. (See the May 2014 issue of the Informer: The Early NY Mafia, An Alternative Theory.)

NICOLO "COLA" SHIRO

Both Nicolo Gentile and Joe Bonanno named Schiro as a Bonanno Boss. He was born in 1872 in Roccamena, in the province of Palermo in Sicily.

According to Schiro, he first arrived in the USA in 1897. A search of records shows a Nicola Schiro of the right age landed in New York on October 22, 1898. The vessel's name was Victoria. Perhaps Schiro was mistaken about the year, or this might not be the same person. The future Bonanno Boss indicated that he left the USA in 1901.

Schiro returned to America, landing in Boston on May 18, 1902, from Naples on the ship Cambroman. He stated that he was single, couldn't read or write, paid for his ticket, and was on his way to New York to live with his uncle Antonio Governale. Included on the same document was the information of his previous visit mentioned above.

CITIZENSHIP

On June 22, 1912, Schiro petitioned for US Citizenship. He indicated that he was 37, 5' 4", 190 pounds, brown hair, and brown eyes. Schiro gave his arrival date to the USA as May 14, 1902, on the vessel Cambroman. That date conflicted with his actual 1902 arrival by four days, but no one noticed. According to Schiro, he was an "agent" living at 42 Troop Avenue in Brooklyn.

Unfortunately for Schiro, the US denied his application on June 11, 1913. However, it was "without prejudice," indicating his lack of knowledge of the US Constitution was the problem.

Less than a year later, on January 7, 1914, Schiro petitioned a second time. Two witnesses asserted that they knew Schiro had lived continuously in Brooklyn since 1907. On April 16, 1914, the United States granted citizenship to the Bonanno Family Boss. Presumably, he now knew more about the Constitution.

DANCING SHOES

During the next two decades, Schiro put on his dancing shoes to survive the seemingly endless conflicts in New York's Mafia milieu. One of the critical events was the conviction of Boss of Bosses, Giuseppe Morello,(Genovese Family) in 1910. His imprisonment opened opportunities for rivals to encroach on his territory. An influential gang leader in East Harlem was one of the first.

Giosue Gallucci had extensive "legitimate" holdings in East Harlem along with political connections. He and his men competed with the Morello group for the same spoils. Hoods made several attempts on his life, finally succeeding in May of 1915. There does not appear to be any evidence that Schiro's Bonanno Family was involved in these events.

Gallucci's death was vital for it temporarily restored the Genovese control of East Harlem. Another rival soon emerged from an alliance of two Brooklyn Camorra gangs. A series of killings took place, but by 1920 the police had decimated the Camorra group with legal proceedings. I have no material to indicate Schiro's participation in this conflict.

TAKING SIDES

There is some evidence that Schiro briefly took sides in the Morello group's (Genovese Family) growing tension with Salvatore D'Aquila, Boss of what we now call the Gambino Family. In 1912, a General Assembly of the Mafia had elected D'Aquila as their new Boss of Bosses to replace the incarcerated Giuseppe Morello. D'Aquila was eager to exercise his new power, and the Morellos were in his sights. Secret Service informer Salvatore Clemente indicated that Schiro initially aligned his organization with the Morellos in 1913.

Interestingly Schiro took a trip to Italy in 1913. This voyage suggests he must have felt secure in his Mafia position to leave New York as things heated up. His purpose for this event remains a mystery. On October 20, 1913, Schiro returned to New York on the ship Martha Washington. The arrival form indicated that he was an Italian citizen, and his occupation was "merchant."

Starting in late 1913, a series of back and forth murders took place between the Morello forces and D'Aquila. There does not seem to be any direct involvement of the Schiro group until 1920 and these events concerned an internal Morello Family dispute.

INTERNAL DISPUTES IN THE MORELLO FAMILY (GENOVESE FAMILY)

In March of 1920, the authorities released Giuseppe Morello from prison. At the time, Salvatore Loiacano led the Morello forces and refused to step down. That was a mistake. Loiacano met his end on December 10, 1920, likely at the hands of Morello loyalists. But Loiacano had allies who might cause trouble. According to later Bonanno informer Bartolomeo Fontana, Morello convinced Schiro to deal with these dissidents. Probably he believed that using outsiders would make the killings easier since the intended victims would not recognize their stalkers. Also, it would not appear that Morello was targeting his members.

Fontana stated that Schiro men committed the killing of Salvatore Mauro, a Loiacano ally, on December 30, 1920. In February of 1921, Schiro men attacked another Loiacano man, Angelo Lagattuta, but only managed to wound him. According to Fontana, the Schiro group carried out the February 28, 1921 hit of yet another Loiacano Associate, Giuseppe Granatelli.

AN INTERESTING MOVE

Nicolo Gentile was influential and well-traveled in Mafia circles. This book is not the place to detail his fascinating life other than how it relates to the Bonanno Family. In 1921, Bosses Salvatore D'Aquila (Gambino Family) convinced the General Assembly to condemn about 11 men, including Giuseppe Morello and Umberto Valenti, a former ally. Bringing these "outlaws" to Mafia justice proved to be complicated. D'Aquila decided to use Gentile to lure his friends into a trap.

With his experience and connections, Gentile quickly realized the reason behind D'Aquila's invitation to join his Family. In a smooth move, Gentile asked for permission from Schiro to join his organization. Schiro granted this request in April 1921, after receiving the obligatory transfer acceptance from Schiro's Porto Empedocle Family. It is improbable that Schiro was unaware of D'Aquila's machinations. From an outsider's perspective, it seems like

Schiro was serving notice that he was not a puppet to the Boss of Bosses. In any case, Gentile dodged a bullet.

THE GOOD KILLERS

Stefano Magaddino came from a long line of Mafioso in Sicily. His blood family was involved in a long-standing feud with the Buccellatos. Among the casualties of that turmoil was one of Magaddino's brothers. This bad blood carried over to the United States when Magaddino joined the Bonanno Family.

I will not retell the long history of this conflict but will focus on one murder with broad-ranging consequences. This event began with discovering the body of Camillo Caizzo in rural New Jersey on August 9, 1921. An investigation revealed that Bartolo Fontana had been the last man seen with the victim. Under police questioning, it was not long before Fontana rolled over and told all on August 15.

According to Fontana, a group of hoods had coerced him into killing his friend. On July 30, 1921, Fontana lured Caizzo over to New Jersey and blasted him with a shotgun. Others later dumped the body in a river where crab fishers discovered it. According to the turncoat, the hit was the result of a long-time feud involving the Bonventre family. Many historians accept that the Bonannos believed Caizzo was involved in the murder of Stefano Magaddino's brother in Sicily. (Unfortunately, Fontana named the prime victim as Vito Bonventre, a baker. He was confused about his history and identified the wrong victim.)

On August 16, Fontana, at police urging, lured Stefano Magaddino to Grand Central Station. Fontana said he needed money to flee the city. Magaddino took the bait, and the police arrested him after a struggle. Later that day, police detained another five men in connection with the hit. Among these was Vito Bonventre, whom Fontana identified as the leader of the gang. Bonventre later went on to become a power in the Family.

Three men, Fontana, Lombardi, and Puma, were extradited to New Jersey to face trial. The authorities dropped charges against the other two after Fontana gave a shaky appearance in the case of a New Jersey man whose farm was the scene of the murder. The jury found that man not guilty. Back in New York, Bonventre, Magaddino, and Mariano Galante were set free. The court convicted sad sack Fontana, and the judge gave him a life sentence.

As unfortunate as the killing of Caizzo was, the real significance was that Stefano Magaddino was now a known figure. According to Joe Bonanno, rivals also targeted Magaddino and his friend Gaspar Milazzo to continue the Buccellato deadly feud. Two innocent bystanders died in this shooting. It appears that the combination of these events led to the decision of Magaddino and Milazzo to move elsewhere in 1921. Magaddino became the Boss in Buffalo, while Milazzo had a brief run as Boss of Detroit around 1930.

The New York media blew Fontana's revelations into a gang of "Good Killers" committing murders all over the USA. It was beyond sensationalism and led to nothing. Fontana had accurately named 17 victims in New York and several in Detroit, where he once lived. No convictions resulted from his tales, partly because the authorities lost confidence in his ability to testify convincingly. Ironically his information proved to be more valuable to mob historians many decades later.

CHAPTER TWO

Cola Shiro's World

In the early 1920s, violence increased between the feuding Morello/Masseria (Genovese Family) group and Salvatore D'Aquila (Gambino Family). On May 8, 1922, D'Aquila forces gunned down Vincent Morello. The same afternoon Joe Masseria and friends attempted to strike back in a wild shootout. The police chased Masseria and arrested him, but no charges stuck.

Early in August 1922, Masseria was the target but miraculously avoided a volley of shots as he danced around. A few days later, On August 11, 1922, D'Aquila's main hitman, Umberto Valente, was gunned down. He had been in and out of favor with D'Aquila in the past. In 1921 Valente was one of those condemned by the General Assembly at D'Aquila's request. The two men reached a deal that required him to kill Masseria. That deal didn't work out too well for Valente.

SCHIRO'S PASSPORT

On April 3, 1923, Schiro applied for his first American passport. The application contained his father's name (Matteo, deceased), his 432 Marcy Ave, Brooklyn address, and his occupation as a salesman and broker. Schiro declared that he was planning a six month trip to Italy, France, and England. The purpose was commercial business, but pleasure would also be part of his

English visit. His ship Giuseppe Verde would depart on April 28, 1923. The authorities quickly issued Schiro's passport on April 5. (Certificate 263840.)

It is probably safe to conclude that Schiro had full control of the Bonanno Family at this time. The lengthy trip strongly suggests that. On the other hand, it wouldn't be the first time a Boss took a trip to avoid the trouble of one kind or another. However, I have been unable to find any evidence of internal Bonanno trouble nor recent outside events that involved them. Schiro was taking one of his reasonably regular voyages.

The Bonanno Boss trip was more than six months. From May 24, 1924, an Ellis Island arrival record shows Schiro docking from the Conte Verde. The document contains the correct information for the date of his naturalization, his address, and his single marital status. We would conclude that he was having a good time and that no pressing Family matters required his earlier return.

Schiro was off again in late 1925. We don't know his departure date, but the Bonanno Boss returned to the US on November 20 on the SS Mauretania via Cherbourg, France. A reasonable guess would be that he was conducting business there, as he had explained in his passport application. What other countries, if any, he visited, are unknown.

D'AQUILA GOES DOWN

On October 10, 1928, a gunman filled Salvatore D'Aquila full of lead ending his 16 years as Boss of Bosses. D'Aquila made it easy for his killer by making daily visits to a doctor for weeks. It was there, on the street, that he met his end. I suggest that his replacement, Manfredi "Al" Mineo, and new Underboss Steve Ferrigno set up the hit. I have no proof. Another guess would be that these two had the support of Joe Masseria in their actions, for the new leaders quickly allied themselves with Masseria.

There is no indication that Schiro was directly involved in this major hit. He may even have been out of the country. Records indicate that he returned to New York by way of Naples on the Conte Grande. The arrival date was November 8, 1928. Unfortunately, we do not know when he left the Big Apple, so his absence during the D'Aquila hit is speculation.

THE RISE OF JOE MASSERIA

With D'Aquila's death, the General Assembly voted Joe Masseria (Genovese Family) as their new Boss of Bosses. It would be a short and tumultuous reign with enormous consequences for Schiro.

Veteran mobster Giuseppe Morello was Masseria's Underboss indicating that the two powers had combined forces. The two would attempt to exert their influence over other New York Families and those in Buffalo, Detroit, and Chicago. These conflicts became known as the Castellammarese War because many of the participants were initially from Castellammare del Golfo. I will explain the war in the next chapter but will conclude the Schiro story here.

In 1928 Schiro moved from his long-time home at 432 Marcy Avenue in Brooklyn. He had been living there since at least 1912. Schiro may have operated a store from that location besides living there.

On January 22, 1929, Schiro was in Los Angles, attending Anthony N. Lanza and Tonena Desimone's wedding. Lanza was a son of San Francisco Boss Francesco Lanza and brother of future San Francisco leader James Lanza. Francesco Lanza and his young family had lived in Brooklyn after emigrating from Italy. They moved west around 1921.

Sometime in 1929, Schiro took yet another trip. Again we do not know when he departed nor the nature of the travel. He returned to New York on October 14, 1929, by way of Naples. His given address was on 436 North 11th Street in Newark, New Jersey. According to his arrival document, Schiro was still single. This status was unusual, especially for a Mafia Boss.

SCHIRO STEPS DOWN

In 1930, tensions rose dramatically in the Mafia world. Some in the Bonanno Family felt that Genovese Boss Joe Masseria was conspiring to subjugate all of them, including the Castellammarese living in Detroit.

According to Joe Bonanno, war frightened Schiro, and he wanted neutrality. He turned to powerful Bonanno Soldier Salvatore Maranzano and asked what they should do. With this query, the reign of Schiro was over, at least unofficially. He quickly faded from the scene and took no part in the hostilities.

RACKETS

The summary below is not an exhaustive list of the Bonanno Family rackets during Schiro's reign. I do not have enough primary sources to detail the various ways his men made their money illegally.

There doesn't seem to be any evidence that the Bonanno Family members participated in counterfeiting to any serious degree. The same conclusion applies to the drug trade.

Gambling would have been common in the Williamsburg section of Brooklyn. Dice and card games would take place in cafes and even private residences. One lucrative form of gambling was "policy," "numbers," or the Italian lottery. The winning three numbers had to be from some source that all the players believed were safe from manipulation. In Italian enclaves in New York, the numbers often came from state lotteries run in Italy. It was cheap to play, but the profits came from the enormous volume of betters.

Joe Bonanno wrote of an extortion attempt on his still operation in the early 1920s. A made member of the Family, Mimi Sabella, approached Bonanno and demanded a payoff for operating in his territory. Luckily for Bonanno, he was well connected, and at a sit-down, rising power Salvatore Maranzano backed Bonanno. A guess would be that Sabella had better luck extorting others.

In the early days, it was common for Mafia hoods to extort fellow Italians under the guise of providing "protection." Street vendors and storekeepers were vulnerable to attack by young street criminals. The young Mafia members or their Associates would visit the potential victims and offer to "protect" them for x amount of dollars. Often the fear of the Mafia was enough. Sometimes more active measures were required. After windows were smashed or carts upturned, the merchant would usually pay up.

Arrest records, newspaper accounts, and the books of Joe Bonanno and Nicolo Gentile clarify that many Bonanno members were involved in bootlegging. They used stills ranging from small units hidden in homes to massive operations involving hundreds of illegal liquor gallons. Probably some of these hoods dabbled in the hijacking of the product of other gangs. A small sample of Bonanno members participating in bootlegging would include Joe Bonanno, the DiGregorio brothers (Gaspare, Nino, and Matteo), Vito Bonventre, Salvatore Maranzano, and Giuseppe Asaro.

SHADOWY SCHIRO

October 25, 1934
Shiro returned to New York on the Conte di Savoia via Naples. He gave his address as 475 Marcy Avenue in Brooklyn.

October 28, 1937
Shiro returned to New York on the Conte di Savoia by way of Naples.

April 27, 1939
Shiro returned to New York on the Conte di Savoia by way of
Naples. He gave his address as 165 North 11th Street in Bloomfield,
NJ.

July 16, 1946
Shiro returned to New York on the Vulcania via Palermo. He
gave his address as 265 North 15th Street, in Bloomfield, NJ.
He was traveling on an American passport issued in Palermo on
June 16, 1946.

April 13, 1948
Shiro returned to New York on the Vulcania via Naples. He gave
his address as 215 15th Street in Bloomfield, NJ. He was traveling
on his American passport issued in 1946 in Palermo.

SHAKY CONCLUSIONS

Information on Schiro's legal pursuits is scant. That is not to say it doesn't
exist, but I have not been able to find it easily. Perhaps others have. What
follows are some minor details that I have dug up.

The United Italian-American Democratic Club listed Nicolo Shiro as one
of its directors in 1916. I cannot prove this is the Bonanno Boss. His political
activities, if any, remain elusive. We know that Schiro operated a store at
Marcy and Walaboute Street in Brooklyn until 1928. The type of commerce
he carried on there remains inaccessible to me.

In the fall of 1931, the Montrose Investment and Loan Corporation
published a summons for Schiro and others in the Times Union and the
Brooklyn Citizen. Those subpoenaed were involved with the Masterbilt
Housing Corporation. Unfortunately, I have no evidence of the dispute's
cause or resolution. However, I am confident that I have the right Schiro
for Joseph Giardelli listed an address on Marcy Avenue near Schiro's former
home after being involved in a dust-up that same year. Giardelli was one of
those subpoenaed with Schiro.

ITALIAN CITIZENSHIP AND DEATH

According to noted Mafia historian David Critchley, the United States
withdrew Schiro's citizenship in 1949. The reason given was that Schiro had

not established permanent residence in the US before 1944. I won't pretend to understand this problem. In any case, Schiro re-establish his Italian citizenship at that point.

On April 29, 1957, Schiro died in Italy. Unfortunately, I have no prime source for this date. I'm slightly embarrassed to say I found it on an internet profile of Schiro.

AN ANALYSIS OF SCHIRO'S MAFIA LIFE

Joe Bonanno painted a very gloomy picture of Schiro. He described Schiro as a bland and compliant man who was extremely reluctant to ruffle anyone. Also, Bonanno alleged that Schiro was but a puppet to Buffalo Boss, Stephano Magaddino, and depending on him for his New York position. Genovese Boss Joe Masseria demanded and received a $10,000 tribute from Schiro as events heated up in 1930. Then Schiro went into hiding. This evaluation was not a pretty picture.

I have a different point of view. To me, Schiro brilliantly maneuvered his way through the Morello/Gallucci conflict, the internal Morello Family (Genovese Family) battles, and the shooting war between Salvatore D'Aquila (Gambino Family) and Joe Masseria (Genovese Family). He survived while fellow Bosses, Tommy Reina (Lucchese Family), Charles Lomonti (Genovese Family), and Salvatore Loiacano (Genovese Family), lost their lives. Bosses Joe Masseria (Genovese Family), Joe Pinzolo (Lucchese Family), and Salvatore Maranzano (Bonanno Family) died during the Castellammarese War. By moving on, Schiro avoided their fates.

While we don't know what Schiro was doing over the next twenty-seven years, there is clear evidence his wallet was full. He traveled back and forth to Italy many times while maintaining residences in both countries. Living well and dying in your bed was an excellent counter to Bonanno's harsh criticisms.

CHAPTER THREE

Salvatore Maranzano: Boss of Bosses

Salvatore Maranzano, a future leader of the Bonanno Family, was born in Castellammare del Golfo on July 31, 1886. At a young age, he became involved with the Mafia Family of that city controlled by the Magaddinos and Bonannos. At some point, his leaders inducted him into the Family, but we have no definite date.

Some information exists of Maranzano's life before coming to America permanently. He married Elisabetta Minore and had four children with her. She was the sister of Salvatore "Don Toto" Minore, a Mafia Boss in Trapani. According to Italian Mafia turncoat Dr. Melchiorre Allegra, Maranzano was both Boss of Castellammare del Golfo and regional Boss of Trapani (a province). Allegra provided this information way back in 1937, but historians could not obtain it for many decades.

Note:
I am uncomfortable with Allegra's labeling of Maranzano. In 1915 Stefano Magaddino (not the Buffalo Boss) became the Boss in Castellammare del Golfo. He visited Joe Bonanno in Palermo between 1921 and 1924. These dates mean Maranzano was not Boss of Castellammare del Golfo at this time. Joe Bonanno described Maranzano as Magaddino's "chief warrior." There was no mention of him being Boss.

Perhaps Allegra meant to say that Maranzano had replaced his father-in-law Toto Minore and Boss of the city of Trapani. This position would have allowed him to become the Boss of the province of Trapani as well.

MARANZANO MOVES TO THE USA

Allegra was involved in politics in 1924 and claimed to have met Maranzano at that time. In June, Italian Fascist leader Mussolini appointed infamous prosecutor Cesar Mori as prefect of the province of Trapani. His mandate was to wipe out the Mafia. It is reasonable to guess that this was a significant reason Maranzano left Sicily later in the year.

At some point, Maranzano ended up in Cuba. How he got there and from where remains elusive. Fortunately, the Miami port's immigration records indicate that Maranzano arrived there on February 18, 1925, aboard the ship City of Seattle.

His immigration form contained a lot of facts of interest to historians. He described himself as 5' 7" with brown hair and eyes. This trip was his first time in the United States, and he had no intention of becoming an American. He planned to stay for six months and claimed to have a return ticket. Maranzano's destination was with the Castro brothers in New York at 2165 First Avenue. Of trivial interest is that the clerk misspelled Maranzano's wife's name as Elizabela instead of Elisabetta.

According to Joe Bonanno, it didn't take long before Maranzano was operating an import-export business, dabbling in real estate, running a major bootlegging racket, a fishing fleet, and a processing plant. Circulating all this income must have been time-consuming as well. The Family gave a big welcome party for the famous Maranzano in late 1925, which Bonanno attended. At some early date, the Schiro Family formally accepted Maranzano as a member. Schiro would have received a letter or telegram from the Castellammare del Golfo Family urging the transfer.

According to immigration records, Maranzano's wife arrived in New York on May 19, 1927, accompanied by her four children. The family traveled first class on the vessel Martha Washington. She stated they were on their way to Hamilton, Ontario, Canada to see her husband. Oddly Elisabetta noted that this was her first trip to the United States. However, records indicate she disembarked in New York on October 27, 1923. It is impossible to know whether this was a deliberate lie or an error, but the former seems more likely. They crossed the Canadian border on May 22, 1927.

MARANZANO RESIDENCES

Joe Bonanno wrote that Maranzano rented a New York apartment until his family arrived in 1927. Bonanno gave a vague location of the building as near Fourteenth Street and Second Avenue in Manhattan.

Records indicate that Maranzano also spent time on his Hamilton area farm. It remains a mystery as to why he had this place and what he would be doing up there. How frequent were his trips into Canada? Unknown. In that era, Canadian border control usually asked travelers their citizenship, where they were going, and how long they would be there. Often no documents were required.

In the same year his wife arrived in America, Maranzano purchased a home at 2706 Avenue J, in Brooklyn. Bonanno described visiting Maranzano there in August of 1931. Valachi related a brief night visit to the house on September 9, 1931, to see Maranzano. At least one young son was present, and it's reasonable to assume the rest of Maranzano's family was too.

Maranzano bought another farm in the fall of 1928. It was in the Wappinger Falls area and would be the location of several important Mafia gatherings in the coming years.

According to Joe Bonanno, Maranzano and his men and some "safe houses" around New York during the Castellammarese War. Joe Stabile owned one of them. Valachi mentions a place in Yonkers but is not more specific. Maranzano's family would not be residing in any of these locations but were probably at the Wappingers Falls farm.

In 1931, Maranzano rented a large apartment behind the Commodore Hotel at 109 East 42nd in Manhattan. Gentile explained that Maranzano used it as a headquarters with six to eight Soldiers present.

James Alescio leased space in the nearby New York Central Building at 230 Park Avenue in 1931. Located on the ninth floor, Alescio's Eagle Building Corporation included offices for Maranzano. (In the mid-seventies, the Helmsley family would purchase the building. Later, Donald Trump would be involved in an ownership partnership.)

THE CASTELLAMMARESE WAR

This interstate Mafia conflict took place between 1930 and 1931. Many members whose roots were in Castellammare del Golfo took part in the mayhem and thus the label. For decades myth or mistakes dominated the analysis of the war. Finally, Mafia historian David Critchley's research brought facts to the table resulting in a new take on the conflict's effects.

After the murder of Salvatore D'Aquila (Gambino Family) in 1925, the General Assembly elected Joe Masseria (Genovese Family) as the new Boss of Bosses. For a variety of reasons, he became involved in the affairs of several Mafia Families.

CHICAGO

At some point, Masseria appointed Chicago's Al Capone as a Capo in his Family. This move was unusual, for there already was a Sicilian Mafia organization in the Windy City. By the time of the Castellammarese War, Joe Aiello headed that Family. To this day, Masseria's decision to back Capone, a Neopolitan, over the Sicilian Aiello remains controversial. The bottom line, however, is that he did.

DETROIT

Much to Masseria's chagrin, Aiello's buddy, Gaspar Milazzo, the new Boss of the Detroit Family, backed the Sicilian. Enraged, Masseria inserted himself into the Detroit leadership turmoil. Boss Gaspar Milazzo's rivals gunned him down and an Associate on May 31, 1930. Milazzo was from Castellammare del Golfo and had been an early member of the Schiro (Bonanno) Family. His many friends demanded revenge.

Note:
Masseria Underboss Giuseppe Morello, admitted to Maranzano that they were behind the Milazzo hit. The reason given was Milazzo's support of Aiello.

BUFFALO

Stefano Magaddino had been Boss of the Buffalo Family from around 1922. Like Milazzo, Magaddino was from Castellammare del Golfo, and they were friends. According to Bonanno, Masseria had summoned Magaddino to New York after Milazzo's death. Stefano refused to budge. Masseria was not pleased.

NEW YORK

Bonanno Family
After Milazzo's death, the mainly Castellammarese Schiro Family (Bonanno Family) were nervous and in a high state of alert. Schiro called a Family meeting to decide their response. Bonanno wrote that Schiro wanted to avoid hostilities. At that point, Maranzano took the floor and inflamed the membership claiming Masseria had condemned all Castellammarese.

Maranzano, Bonanno, and Gaspar DiGregorio traveled to Buffalo to consult Stefano Magaddino. Other Castellammarese Mafia members recognized him as their senior leader. After discussions, Magaddino agreed that Maranzano would lead the struggle against Masseria. In effect, Magaddino had appointed Maranzano as the new Schiro Family (Bonanno Family) Boss. Schiro went into hiding without any protest.

Lucchese Family
At this time, some members of the Lucchese Family were eager for revenge as well. A rebel group in their organization, led by Joe Pinzolo, had plotted and killed Boss Gaetano Reina on February 26, 1930. To these loyalists, Pinzolo would not have made his move without the backing and blessing of Masseria. In time they would ally with the Maranzano forces in battling Masseria.

Profaci Family
According to Bonanno, the Joe Profaci Family (Colombo Family) remained neutral. However, Valachi wrote that Profaci was at least once in his presence on a stakeout. It is safe to say that, at the very least, Masseria didn't have Profaci actively on his side.

Gambino Family
The Gambino Family, then lead by Al Mineo, was solidly behind Masseria. In 1925, Mineo and others killed Boss of Bosses Salvatore D'Aquila and took over the Family. Masseria most likely backed their move. Bonanno wrote that Gambino powers such as Vince Mangano and Frank Scalise eventually deserted to the Maranzano side.

PHILADELPHIA

In 1930, Salvatore Sabella was the Family Boss. He was from Castellammare del Golfo and friends with men from the Bonanno Family.

Documents show that Sabella and a handful of men moved to New York presumably to aid Maranzano. Strangely he took his family with him.

To date, no evidence has emerged to show his men were active in any shootings.

MAJOR EVENTS

After the Milazzo hit

VITO BONVENTRE

On July 15, 1930, shooters hit veteran Bonanno mobster Vito Bonventre outside his garage on 69 Orient Avenue. Bonventre was well established in Brooklyn, having arrived in the United States back in 1905. Along the way, he had become an American citizen and carried an American passport issued in 1919. Bonventre was a baker for a time, but his wealth didn't come from that enterprise located at 115 Roebling Street. Like many others, Prohibition filled his wallet.

OPINION

To date, most mob historians place Bonventre in the list of Masseria victims. For decades I have been suspicious that the real culprit was Maranzano. I have zero evidence to back up that theory. However, it was clear that Maranzano coveted power and didn't hesitate to push aside his Boss Nicolo Schiro when the opportunity arose. Perhaps Maranzano saw the wealthy and successful Bonventre as a possible rival to his ambitions. In any event, Bonventre ended up dead in his mid-fifties, leaving a wife and five children.

After this killing, Maranzano called a Bonanno Family meeting. In a fiery speech, he urged total war against Masseria. Not surprisingly, the Family members elected Maranzano as their new Boss confirming Magaddino's unofficial early blessing.

Note:
The police arrested the widow Bonventre and her son Gaspar on April 23, 1940. The charge was that they were involved in a significant still operation. Perhaps the money from Vito had run out by this time.

JOE PINZOLO

Pinzolo became the Lucchese Family Boss after the murder of Gaetano Reina back in February of 1930. A group of Reina loyalist secretly plotted to kill Pinzolo, an ally or puppet perhaps of Masseria. On September 5, 1930, they caught him and two others in an office, bringing their lives to an end. The Lucchese Family, under Tommy Gagliano, allied with the Maranzano group to fight Masseria.

GIUSEPPE MORELLO

After being released from prison in 1920, Morello eventually joined forces with Masseria and became his Underboss. According to Bonanno, Morello was the chief strategist of the Masseria forces (Genovese Family) and was a prime target of Maranzano's men.

On August 15, 1930, Joe Valachi claimed that famous Bonanno shooter "Buster from Chicago" (Bastiano Domingo) killed Maranzano and another man in an office. Interestingly Tommy Lucchese had rented that space. He was a loyalist for the late Tommy Reina (Lucchese Family, and that Family's future Boss.) This event feels like a setup, but there is no concrete proof. I'd bet on it, however.

JOE AIELLO

Aiello was a long-time foe of Al Capone and headed the Sicilian Family in Chicago. Frustrated by Masseria's support of Capone, Aiello reportedly sent $5000 a week to the Maranzano forces hoping for the end of Masseria. He did not live to see the outcome of his payments. On October 23, 1930, Capone shooters riddled Aiello with machine-gun bullets as he exited a hideout apartment. Maranzano lost both an ally and five grand a week.

AL MINEO

Mineo became Boss of the Gambino Family after the murder of Salvatore D'Aquila back in 1925. He and his Underboss Stefano Ferrigno were firm Masseria supporters. This fact made them prime targets of the Maranzano forces.

Informants told Maranzano that Masseria and his main men would be holding a meeting at the Alhambra apartment complex on Pelham Parkway. Accordingly, they set up Joe Valachi, a new Lucchese recruit in the same building. He spotted Masseria arriving and quickly summoned shooters.

Note:
The Alhambra apartments still stand at 750-760 Pelham Parkway South. A visit there helps visualize the Mineo/Ferrigno hits.

On November 5, 1930, Mineo and Ferrigno were two of the last exiting the meeting. Although the prime target was Masseria, the gunmen decided they couldn't pass up the two Gambino leaders. Mineo and Ferrigno were blasted by shotgun fire as they passed an apartment window. A dramatic photo exists of the two bodies lying in the courtyard. From that point on, more Gambino Family members began moving to the Maranzano camp.

POLITICAL MANEUVERING

GENERAL ASSEMBLY ONE

By late 1930 Masseria's position was weak. He had lost essential allies, and according to Nicolo Gentile, the chief of the New York police had warned him to cease hostilities. He ordered his men to stand down. Many of them were not pleased.

Concerned Mafia leaders called a General Assembly in Boston, on December 30, 1930, to discuss the conflict. The powers (neither Maranzano nor Masseria were present) decided to appoint Boston Boss Gaspar Messina as the temporary Boss of Bosses. Masseria had lost his position.

COMMITTEE ONE

The Assembly formed a five-person commission, headed by Gambino Family power Giuseppe Traina, to meet with Maranzano in the hopes of negotiating an end to the war. The commission met in the Hotel Pennsylvania in New York early in January of 1931. Their mandate was to arrange peace and new elections for Boss of Bosses. According to Nicolo Gentile, Maranzano kept them waiting and waiting.

Finally, Maranzano summoned the committee to his Wappinger Falls area farm. According to Gentile, Maranzano tried to intimidate everyone with a host of observers armed to the teeth. The Bonanno Boss was not interested in a discussion but went on a four-day rant about the ills committed by Masseria and his allies. Maranzano was not interested in a peace deal now that he had Masseria on the run.

GENERAL ASSEMBLY TWO

With the committee's mission a failure, Mafia leaders decided to convene another General Assembly. The hope was that Masseria would revoke the various death sentences he had decreed while Boss of Bosses. Boston Boss Gaspar Messina was supposed to preside, but Maranzano dominated. (Masseria was not present.)

According to Gentile's possible biased account, only he spoke up against Maranzano's wish for a death sentence on Masseria. The Assembly appointed another commission, but Maranzano never got his death sentence approved.

MASSERIA FAMILY REVOLT

Reportedly, despite the urging of some of his leaders, Masseria refused to give his blessing to a return to hostilities. He must have been hoping for a peace agreement. It was a mistake.

Masseria powers Lucky Luciano, Al Capone, and others decided that Masseria's death was their only way out of the mess. According to Joe Bonanno, Luciano met with Maranzano, who indicated peace would come with the end of Masseria. It didn't take the Luciano plotters long to accomplish that goal.

MASSERIA'S END

Feeling safe since he believed peace negotiations were underway, Masseria agreed to a meeting at the Nuova Villa Tammaro restaurant at 2715 West 15th Street in Coney Island. It was a mistake.

To this day, we don't know the identities of the perhaps three men who sat down with Masseria. Police found his vehicle parked nearby, so at least one of the men drove the Boss to the restaurant. Around two pm, witnesses heard gunshots. One found Masseria lying dead on the floor, surrounded by a scattered deck of cards. Although contemporary pictures show a card in his hand, it was placed there after death by an enterprising photographer.

The fact there were no other casualties indicates the hit was a setup. There has been lots of speculation about the shooter's identities, but there is no need to examine the theories here. I will state that despite accounts to this present day, there is no evidence that Lucky Luciano was present, let alone taking a timely bathroom break just before the shooters arrived.

It's interesting to note that Gentile claimed that he, Vito Genovese, Toto LoVerde (Chicago hood), Joe Biondo (Gambino), and Vince Mangano (Gambino) were on their way to the restaurant for a meeting that same day. They arrived late and missed the shooting. Gentile wrote that he and Vince Troia met with Luciano, who told them his men had killed Masseria. There is little reason to doubt this account.

MAFIA MEETINGS

WAPPINGERS FALLS

Joe Bonanno wrote that Maranzano held a series of meetings to bring all the Mafia members up to date on their current affairs. In May, one took place at a resort near Wappingers Falls north of New York. (This area was also the location of Maranzano's farm.) Here Maranzano outlined his version of the causes and events of the Castellammarese War. Also, Maranzano spoke to each leader, attempting to form an opinion of them.

THE BRONX

Valachi describes attending another Maranzano meeting in a big hall in the Bronx. This gathering was also in May. About 300 men packed the joint eager to learn what Maranzano had to say. For the newcomers to Mafia life, Maranzano outlined the Families' structure and who their leaders were. Valachi mistakenly thought this was a new method of organizing the Families. Maranzano also explained the "rules" of La Cosa Nostra. Then Maranzano addressed the men inducted into the Lucchese and Bonanno organizations during the hostilities. He gave them a choice to stay with him or go with Tom Gagliano, Boss of the Lucchese Family. Valachi chose to remain with Maranzano. It was a decision Valachi came to regret.

PRIVATE MEETING

Bonanno wrote that Maranzano and Al Capone reached an agreement for the future. Maranzano would recognize Capone as the Boss of Chicago's only Mafia Family, while Capone would salute Maranzano as Boss of Bosses. Capone offered to host all Mafia leaders in Chicago to inform everyone of the new state of affairs.

GENERAL ASSEMBLY THREE

In late May of 1931, at the Hotel Congress in Chicago, Maranzano introduced all the Mafia Bosses and publicly recognized Capone as the top dog of Chicago. After Maranzano fought off an attempt by a few members to replace the Boss of Boss system with a Commission, the Assembly recognized Maranzano as the new Boss of Bosses. He was at the height of his powers.

VICTORY BANQUET

From August 1-3, 1931, Maranzano's allies held a victory banquet to honor their new leader. Ironically the affair took place in the Nuova Villa Tammaro restaurant in Coney Island, the same place where they whacked out Masseria. The Maranzano forces expected everyone attending to make a financial contribution to offset Maranzano's cost in conducting the war. Reportedly Capone sent in $6000. Valachi and Gentile both reported that the take was around $100,000. (About $1,700,000 in 2020.)

MARANZANO'S DOWNFALL

Gentile wrote that Maranzano approved Frank Scalise as the new Gambino Boss as long as he killed Vincent Mangano. When Scalise hesitated, he became a target. The fearful Scalise consulted with fellow Gambino member Joe Biondo, Lucky Luciano, and Al Capone. They decided to strike first and hit Maranzano.

Joe Bonanno's book confirms that there was tension in the ranks surrounding Maranzano. Some men, like Gaspar DiGregorio, complained about not receiving a piece of the banquet windfall. According to Bonanno, Maranzano was under constant tension, including frosty relations with Buffalo Boss Stefano Magaddino.

Joe Valachi's writings confirmed the Boss of Bosses' intention to murder other leaders. On September 9, 1931, Maranzano ordered Valachi to visit him at his residence at 2706, Avenue J in Brooklyn. Maranzano explained that he had not distributed the take from the victory banquet because the Family would probably go to war again. According to Valachi, Maranzano's hit list included: Lucky Luciano, Vito Genovese, Al Capone, Willie Moretti, Joe Adonis, and Dutch Schultz. Valachi was stunned and sick at heart. Maranzano told Valachi he would have one last meeting with Luciano and Genovese the next day at two PM.

MARANZANO DIES

The day after Valachi visited Maranzano's Avenue J residence, Charles "Charlie Buffalo" DiBenedetto told Valachi not to come to Maranzano's office as he usually did. It was September 10, 1931.

Gentile related that six plain-clothed men, accompanied by a lone Italian, entered Maranzano's ninth-floor offices in the New York Central Building and announced that they were federal agents. (Valachi and police records said there were four.) They lined up everyone present and asked the Italian which one was Maranzano. Two of the hitmen marched Maranzano into his private office to kill him. The warrior fought back desperately. He succumbed to stabbing and bullet wounds. The last Boss of Bosses was dead.

Gentile didn't name the fake agents. Valachi identified one as Red Levine and another as a Dutch Schultz man, Abe "Bo" Weinberg." Bonanno didn't mention the monikers of any of the hitmen, but Stefano Magaddino told him Luciano had taken responsibility for Maranzano's death.

MURDER INVESTIGATION

The police investigation into the hit didn't get anywhere. Witnesses had seen a tan Studebaker fleeing the scene. When the authorities tracked down the vehicle, they arrested three men, including James F Alescio. After learning his Eagle Building Corp rented the offices, they released him. Police also let the other two go as well.

At the scene of the murder, police detained Girolamo "Bobby Doyle" Santucci. Doyle stated that he had come to the offices to see James Alescio. Santucci later told Valachi that he was in the outer office when the hit went down. After the killers fled, he went in to see how Maranzano was. Boss Tom Gagliano (Lucchese Family) was present along with his Underboss Tom

Lucchese. Decades later, Lucchese testified about his experience before the New York State Crime Commission.

ALIEN SMUGGLING

Initially, police told the press that the killing had to do with a vast alien smuggling ring operated by Maranzano. That theory quickly went out of the door.

BOOTLEGGING

News reports mentioned that bootlegging competition might have played a role in the hit. This lead led nowhere but may have been partially correct.

PRIVATE MOB JUSTIFICATIONS

After the murder, Valachi went into hiding. He then contacted Tommy Lucchese, the Underboss for Tom Gagliano (Lucchese Family.) Lucchese told Valachi that Maranzano had been hijacking Luciano's liquor trucks. Furthermore, he stated that Maranzano had hired wild mobster Vincent "Mad Dog" Coll to kill Luciano and Vito Genovese.

When Valachi later met with Vito Genovese, the Underboss confirmed the Coll story. He added drama to the report by claiming that he and Lucky were to meet Maranzano in his offices the day of the murder. Coll was on his way up to the ninth floor when the fleeing killers told him to make himself scarce.

Joe Bonanno suggested the conflict might have been over influence in the garment center. This theory was a reasonable explanation considering that racketeering in the garment center was a gold mine for many decades.

There were probably several reasons that Luciano et al. plotted against Maranzano. For an outsider, it seems clear that the major one was Maranzano's plan to whack out Luciano and many others. Kill or be killed. Luciano moved first. Game over.

OPINION

Maranzano probably hired or was going to hire Coll to whack Luciano and Genovese. They were on his well-known hit list. However, I find it difficult to believe that Maranzano planned the hit for his own offices. That would have involved witnesses and a mess. I suspect that Genovese was exaggerating as part of the justification for the murder of Maranzano.

AFTER MARANZANO

THE WILL

Maranzano's will indicated he had a gross worth of $87,595 with a net of $54,056. His wife received $18,018 while $9,008 went to each of the four children. The net worth of $54,056 translates into approximately

$925,450 in 2020. The Maranzano family fared much better than many other mob victims.

We catch a glimpse of the widow and two of her children in February of 1937. On February 9, they arrived in New York aboard the American Oriente. They had been in Cuba. Whether it was just a vacation or, more interestingly, a visit to relatives/friends in Cuba is unknown. You'll recall that Maranzano made his entrance into the USA from Cuba back in 1925.

THE EFFECTS OF THE CASTELLAMMARESE WAR

For many decades historians viewed the end of the conflict as a watershed event in American Mafia history. For them, La Cosa Nostra emerged with its structure of Families headed by a Boss, Underboss, Consigliere, and Capos. The Mafia created a Commission to arbitrate disputes, set rules, and the like. They eliminated the old Boss of Bosses system. Furthermore, 1931 signified the Americanization of the Mafia with new young leaders.

Some of that analysis was incorrect. With the benefit of new primary sources and further investigation, researchers like David Critchley came to a different view. I agree with him. What follows is a quick summary of the history.

The structure of the Families did not change after the war. Going back to Sicily in the 1800s, the Families had a Boss, Underboss, Consigliere, Capos, and Soldiers. Luciano did not create this model.

Critchley also rejects the notion that the mob became "Americanized" after 1931. In an excellent examination, he shows that Sicilian-born hoods maintained control of many of the Families for decades after the war. A sample of names would include Bosses; Joe Bonanno, Joe Profaci, Vince Mangano, and Tommy Gagliano. Outside New York reigned Stefano Magaddino of Buffalo, Sal Sabella of Philadelphia, Gaspar Messino in Boston, etc. Luciano did not "Americanize" La Cosa Nostra after 1931.

THE PURGE

One of the Americanization theory's fundamental building blocks was the claim that Luciano et al. whacked out many old-timers after Maranzano. Supposed body counts ranged from 40 up to 100. It was all nonsense. Research by Alan Block, Albini, Critchley, and others proved the purge theory is a myth. Most serious mob historians and researchers like myself adopted this view.

THE COMMISSION

The primary outcome of the war was the creation of a Commission. The Mafia leaders agreed to this concept at a General Assembly held in Chicago's Hotel Congress in September of 1931.

The Boss of Bosses system had not worked, as proved by the endless conflicts leading up to 1931. The Bosses created a seven-man Commission with a five-year mandate. The Bosses of the five New York Families would have a seat. Stefano Magaddino of Buffalo joined them along with Capone of Chicago. It was essential to have an odd number of members to facilitate tie-breaking.

The Commission would approve new members and Bosses. They would arbitrate inter-family disputes and clarify Mafia rules. In a previous book, "The Mafia Commission," I provide much more detail on the Commission and its history.

1931 LEADERSHIP

After the death of Maranzano, the leadership of the New York Families was as follows:

Gambino: Vincent Mangano
Lucchese: Tom Gagliano
Genovese: Lucky Luciano

Colombo: Joe Profaci
Bonanno: Joe Bonanno

1931 Commission Membership
Vince Mangano, Tom Gagliano, Lucky Luciano, Joe Profaci, Joe Bonanno, Al Capone, Stefano Magaddino.

The next chapter will examine the early years of Bonanno's life.

CHAPTER FOUR

Bonanno's World Part One

Bonanno was born in Castellammare del Golfo on January 18, 1905, into a Mafia milieu. His paternal grandfather, uncle, father, and second cousin, Stefano Magaddino, headed the city's Mafia Family in succession.

Note:
This Stefano Magaddino was an uncle to the future Buffalo Boss of the same name.

Under legal pressure, Bonanno's family fled to the United States in 1908. The family resided in Brooklyn, where his father operated a small pasta factory and a tavern. Four years later, they returned to Sicily after conflict re-erupted with the rival Buccellato clan.

According to Bonanno, his father served in the Italian Army during World War 1. Due to a severe wound, he died at his home in early 1916. New Boss Stefano Magaddino took Bonanno under his wing and further schooled him in the Mafia ways. After Bonanno's mother died in 1920, he moved in with her family, the Bonventres.

BONANNO'S FATHER'S CHARACTER

From Bonanno's writings, it is clear that he loved and respected his father. However, he related a couple of instances in his autobiography that makes me question his respect and honor criteria.

Under the influence of his mother, Salvatore Bonanno joined a seminary to become a priest. Joe Bonanno wrote that when a family emergency arose, his father devised a method to get out of his church obligation. Salvatore stole a gold candelabrum from the monsignor who expelled him.

A second incident occurred after the Bonannos returned to Sicily in 1912. The police accused Bonanno's father of murder and had a witness to testify against him. Salvatore protested his innocence and argued that the witness felt jealousy towards him.

Bonanno wrote that his father used a relative to trick the witness's wife into having a physical examination of her private parts by a midwife. Salvatore Bonanno received the results. At trial, the father protested that the witness was falsely testifying because he had an affair with his wife. The witness was enraged to be humiliated in public. Bonanno's father then "proved" his story by revealing that the wife had a mole near her private parts. He was quickly acquitted.

Salvatore Bonanno had always told his family that he never had an affair with the witness's wife. Yet, he publicly humiliated the innocent woman and destroyed her reputation. It would have been impossible for her to regain her standing in that era.

The two tales Joe Bonanno related caused me to think less of the father. Secondly, I find it very strange that Bonanno told these events and seemed to have had no empathy for the woman, nor did he condemn his father's stealing from a church.

LEAVING FOR AMERICA

During 1921-1924, Bonanno was in Palermo, attending nautical school, hoping to become a captain. Fascism, under Benito Mussolini, dominated every phase of Italian life. Bonanno wrote that he resisted their indoctrination attempts, and the school suspended him in 1924. Not long afterward, he began his way to America.

Initially, Bonanno traveled to Tunis, where his cousin Peter Bonventre joined him. Next, they went to France then to Cuba by boat. In December of 1924, a small boat took them to the Tampa area. He revealed these details at the time of his May 18, 1938 entrance into the US via Detroit.

After being briefly detained by immigration officers in Jacksonville, the two men made their way to New York. Bonanno settled in with his mother's brother, Peter Bonventre, at his home in Brooklyn. Not long afterward, he was deep into the bootlegging business with future long-time friends the DiGregorio brothers. Unfortunately, an accident killed one of their partners, so they shut down the enterprise.

For a year, Bonanno worked as a salesman/promoter in an uncle's bakery business. But the arrival of Salvatore Maranzano in 1925 dramatically changed his life.

According to Bonanno, his main job with Maranzano was to supervise a vast bootlegging operation that included numerous large stills located in rural areas. Duties ranged from making sure supplies arrived on time and that the men made their deliveries. As with most such operations, hoods occasionally tried to hijack the moonshine. At times Bonanno would have to resort to violence, but he spared the details. For the young man, these were exciting times.

I won't relate the details of the Castellammarese War again. But Bonanno's role is essential to this history. He was part of Maranzano's palace guard and described himself as "chief of staff." There would be countless details to be looked after, such as arranging meetings and setting up hits. Interestingly Bonanno never admitted taking part in any murders.

After the Maranzano forces were victorious, Bonanno's daily connection with Maranzano began to fade. He wrote about Maranzano's difficulty with peacetime and his death but in a detached way. I think this was disingenuous. Here's why.

OPINION

La Cosa Nostra's long history shows that when a Boss is whacked, his successor was often in on the plotting. Some samples include Reina-Pinzolo, D'Aquila-Reina, Milazzo-LaMare (Detroit), Mangano-Anastasia, Anastasia-Gambino, and Castellano-Gotti. I believe this pattern includes Maranzano-Bonanno.

Lucky Luciano, with the support of other Mafia leaders, arranged to kill Maranzano. He used Jewish hitmen in the hopes the Maranzano forces wouldn't recognize them. Buffalo's Stefano Magaddino would have had to have been in on the plotting due to his power. Luciano wouldn't have proceeded without his blessing, for he didn't wish to start another war.

Before killing the Boss of Bosses, it would have been prudent for Maranzano and his fellow plotters to have a Maranzano man willing to take over. They would have to have believed that this new man would be willing to toe the line. Stefano Magaddino probably suggested Bonanno figuring he would be able to control the young man. If my theory is correct, Joe Bonanno must have been in on the planning.

Supporting my position are the mysterious words that Nicolo Gentile claimed Maranzano spoke as the phony agents took over his office on that fateful day in September 1931. When the killers demanded to have Maranzano identified, the unsuspecting Boss turned to one man and said, "Peppino, you know I am Maranzano..." Peppino is a common nickname for Giuseppe, and in his autobiography, Bonanno noted that friends called him Peppino. I think Bonanno was there, along with Gagliano and Lucchese. They were all in on the plot, in my opinion.

Note:
The date of Bonanno's marriage license undermines my opinion somewhat. New York City issued the paper on September 9, 1931. The day before the Maranzano hit. It seems unlikely that Bonanno would be doing marriage paperwork that day. Ah well.

NEW BOSS

Not long after Maranzano's death, the Bonanno Family met to select a new Boss. By Bonanno's account, he was the clear favorite, especially with the backing of Magaddino. He received 300 votes while an opponent polled seven. Of interest here is the number indicating the Family was much larger than it would be in the distant future.

Bonanno selected relative John Bonventre as his Underboss, and theoretically, the membership voted in Frank Italiano as Consigliere. He was the lone opponent in the leadership election. I have been unable to find my sources for Italiano's selection from my list of 30 years ago, so Consigliere should have a question mark.

MARRIAGE

From Bonanno's autobiography, we learn that he married Fay LaBruzzo on November 15, 1931, at St Joseph's Church in Brooklyn. Guests gathered at the Knights of Columbus Hall on Grand Avenue to celebrate the union. As was the custom, the males invited gave cash gifts in envelopes. Al Capone, although not present, passed along $5000. (Nearly $80,000 in 2020.)

The couple had three children, Salvatore (Bill) (1932), Catherine (1934), and Joseph Jr (1945.) It is clear from his writings that Bonanno adored his wife Fay and all his children and grandchildren.

The men in his wedding party are interesting and well known to most mob researchers. What follows are brief outlines of their Mafia careers. I'll provide more detail on some of the men later.

GASPARE DIGREGORIO

He was the best man and one of Maranzano's key bodyguards. Through his late wife Maria (Died 1927), Stefano Magaddino was his brother-in-law. DiGregorio operated for decades as a Capo in the Bonanno Family.

BASTIANO "BUSTER FROM CHICAGO" DOMINGO

Domingo was a prolific hitman for Maranzano, with several big names as victims. Valachi wrote about Buster, who remained mysterious until terrific research by David Critchley finally identified him in the 2000s.

VINCENT "THE DOCTOR" DANNA

Danna was another of "The Boys of the First Day," as Maranzano's bodyguard troop referred to themselves. According to Bonanno, Danna's father was a pharmacist and his uncle a doctor, hence the nickname.

Danna remained friends with Bonanno for decades and is present in several pictures from later happy times.

CHARLIE "CHARLIE BUFFALO" DIBENEDETTO

DiBenedetto came from a Mafia family in Sicily. He moved to Buffalo to live with an uncle after the killing of his father. Stefano Magaddino must have sent him to New York to become part of Maranzano's palace guard. It was DiBenedetto who told Valachi that Maranzano didn't need him at the office. Later that day, hitters whacked the Boss of Bosses. Charlie Buffalo was probably in on the hit. He returned to live in Buffalo after the war.

NATALE EVOLA

Evola was born in New York City in 1907. He and Joe Bonanno were friends for decades after the marriage ceremony. With interests in the garment center, Evola also had his fingers in other rackets, including drug dealing in the 1950s. In the early seventies, Evola had a three year run as Bonanno Family Boss.

SALVATORE PROFACI

Profaci was a brother of Colombo Family Boss Joe Profaci. He and Bonanno became fast friends after Bonanno helped smuggle Profaci into the US from Canada in 1926. According to Profaci's daughter Rosalie, the two men spend a few months bootlegging in the Buffalo area before going to New York. To date, there isn't any evidence that he participated in the Castellammarese War. His claim to fame for our purposes is that Rosalie married Bonanno's eldest son Salvatore. Profaci died a few weeks after suffering burns in a fire on his pleasure boat in the summer of 1954.

MARTIN BRUNO

Unfortunately, I do not know anything about this man. He does not appear on Bonanno member lists starting in 1963 or later.

JOE STABILE

Bonanno wrote that Stabile was one of the prime Maranzano bodyguards and gunmen. During the war, the Maranzano crew used his residence as one of their safe houses. Hoods killed a Joe Stabile, a tavern keeper, on February 8, 1944, but I have no idea if this is the same man. Other than Bonanno describing him as a short man, I have nothing else at this date.

THE EARLY 1930S

POLITICAL EFFORTS

Bonanno wrote that early in his career as Boss, he formed the Abraham Lincoln Independent Political Club on Metropolitan Avenue in Williamsburg, Brooklyn. Bonanno had a private office in the rear. According to Bonanno, multitudes of politicians would come to seek favors due to the fact he was an important man. His Capos would also make appearances to get their orders and pass on money to Bonanno.

In that era, Mafia involvement in politics through political clubs was quite common.

LEGITIMATE INCOME FOR BONANNO

It would take countless hours to run down all the details on Bonanno's various legitimate businesses over his lifetime. I have not done that with a few exceptions.

B&D Coat Company (Bonanno and DiPasquale)
From 1947-1955 it was located at 47-52 Thames Street in Brooklyn.
The product was women's coats.

Morgan Coat Company
1936-1942
109 Ingram Avenue in Brooklyn
Brothers Vincent and Natale DiPasquale were partners in this firm as well. On November 4, 1944, someone discovered Fillipo Rapa's body (57) in a culvert leading into Jamaica Bay in Ozone Park, Queens. He was another partner with Bonanno in the company. It appeared to be an accident.

Note:
In 1942 a court found Bonanno guilty of wage and hour violations at both of his garment companies. He received small fines and probation. These convictions would come back to haunt him a decade later. I'll provide more detail in a later chapter.

The Anello and Bonanno Funeral Home
273 Central Avenue in Brooklyn.

The Brunswick Laundry
39-45 Central Avenue in Brooklyn.
Bonanno was second vice president.
He probably became involved in 1933 and continued to have an interest until at least 1954.
Unsupported allegations suggested Bonanno harassed the owners, including stealing one of their trucks. He then became a partner.

Miss Youth Clothing Company
Manhattan
Bonanno wrote that he was partners with another Family member in this firm. Its workers cut out the patterns from cloth (A jobber operation). Another company would sew the pieces into clothing.

Sunshine Dairy Farm
Located near Middletown, NY, this enterprise was a 280-acre farm with about 75 dairy cattle and assorted other animals. Bonanno wrote that the US military did not draft him during World War Two since the farm was an essential business. That label is probably the reason he bought the place in the early 1940s.

The Grande Cheese Company (Fond de Lac, Wisconsin)
Initially started in Chicago in 1941, its stated purpose was to develop dairies, dairy farms, and creameries on a national scale. Notorious Chicago hood Ross Prio held control of the firm. Several men associated with the company lost their lives, giving it an infamous reputation from the start.

In 1950, an experienced businessman from Brooklyn investigated buying the company. John DiBella knew Joe Bonanno's wife's family well and decided to consult Bonanno on his intentions. He hoped that Bonanno's name would scare off any other hoods from muscling in on Grande. Under his wife's name, Bonanno invested in Grande. Fay received payments for years afterward. John DiBella died in 1964, with his shares going to his partner, his sister Rose. She sold out in 1967. Unfortunately for DiBella, the Bonanno connection blackened his reputation for the rest of his life and beyond.

Saputo Cheese Company (Montreal, Canada)
Giuseppe Saputo immigrated to Montreal from Sicily and started a small cheese company. He was friends with John DiBella of Grande Cheese. On

a 1964 trip to Montreal, Bonanno met with Saputo. He agreed to invest $8000 in the company in return for 20% of its stock. Whether this deal was ever fully consummated remains controversial to this day. Saputo is now a 15 billion-dollar conglomerate. I will detail this story in the chapter on the Canadian arm of the Bonanno Family.

Airport Motel
Bay Avenue, Newark, NJ
Joe Bonanno and Soldier Anthony "Tony" Riela opened the motel in 1953. In November of 1957, two men, James Colletti and Frank Zito, who attended the infamous Apalachin gathering of Mafia hoods, used the motel as a waystation. On December 2, 1958, Riela told the FBI that Bonanno owned one-third of the place. Riela and the Marino family, who ran the business, each had a third.

Cortaro Cotton Farm
Marano, Arizona

Sciortino Italian-American Bakery
Tucson, Arizona

Five Bar B Ranch
Tucson, Arizona area

Parking lot
Downtown Tucson, Arizona
Bonanno owned this property from the early fifties until at least 1983.

Alliance Realty and Insurance (Tucson)
3931 E Broadway, Tucson, Arizona
The company was primarily a realtor from 1953 through to at least 1960. Many advertisements for housing developments included their name as the primary agent. Whether they were involved in the April 1955 sale of about 200 acres of Tucson area land belonging to Bonanno and John DiBella of Grande Cheese to Chesin Construction Company is unclear.

In the 1950s, Bonanno and his wife were involved in numerous land transactions. One was the purchase of land from Cortaro Farms Company. Another was selling two parcels of land to the Mutual Life Insurance Company for about $22,000 in 1952.

In the early sixties, the feds called Alliance and three other realty firms before a grand jury investigating Bonanno's income taxes. I have been unable to discover what stake Bonanno held in the firm, either publicly or privately.

Colorado Cheese Company

Trinidad, Colorado

The Chicago Crime Commission's Executive Director testified before the Kefauver Hearings (1950-1951). He claimed that Bonanno had an ownership position in the Colorado Cheese Company with John Spadero and Robert Donisis. Later investigations showed that Colorado Mafia Boss James Colletti also held a stake. Bonanno never mentioned this enterprise in his book.

It is more than likely that Bonanno had his fingers in many more businesses. However, these few examples demonstrate that he had a wide range of interests over the decades. A reasonable guess is that many of the funds came from illegal means.

CITIZENSHIP WAR PART ONE

As related earlier, in December of 1924, Bonanno illegally entered the US near Tampa after traveling in a small motorboat from Cuba. By 1938 his concern about his illegal status caused him to meet with immigration people. Their advice was for Bonanno to leave the country then re-enter legally.

Bonanno left the United States on February 1, 1938, then spent the next three-plus months in Canada waiting to re-enter the US. On May 18, 1938, Bonanno crossed into Detroit by bus from Windsor, Ontario. He stated that his purpose in coming to the United States was to obtain a resident permit. The form detailed his earlier time in the US (March 1908-1912) and December 1924 until January 31, 1938. He explained that he arrived in Tampa in December of 1924 via a small motorboat. Bonanno gave his wife's (Felippe/fannie) name and provided his permanent US address as 208 Union Street in Brooklyn. As for his physical description, Bonanno stated that he had a dark complexion, brown hair, and brown eyes and stood 5' 10". Interestingly his birthdate was incorrect. Instead of January 18, 1905, the border agent noted it as January 21, 1905. Bingo! Immigration issued Bonanno an admission permit.

Bonanno registered for the draft on October 16, 1940. A reasonable guess would be that his lawyers advised him that this move would help his attempt to get citizenship. They would have also told Bonanno that his ownership of a dairy farm would exempt him from ever being called up.

On July 17, 1942, immigration officials interviewed Bonanno as part of his citizenship process. More than a year later, on October 13, 1943, immigration thought it best to check with the FBI about Bonanno's background. The feds told them that a Giuseppe Bonanno in New York allegedly was a member of the Grand Council of the Sicilian Underworld. Not surprisingly, immigration called Bonanno in for a second interview. In May of 1944, Bonanno played innocent and denied the alleged mob connection. The immigration boys bought his story! Bonanno was on his way to full citizenship.

On May 17, 1945, Bonanno was in a Brooklyn Court on the verge of receiving his citizenship. The judge asked him what he would do if he had to fight Italians. Bonanno replied that he would do so, but he would feel bad. The judge praised his answer and granted him citizenship. Bonanno wrote that this was "one of the proudest moments of his life."

CITIZENSHIP WAR PART TWO

During and after the Kefauver Hearings of 1951-1952, it seemed to the public that the bad guys were immune from prosecution. The fact that many of them refused to testify under their Fifth Amendment rights compounded the frustration. Among other steps, the federal government adopted the tactic of deporting as many of these men as possible. The 1952 McCarran Act permitted denaturalization if the government could prove the person concealed facts or misrepresented them. They put a target on Joe Bonanno's back.

Representatives of US Attorney General Brownell filed denaturalization proceedings in the Tucson federal court. The initial complaint was that Bonanno failed to disclose several convictions when he applied for citizenship. The alleged charges included possession of a revolver, theft of a car, and the two wage and hour convictions mentioned earlier. On or about March 12, 1953, federal marshals served Bonanno with a civil complaint summons. The feds amended the denaturalization petition on September 10, 1953, clarifying the criminal charges Bonanno avoided disclosing. The petition dropped gun possession and car theft charges.

The feds held a one day trial on December 16, 1954. Judge James A Walsh presided with no jury. The prosecution outlined their case; then, the defense presented their witnesses.

Bonanno took the stand and played innocent. He testified that he had little to do with the day to day operation of the two clothing firms. Bonanno believed that the convictions were for the company and not him personally. The fact that he turned up in court to face the charges weakened his position.

The DiPasquale brothers, Bonanno's partners in the two garment firms, fell on their swords. They took all the blame for the fiasco and confirmed that Bonanno operated at a distance from their operation. Bonanno also lined up a prestigious group of character witnesses, including Judge Evo DeConcini, Congressman Harold R Patten, and auxiliary Bishop Francis Green. A clerk read their testimony in the court. Four other supporters testified in person.

After the court cleared up legal issues on January 24, 1955, Bonanno had to wait till April 1, 1955, to learn his fate. Much to the delight of him and his supporters, Judge Walsh ruled that the government had not proved Bonanno intentionally deceived the immigration authorities. This ruling meant the McCarren Act didn't apply to Bonanno. He no longer had to fear deportation.

RESIDENCES

I included some information on the various addresses that Bonanno called home over his long life. The list is not complete, but some mob fans might enjoy using Google Maps to look at the buildings. I only used dates from official government documents and didn't guess and fill in the gaps.

1925
4009 Church Street, Brooklyn
A narrow two-story brick building with commercial space on the first floor and an apartment or two above. This location was the home and barbershop of Bonanno's uncle Peter Bonventre. Bonanno lived there when he returned to New York in 1925.

1935
208 Union Avenue, Brooklyn
A three-story brick apartment building.

1942-1943 (Winter season)
1122 North First Avenue, Tucson
A small stucco bungalow with the front porch covered by the roof which Bonanno rented.

1943-1944 (Winter season)
1637 East Speedway, Tucson
This address was the home of Andrea Cracchiolo, a friend of Bonanno. They stayed there as guests.

1945, 1946
61 Clermont Avenue, Hempstead, Long Island
A narrow two-story brick building with a large chimney on the front. It has a detached garage.

1952
1247 Warren Avenue, Tucson, Arizona
The structure is gone and replaced by University of Arizona buildings.

1953-1972
1847 Elm Ave, Tucson, Arizona
Lowlife associates of a rogue FBI Agent bombed the Bonanno residence on July 22, 1968. They placed one explosive against the back fence and threw another into the back yard. Both exploded. The city of Tucson leveled this residence to make way for a road widening.

1973-2002
255 North Sierra Vista, Tucson, Arizona
This address is where the Arizona Narcotics Strike Force ran a garbage cover from December 1975 until April 1979. (Hoping to find incriminating evidence.) On March 17, 1979, they raided the residence and confiscated materials. In October of 1979, they tapped Bonanno's phone.

Bonanno died in 2002. The family put the home for sale on eBay in 2004, asking nearly $500,000. It was/is a 2,100 square foot brick adobe bungalow with three bedrooms. Other features included a bocce court, an inground pool, and a basement. (Concrete slabs are the standard foundation for Arizona homes.)

In the next chapter, I will cover Bonanno's history with the Mafia since 1931.

CHAPTER FIVE

Bonanno's World Part Two

Note:
Nicole Gentile labeled a gathering of all the Mafia Bosses in the US a General Assembly. Following the lead of Joe Bonanno, starting in 1931, I will use the term National Meeting for such gatherings.

In this chapter, I will summarize major Mafia events that would have come to Bonanno's attention. Some would require direct action, while others would have only been of interest to the mob Boss.

1931
Joe Bonanno and Lucky Luciano

According to Bonanno, Luciano offered to cut him in on a garment district racket. Bonanno would be able to place some of his men in the Amalgamated Clothing Union. From that position, they would have influence over jobs and most likely kickbacks as well. Without offending Luciano, Bonanno rejected the idea, not wanting to owe a favor.

Bonanno also wrote that he did not take Luciano's bait to put down Salvatore Maranzano, hoping to gain Lucky's favor. He said that

Luciano approved of his loyalty. I don't buy it for a minute. The two plotted against Maranzano, in my opinion.

October 15, 1931
JOE ARDIZZONE

Ardizzone had become the LA Boss after the May 22, 1922 murder of Boss Vito DiGiorgio. Newspapers described him as a wealthy vineland owner. He and the powerful Jack Dragna had a falling out. According to Nicole Gentile, Dragna complained about Ardizzone while they were both at the first National Meeting in Chicago when the Bosses formed the Commission in September of 1931. Gentile related that Capone told Dragna to take an early train back to LA and whack out Ardizzone. He did.

Bonanno and the other six Commission members must have approved this hit for one of the new body's key mandates was the approval of the murder of any Boss.

October 24, 1931
AL CAPONE

The feds convicted Capone of income tax evasion on October 24, 1931. He would receive a total of 11 years on various counts. In May of the following year, he lost his appeal to the Supreme Court, and the authorities shipped him off to Atlanta. Frank Nitti stepped in as Boss of Chicago and took Capone's Commission seat.

1932
PHIL BUCCOLA

The Commission approved Phil Buccola as the Boss of New England, replacing veteran mobster Gaspare Messina.

1932
SAVERIO POLLACCIA

Pollaccia acted as Consigliere to the late Joe Masseria. Vito Genovese did not trust him and called in a few favors to take care of the problem. According to Gentile, Chicago power Paul Ricca helped Genovese eliminate Pollaccia while on a trip to Chicago.

Due to Pollaccia's former position and contacts, Bonanno and the Commission most likely approved the hit.

May 16, 1932
JAMES ALASCIA

James Alascia was a Maranzano confidant. It was he who rented the suite of offices where shooters ended Maranzano's life. A few days after, police arrested Alascia and two others, suspecting them of being part of the hit squad. They never laid charges.

The 1930 census located Alascia's residence at 335 20th Street, New York City. It stated that his occupation was a real estate salesman. It is unclear whether it was a personal or Mafia matter that caused a shooter to open up on Alascia on a crowded sidewalk in the late afternoon of May 16, 1932. Alascia was hit three times and died later that day in the hospital. A news report stated that Alascia knew someone had targeted him. It added that his chief lieutenant, Vincent Bamiano, met a similar death on May 12. Even if he was not involved, Bonanno must have been mildly interested in Maranzano's partner's fate.

July 29, 1932
THE VOLPE BROTHERS

The Volpe family had a strong presence in the Pittsburgh Family. Boss John Bazzano saw them as a threat to his continued control. Without consulting the Commission, Bazzano organized a hit that killed three brothers in his own Roma Coffee Shop. Victims John, James, and Arthur Volpe had powerful friends who demanded justice. The Commission ordered Bazzano to New York to explain his actions.

August 7, 1932
JOHN BAZZANO

Vito Genovese, a good friend of the Volpe brothers, was convinced that Albert Anastasia, Vincent Mangano, Joe Biondo, and Nicole Gentile were in on the massacre. Anastasia was a Bazzano friend while some of Gentile's men carried out the hit. Luckily for them, Anastasia convinced Genovese they were innocent and promised to interrogate Bazzano. Not long afterward, the police found the strangled and shot Bazzano in a sack. The Commission would have ruled on the murder of this sitting Boss.

February 18, 1933
JOE ROMA
JAMES COLLETTI

On February 18, 1933, Denver Boss Joe Roma was entertaining Eugene Smaldone, his father Ralph, and two other men in his home. About two hours later, his wife returned from a short excursion and found him lying dead in his chair. The visitors were long gone.

In March, the police arrested four Smaldones and three others concerning the murder, but nothing came of the inquiries. The Commission made no move on the Smaldones, strongly suggesting they had approved the hit. The Smaldones were long time powers in the Family for decades. Bonanno and the Commission red-lighted James Colletti as the new Boss.

May 30, 1933
SEBASTIANO "BUSTER FROM CHICAGO" DOMINGO

Joe Valachi introduced us to Domingo in the book "The Valachi Papers." Known to Valachi as "Buster from Chicago," Domingo was a daring and prolific shooter for Maranzano during the Castellammarese War. But his full identity remained elusive until noted mob historian David Critchley tracked down the details.

Domingo was born in Castellammare del Golfo in 1910. Three years later, he and his family moved to Chicago, finally settling in Benton Harbor, Michigan. In the 1920s, Sebastiano and his brother Tony were involved in bootlegging, which always created rivals. On October 22, 1927, someone blew up Tony's wife as she was driving his car. The husband must have been the real target.

Sebastiano and Tony attempted revenge but missed their target in a wild shootout. Two years later, the brothers were residing in Chicago, but trouble found Tony again. On August 29, 1929, nine shots hit him, ending his life. By April of 1930, the census showed that Bastiano lived in Newcastle Township, near New York. Whether a Maranzano ally had summoned his aid remains unclear.

Sebastiano Domingo survived the Castellammarese War and served as an usher at Bonanno's 1931 wedding. Something had to have gone wrong two years later. On May 30, 1933, Domingo played cards with about ten other men in the Castle Cafe at 72 1ˢᵗ Street in Manhattan. Four shooters barged in, blasting shots at Buster as everyone scrambled. The bullets wounded several men, with Buster falling dead in the street. His mother quickly arrived on the scene, wailing away. Looking at her dead son, very well dressed in a suit, she remarked that he was a good boy although he was out of work.

From the witness's reports, it was clear the gunmen had targeted Domingo. It is unlikely the killing was a private affair since there were four shooters. The hit had all the appearances of a Mafia hit. The question was who was behind it?

OPINION

Without any evidence, I suggest that Bonanno must have been in on the murder. It seems highly unlikely that another Family would order an unsanctioned hit. If that were the case, Bonanno would have had to respond with revenge to maintain his prestige. There is no evidence that I am aware of that supports such action. Domingo might have been unhappy with his position and income. Perhaps he muscled in on the territory of someone else, forcing Bonanno to approve his demise. We will never know the truth, but it is fun to speculate.

July 10, 1934
JOHN LAZIA
CHARLES CARROLLO

Lazia rose from a street hood to be the politically well-connected Boss of Kansas City by the late 1920s. Boss of Bosses Salvatore Maranzano would have acknowledged his position at the General Assembly in May of 1931. The newly formed Commission would have done the same in September of the same year. With political and police protection, Lazia gathered wealth and seemed untouchable. That assessment proved wrong.

There is rarely only one reason for the murder of a Mafia Boss. Jealousy and envy usually play a role. With Lazia, the infamous Union Station Massacre on June 17, 1933, appears to have been the straw that broke the camel's back. On that day, four lawmen died in a botched attempted to free a notorious mobster. A national outcry erupted, resulting in a massive embarrassment to the Kansas City political machine. Lazia's protection faded away.

Indictments followed, and a one-year tax sentence was pending. The Family must have decided that they needed a Boss with a lower profile. On February 22, 1937, a driver dropped Lazia and his wife off at their apartment. Two gunmen opened up with a machine gun and shotgun. Lazia was mortally wounded and died in the hospital later that night. Thankfully his wife escaped harm.

The Boss of the Chicago Outfit, Frank Nitti, would have approved this hit in advance if the Kansas City plotters followed Mafia protocol. Unfortunately, no prime evidence of this blessing exists. At the very least, Nitti would have informed the other six Commission members of the hit and that the Kansas City members had elected Charles Carrollo as the new Boss.

September 19, 1934
FERNAND BOCCIA

A gunman killed Ferdinand "The Shadow" Boccia in the Circolo Christofolo Club on Metropolitan Avenue in Brooklyn. This act remained unknown to the police until they found the body in the Hudson River on May 11, 1937.
Not too long afterward, when police started investigating, Vito Genovese took an extended trip to Italy. I'll write more on that in a later chapter.

August 22, 1935
VINCENT TROIA

Although I am uncertain about which Family Troia belonged to, Gentile described him as a significant player. When the General

Assembly formed a special commission in December of 1930 to approach Maranzano about making peace, Troia joined Gentile on the five-person group. Gentile felt that Troia, rather than being neutral, toed Maranzano's line and was a good friend. This allegiance MAY have played a role in the event I outline below.

On August 22, 1935, Troia and a group of men played cards in a Newark, NJ, candy store. Three gunmen barged in, slinging lead. Troia, his son Joseph and another man ended up dead while three others were wounded. It was a successful hit. A newspaper account stated that Troia ran the Two Eagles lottery.

Without knowing Troia's Mafia position, it is impossible to classify his murder as a sanctioned Commission move or an internal Family matter. A 1988 chronological history of the Mafia, produced by the FBI, listed this killing. The agency speculated that it was due to Troia's alleged attempt to take over the Newark Family. If this conclusion is correct, we may tentatively conclude that Bonanno and the Commission gave the attack OK. (See February 22, 1937 entry below.)

October 23, 1935
DUTCH SCHULTZ

Over the years, Schultz developed a lucrative policy (gambling) operation in Harlem. He never hesitated to use violence to get his way. When the newspapers focused on Schultz, he became a prime target for ambitious prosecutor Thomas Dewey. In response, Schultz proposed to the other New York Bosses that they eliminate Dewey. Wiser heads prevailed. The Commission refused to sanction the hit. When Schultz insisted he would go it alone, they leveled a death sentence. The realization that the Genovese Family would take over the numbers operation influenced their vote, in my opinion.

On October 23, 1935, Charles Workman and Mendy Weiss walked into the back dining room of the Palace Chop House in Newark, intending to kill Schultz. ("Piggy" stayed outside.) They had been enforcers for prominent Jewish hood Lepke Buchalter for years. The target was not in the back dining room as expected, so Workman and Weiss opened fire on the three men sitting there.

Despite being severely wounded, two of the men returned shots. The gunmen retreated, but Workman stopped at the washroom where he found Schultz. Using his backup .45 semi-automatic, Workman hit the Dutchman with one shot but missed with the second. Schultz died in the hospital later.

Note:
Famous turncoat Allie Tannenbaum had a somewhat different version of the events in the hit. He told the cops that he had heard Workman telling the story.

Workman made it to the street while still under fire by two pursuing wounded men. Unfortunately for Workman, Weiss and the driver had driven off, leaving him to make his way home. He was not a happy camper, but Schultz and his three men died.

Years later, in 1941, Workman took a plea deal to avoid a death sentence after being charged with the Schultz hit. In the 1960s, an illegal bug in a Genovese Capo's office revealed that the Genovese mob had been paying Workman during his time in prison.

May 19, 1936
ARCANGELA LONGO

Arcangela Longo and her husband lived at 1651 Whitney Avenue, in Niagara Falls, NY, next door to her brother Stefano Magaddino. Shortly after 5 AM on May 19, 1936, someone threw a bomb through her door window. Awoken by the breaking glass Arcangela walked down the stairs only to be right in the way of the exploding bomb. She would die a short while later from burns and injuries. Two of her three kids had minor hurts.

The police conducted a thorough investigation focusing on Mr. Longo and any enemies he might have had. The fact that he was in New York when the bombing happened initially raised some eyebrows. However, the authorities could find no connection to Longo.

Decades later, informer Joe Valachi told the FBI that the intended target was Magaddino. Unfortunately, he had no direct knowledge as to the identity of the bomber(s), but his theory was reasonable. Later research demonstrated that Magaddino attempted to impose a tax on all gamblers within his territory. Not all went along happily with this new plan, and they may have been behind the bombing. Magaddino men wiped out some rivals from Batavia, New York after the bombing. Whether this was revenge or business remains unclear. Perhaps it was a bit of both.

June 7, 1936
LUCKY LUCIANO

With Schultz dead, Luciano became the prime target of Tom Dewey. In a controversial trial, the jury convicted Luciano and others of running a compulsory prostitution ring. Later the judge gave Luciano an unheard-of sentence of 30 to 50 years. The Genovese Mob Boss's appeals would fail, and he'd rot in prison for another ten years. His replacement would remain uncertain, which would have troubled Bonanno and the Commission.

August 6, 1936.
DOMINICK "TERRY BURNS" DIDATO

According to Nicolo Gentile, Terry Burns was a powerful Genovese Capo who had his sights on being Luciano's replacement as Boss. This desire threatened the aspirations of Underboss Vito Genovese, who decided to remove his rival. Gentile admitted that he played a role in Didato's murder on behalf of Genovese, who became the unchallenged Acting Boss.
August 17, 1936
JOHN AVENA

Avena had become Boss of Philadelphia when his predecessor, Salvatore Sabella, retired in 1931. The two men were among a group of seven arrested for the 1927 murder of two men. They did not go to trial until 1933, when a jury rendered a not guilty verdict on May 7. Unfortunately for Avena, a rivalry with the Lanzetti brothers (Not Mafia members) led to his murder on August 17, 1936. Since this was a non-Mafia murder, Bonanno and the Commission would have played no role in the plot. However, it is reasonable to assume they made inquiries about the culprits and no doubt urged revenge.

Fall 1936
2ND NATIONAL MEETING OF LA COSA NOSTRA

Mafia Bosses from across America would have gathered in the fall of 1936 for their scheduled National Meeting. Unfortunately, we do not know the location they chose. The Bosses' main order of business would have been the ratification of the seven Commission members who would serve a five-year term. Below is a list of the membership.

Bonanno Family-Joe Bonanno
Lucchese Family-Tom Gagliano
Colombo Family-Joe Profaci
Gambino Family-Vincent Mangano
Genovese Family-Vito Genovese for the jailed Lucky Luciano
Chicago Outfit-Frank Nitti
Buffalo Family-Stefano Magaddino

February 22, 1937
GASPAR D'AMICO

Many mob historians believe D'Amico headed his own Family based in Newark, New Jersey. Primary evidence to support this conclusion remains elusive, at least for me.

D'Amico spent his life running a macaroni business in Newark. City directories, a draft record, and census information indicate he began this pursuit around 1917 and continued uninterrupted till 1937. Things changed that year.

On February 22, 1937, a gunman entered D'Amico's macaroni factory at 34 Drift Street in Newark, firing a gun. In the end, D'Amico's father, Domenico (78), died, but Gaspar survived despite wounds in his gut and leg. The FBI concluded that Joe Profaci (Colombo Family), a Commission member, ordered this hit and the Newark Family's dissolution. At this point, D'Amico fled to Italy. Usually, the agency doesn't pull these conclusions out of their hat, so I assume they had some evidence to support their position.

Assuming the FBI is correct, we have to conclude that this would have been a Commission matter. Not only was a Boss attacked, but his Family's existence ended. Bonanno and the others must have had numerous discussions as to how to handle D'Amico. Unfortunately, he never mentions anything about this matter in his book.

June 14, 1937
FRANCESCO LANZA

Lanza immigrated to the United States in 1904. Over the next sixteen years, many businesses, including a wine store, a realty company, and a contracting enterprise, occupied his time. Whether the Bonanno leadership inducted Lanza is unknown.

In 1921 Lanza and his family moved west to San Francisco. During the next sixteen years, records indicate that Lanza ran a grape farm, the Lucca Olive Oil Company, and some other businesses. Probably before 1930, the small membership elected him Boss of the San Francisco Family.

Lanza is of interest to this book due to his death from natural causes on June 14, 1937. The Commission, including Bonanno, would have been informed of his death and Tony Lima's election as the new Boss. It remains unclear whether the approval would have come from the Chicago Boss or the entire Commission.

October 30, 1939
CHARLES CARROLLO
CHARLES BINAGGIO

Carrollo had been the Boss of Kansas City since the 1934 murder of his predecessor John Lazia. Like Lazia, the corrupt Tom Pendergast political machine protected him in return for a piece of his illegal rackets. Unfortunately for Carrollo, a reform movement destroyed the Pendergast machine and its protection. The courts convicted Carrollo on various charges with the result a judge sentenced him to eight years in the slammer. Underboss Charles Binaggio became the new Boss.

Either Chicago Boss Frank Nitti or the entire Commission would have approved Binaggio's rise if the Kansas City Family followed Mafia rules.

Unfortunately, I have no prime sources to support either option but have to rely on Mob history from a much later era.

For Bonanno, the 1930s were part of his "balmy days." that would continue in the next decade. However, other Mafioso did not have such a good time, as described in the next chapter.

CHAPTER SIX

Bonanno's World Part Three

Fall 1941
3RD NATIONAL MEETING OF LA COSA NOSTRA

There is no evidence about this meeting other than Joe Bonanno wrote that it took place. The location and topics of discussion remain a mystery, but we can produce the Commission membership from other evidence.

Bonanno Family-Joe Bonanno
Colombo Family-Joe Profaci
Gambino-Vince Mangano
Genovese-Frank Costello
Lucchese-Tom Gagliano
Chicago-Frank Nitti
Buffalo-Stefano Magaddino

March 19, 1943
Frank Nitti
Paul Ricca
On March 19, 1943, Nitti awaited a grand jury appearance concerning extortion in the movie business. The investigations had caused great turmoil in the Family, with some leaders criticizing

Nitti's handling of the racket. Nitti's nerves broke, and fueled by alcohol; he shot himself along a rail line. Paul Ricca, the Underboss, became his replacement. The new Chicago Boss would have informed the other Commission members of these changes. Bonanno never commented publicly about them.

December 22, 1943
Paul Ricca
Anthony Accardo
A judge sentenced Chicago Boss Paul Rica and three others to ten years each after a jury convicted them of a movie industry extortion. Powerful veteran mobster Anthony Accardo stepped up as Acting Boss.

June 15, 1944
Ernest "The Hawk" Rupolo
The police jammed up Rupolo on an attempted murder charge. He made a deal on this date to plead guilty to wounding. One of the plea conditions was that Rupolo would disclose his past misdeeds. Much to the police's shock, Rupolo claimed that Vito Genovese had ordered the 1934 Ferdinand "The Shadow" Boccia hit.

July 5, 1944
Peter LaTempa
To confirm his accusation, Rupolo told the police that Peter LaTempa was present when Genovese gave the murder contract. The officers quickly rounded up LaTempa and placed him in the Brooklyn Civil Prison as a material witness. A magistrate set his bail at $50,000.

August 6, 1944
Vito Genovese et al.
On this date, a King's County Grand Jury indicted Genovese and others for the Boccia murder.

August 27, 1944
Vito Genovese
US Military Police arrested Genovese on suspicion of running a sizeable black market racket involving stolen army goods. Agent Orange C Dickey dug into Genovese's background and found the

early murder indictment. He began planning to return Genovese to New York.

December 6, 1944
Peter LaTempa
LaTempa attempted to hang himself in the Brooklyn Civil Jail. A reasonable guess why would be that he heard that the military police had arrested Genovese in Italy and that he might be home soon.

January 15, 1945
Peter LaTempa
While out on a walk accompanied by a guard, LaTempa stopped at a drug store.

January 16, 1945
Peter LaTempa
Guards found LaTempa dead in his cell. Rumors quickly spread that the mob had poisoned him.

February 15, 1945
Peter LaTempa
Assistant DA Edward Hefferman told the press that the report from City Toxicologist Dr. Alexander Gettler said that LaTempa died from an overdose of sleeping pills. A reasonable explanation would be that LaTempa hoarded pills brought by his brother plus purchased more from his drug store visit the day before. Add the attempted suicide from December 6, 1944, and you have all the makings of suicide rather than a mob poisoning.

May 17, 1945
Vito Genovese
Genovese and his escort, Agent Orange C Dickey boarded the SS James in Bari, Italy, headed for New York.

June 1, 1945
Vito Genovese
After arriving in New York, Dickey escorted Genovese to Brooklyn authorities.

June 2, 1945
Vito Genovese
The District Attorney arraigned Genovese in Brooklyn on the Boccia murder charge. He pled, not guilty.

January 4, 1946
Lucky Luciano
Much to everyone's surprise, New York State Governor Thomas Dewey commuted Luciano's sentence, following the parole board's recommendation. They made no mention of Luciano's wartime co-operation. The commutation's prime condition was that Luciano would accept deportation. To Bonanno and the Commission, this seemed like the end of Luciano. They were wrong.

February 2, 1946
Lucky Luciano
Immigration authorities picked up Luciano at Sing Sing prison and transported him to Ellis Island.

February 8, 1946
Lucky Luciano
Immigration agents transferred Luciano to Pier 7, where longshoremen were loading the freighter, Laura Keene.

February 10, 1946
Lucky Luciano
After completing loading, the Laura Keene set sail for the Canary Islands then Genoa, Italy.

February 28, 1946
Lucky Luciano
Luciano arrived in Italy. His activities there are not crucial for our purposes.

June 7, 1946
Vito Genovese
Informant Ernest Rupolo identified Genovese in court and testified that he ordered the killing of Ferdinand Boccia.

June 10, 1946
Vito Genovese
After a short trial, Judge Sam Leibowitz dismissed Genovese's murder charge. The fatal flaw was that the prosecution couldn't produce the necessary corroborating witness. Their only one, Peter LaTempa, was in his grave.

June 11, 1946
Vito Genovese
Officials released Genovese, and he quickly started making careful moves to gain the Genovese Family throne.

September 2, 1946
Lucky Luciano
Sources told the New York Daily News that Luciano had taken a freighter to Mexico.

October 29, 1946
Lucky Luciano
Luciano arrived in Cuba by plane with $4,000 and a 60-day tourist visa.

Fall 1946
4ᵀᴴ NATIONAL MEETING OF LA COSA NOSTRA

In the fall of 1946, the Commission's five-year mandate was ending, and a National Meeting was required to renew it. This event was probably the prime reason Luciano snuck out of Italy. He still wanted to be a power in La Cosa Nostra, and by attending or being near the meeting, he might be able to do so. Gaining permanent residency in Cuba would have been another requisite.

With Luciano in Cuba, the leadership of the Genovese Family was uncertain. Vito's return from Italy shook Frank Costello, and Luciano's closeness to the US must have done the same. Bonanno and the Commission must have had many in-depth discussions about the situation.

The location of this National Meeting has been in dispute for many decades. I reject the theory that the Bosses held it in Havana during the Christmas holidays. No self-respecting Boss would be away from his wife and kids at that time. Indeed not 26 of them! Secondly, there is no evidence of an influx of Mafia Bosses into Havana. Thirdly there is no way the Bosses would have chanced having to cross borders, both coming and going. That would have inevitably drawn attention to themselves and disastrous publicity. Hazy evidence suggests Florida was the setting for the meeting.

Below is a list of the Commission members approved for 1946-1951.

Bonanno Family-Joe Bonanno
Colombo Family-Joe Profaci
Gambino Family-Vincent Mangano
Genovese Family-Frank Costello
Buffalo Family-Stefano Magaddino
Chicago Outfit-Acting Boss Tony Accardo for the imprisoned Paul Ricca

It would be fascinating to know what input, if any, Luciano had at this gathering. While there is no evidence he secretly traveled to Florida by boat, the phones still worked. The bottom line was that Costello would continue as Boss and the Genovese Family's representative on the Commission. Future events would clear up any uncertainty in Luciano's status.

February 11, 1947
Frank Sinatra
Frank Sinatra, Rocco, and Joe Fischetti, two Chicago Mafia members, flew into Havana to visit Luciano. A cameraman either filmed or snapped a picture of their arrival. This trip would cause Sinatra headaches for decades to come.

Note
In an "Ask Andy" piece I did for Ganglandnews a few years ago, I demonstrated that Sinatra could not have been at a wild, 1946, New Year's Eve party with Lucky. That story is a myth.

February 14, 1947
Lucky Luciano
The Havana newspaper, Tiepo En Cuba, carried an article by Ronald Masferrer, revealing Luciano's presence in Cuba. American columnist Robert Ruark picked up the sensational story for his national column. All hell broke loose!

February 22, 1947
Lucky Luciano
After much public outcry in the US and secret US government pressure, Cuban authorities arrested Luciano and stuck him in an immigration prison.

February 27, 1947
Lucky Luciano
Cuban President Ramon Grau San Martin labeled Luciano an undesirable and ordered his deportation.

March 20, 1947
Lucky Luciano
Luciano boarded a freighter bound for Italy. Any dreams of regaining his Mafia power were over. Genovese Boss Frank Costello was relieved of one headache, but the ambitious Vito Genovese was peering over his shoulder. Bonanno and the Commission would be very busy in the future.

CHAPTER SEVEN

The Mafia Comes in from the Cold

By the late 1940s, public worries about organized crime began to sweep the nation. Crime Commissions in California, Chicago, Miami, and other places fed their take on crime to willing newspapers. It soon became apparent that gambling had become the bogeyman replacing alcohol.

To bet on a horse race without being at the track required a bookie who took the wagers and paid the winners. The bookie needed information and results from significant thoroughbred racecourses around the nation so that betting could take place all day long.

In that era, the only way to gain this information was through telegraph lines. The Chicago Outfit helped form companies that rented time on the established telegraph company's wires. These mob enterprises would obtain and distribute race information to the bookies. Of course, the bookies would pay for this vital service making the racket extremely lucrative.

It soon became apparent to the good guys that the hoods had created a nationwide gambling enterprise. The concern was that this goldmine would lead to more political and police corruption. A central turning point occurred on April 5, 1950. Rivals killed Kansas City Boss Charles Binaggio and a companion in his office. Binaggio's deep open involvement in politics became widely known to the public after his death. Fear of a connection between mobsters and politicians grew exponentially. The US Senate gave in to this pressure and created a select committee to investigate organized crime.

May 3, 1950
Kefauver Committee
After much political maneuvering, the US Senate formed a "Special Committee to Investigate Crime in Interstate Commerce." The Committee elected ambitious Kentucky Senator Estes Kefauver as its chairman. The Committee hoped to determine if the bad guys were using interstate commerce to carry out their illegal activities by holding hearings around the nation. It would turn out to be quite a show lasting until September 1, 1951. Fortunately for Bonanno, he was far below the radar during this period and never appeared before the Committee. Others weren't so lucky. I'll only mention the few who had direct connections to Bonanno.

December 12, 1950
Washington, DC
Willie Moretti
Moretti, the Underboss of the Genovese Family, was a big hit when he appeared before the Kefauver Hearings in Washington. Two samples from newspaper accounts said, "One of the most amusing episodes" and a "most refreshing witness." Unlike many other witnesses, Moretti readily acknowledged that he knew people like Frank Costello, Joe Adonis, Lucky Luciano, Tony Accardo, and others. However, he smartly denied ever doing business with any of them. Moretti also admitted to making a living gambling but on his own. The gangster was a hit with the Senators and newspapers but not the mob Bosses.

February 16, 1951
Tom Gagliano
According to an FBI report from 1988, Gagliano died on February 16, 1951, of natural causes. Long-time Underboss Tommy Lucchese filled Gagliano's positions as the Lucchese Family Boss and Commission member.

March 13, 14, 15, 19, 20, 21, 1951
Frank Costello
Costello made seven notable public appearances before the Kefauver Committee. Costello won the right not to have his face televised in his first appearance. The cameras focused on his hands, which intrigued the public. The tactic to remain unrecognizable backfired. Thanks to television, the ups and downs of his testimony

captured the nation. Costello became a nationally famous person. Costello's significant notoriety must have shocked Bonanno and contributed to his lifelong aversion to public testimony.

March 30, 1951
US Senate
On this date, the full Senate voted to cite Costello and others for contempt for not fully testifying truthfully before the Kefauver Committee. Realizing that convictions, more publicity, and prison time could result from these citations, Bonanno must have redoubled his plan to remain unknown. It didn't work.

April 19, 1951
Vincent Mangano
According to Joe Bonanno, Mangano and his Underboss Albert Anastasia had conspired against each other for some time. In April of 1951, Mangano disappeared, and hitmen murdered his brother. In his autobiography (1983), Bonanno acted as if he played no part in these actions and that he was in Arizona at the time. I don't believe him.

Bonanno was an original member of the Commission. One of its prime rules was that no one could eliminate a Boss without Commission approval. A more likely scenario for Bonanno would be that he voted against killing Mangano and lost. He then took off for Arizona to distance himself from the inevitable publicity.

After Mangano disappeared, the Commission met. Anastasia didn't admit guilt but said he had proof Mangano was plotting his death. Frank Costello confirmed Anastasia's story. The Gambino Family had a new Boss and the Commission a new member.

October 4, 1951
Willie Moretti
According to Bonanno, Moretti had fallen out of favor with his Boss Frank Costello. Although they were friends, Costello had begun to lean on Gambino Boss Albert Anastasia, for he feared Vito Genovese's ambitions.

Moretti was unhappy with his loss of influence and openly complained about it. Moretti claimed that he had never heard of Mangano plotting against Anastasia. Costello was not pleased.

Part of Genovese's strategy to gain the Family throne was to eliminate Moretti. He began spreading stories that Moretti had lost his mind, as evidenced by his Kefauver appearance and his mouthy complaints about Costello. Bonanno wrote that Moretti was suffering from syphilis and his mind was rapidly deteriorating.

October 4, 1951
Willie Moretti
Moretti and four men were in Joe's Elbow Room in Cliffside, NJ. When the lone waitress went to the kitchen, his companions filled Moretti full of lead and fled. Bonanno wrote that at the next Commission meeting, Anastasia and Costello said Moretti was sick. The other members could not disagree. Bonanno left out that the Commission, including Bonanno, approved the hit. There is no evidence to support that conclusion, but it is a reasonable one.

Interestingly, the Bergin County Medical Examiner, Dr. Ralph Gilday, later revealed that Moretti's autopsy showed no sign of brain damage. Costello and Anastasia probably began floating this false tale as they undermined Moretti. No doubt, his appearance before the Kefauver Committee helped convince those on the fence. Unfortunately, the myth of Moretti's syphilis lives on to this day.

Fall 1951
5TH NATIONAL MEETING OF LA COSA NOSTRA
Location Unknown

Below is a list of Commission members approved for 1951-1956

Bonanno Family-Joe Bonanno
Colombo Family-Joe Profaci
Gambino Family-Albert Anastasia
Genovese Family-Frank Costello
Lucchese Family-Tom Lucchese
Chicago Outfit-Tony Accardo
Buffalo Family-Stefano Magaddino

The early 1950s (An estimate)
A Commission Meeting
Bonanno wrote that new Boss Tommy Lucchese allied with
Vito Genovese against Costello and Anastasia. Genovese envied
Costello's throne while Lucchese desired more political clout,
which Costello possessed. The result, according to Bonanno, was
a war of nerves and scheming. As per usual, Bonanno claimed not
to be directly involved.

At some point, Costello came before the Commission to complain
that Lucchese was plotting against Anastasia. Two Lucchese
insiders had revealed the secret and then appeared before the
Commission to confirm what they had heard. Costello hoped that
the Commission would censure Lucchese in some way, perhaps
even kill him.

Bonanno described the showdown by showering himself with
praise for his political moves. In the end, Lucchese admitted he had
been plotting and left his fate in Anastasia's hands. The Gambino
Boss forgave Lucchese, which turned out to be a mistake.

The primary outcome of this sit-down, for Bonanno at least,
was that the decision maintained the balance of power on
the Commission. He said there were conservative and liberal
factions. The former included himself, Stefano Magaddino, Albert
Anastasia, and Joe Profaci. Tommy Lucchese and Frank Costello
were liberals, but as demonstrated above, they were not united.
Bonanno and his allies typically dominated Commission decisions.
That status would not last forever.

August 18, 1956
Salvatore "Bill" Bonanno
Bill Bonanno married Rosalie Profaci on this date in St Bernadette
Church in Brooklyn. His father put on a massive reception for
3,000 guests at the Sheraton Astor Hotel in Manhattan. Hotel
staff set up separate tables for each of the 26 Mafia Families from
around the nation. Rosalie Bonanno wrote Joe Bonanno had
the guest list drawn up in code to thwart any law enforcement
snooping. For Bonanno, this event was one of his life highlights,
but he added that he sensed that his cousin Stefano Magaddino
was jealous. He was right.

Fall 1956
6ᵀᴴ NATIONAL MEETING OF LA COSA NOSTRA
In Apalachin, New York, at Joe Barbara's estate

Bonanno wrote about the year and place of this meeting. New York State Troopers arrested one of his Capos, Carmine Galante, in the vicinity supporting Bonanno's version. According to Bonanno, the issue of drugs was on the menu. The Bosses approved the new Commission membership but decided to include Philadelphia and Detroit's leaders starting in 1961.

Below is a list of Commission members approved for 1956-1961

Bonanno-Joe Bonanno
Colombo-Joe Profaci
Gambino-Albert Anastasia
Genovese-Frank Costello
Lucchese-Tommy Lucchese
Chicago-Tony Accardo
Buffalo-Stefano Magaddino

1957 (Exact date unknown)
Tony Accardo
Sam Giancanna
Chicago Boss Tony Accardo stepped aside to let his Underboss Sam Giancanna take the reins in a peaceful move. In reality, Accardo continued to hold power from his Consigliere position.

May 2, 1957
Frank Costello
Vito Genovese
During the 1950s, the government, in its various forms, harassed Frank Costello endlessly. He was in and out of prison on numerous charges, from contempt to income tax misdeeds to the threat of deportation. These events diverted his attention from the Family business. To the shark, Vito Genovese, there was blood in the water, and he made a move.

On May 2, 1957, Costello entered his apartment building when Vincent "The Chin" Gigante fired one shot at his head. Luckily for Costello, the slug only grazed him, but the message was clear.

He stepped down, and the Capos elected Genovese as the new Boss. The unresolved question is whether Genovese sought Commission approval for his attack. A reasonable guess would be that he privately polled several Bosses rather than putting the question formally before the Commission.

Summer 1957 (Estimated date)
Joe Bonanno
After Costello's wounding, Bonanno claimed that even though Anastasia wanted to go to war with Genovese, he talked Anastasia out of it. Bonanno arranged a meeting between the two with other Bosses present. The two rivals kissed and made up. Bonanno boasted of his "Pax Bonanno." The treaty had no substance to it, as events will show.

June 17, 1957
Frank Scalise
Scalise was a long-time power in the Gambino Family. After the 1930 murder of Boss Al Mineo, Scalise took over the leadership with Salvatore Maranzano's support. When an alliance killed Maranzano in 1931, the Gambino Family decided they needed a Boss not closely connected to the fallen Boss of Bosses. Vincent Mangano took over while Scalise moved down to a Capo position.

Anastasia appointed Scalise as his Underboss when he murdered his way to the Family's top in 1951. Something went south in the relationship by 1957. On June 17, 1957, two gunmen blasted Scalise with four shots just as he was about to exit a vegetable store in the Bronx. They jumped into a waiting automobile and escaped into history.

Valachi told the FBI that Anastasia had his Underboss killed because he was selling Mafia memberships. While this may be true, it is my opinion that Valachi was repeating a justification that Anastasia floated for the killing. Anastasia realized he was under threat by a variety of forces, according to Bonanno. Taking out a Boss usually meant secret dissidents within the Family conspired with outside powers first. Whether or not Scalise was a member of the conspiracy is unknown, but the critical fact is that Anastasia thought it was possible. That belief meant it was game over for Scalise.

August 1957
Joe Bonanno
At the invitation of newspaper publisher Fortune Pope, Bonanno took a trip to Italy in the fall of 1957. Bonanno wrote that he felt his Mafia world was at peace so that a trip would be reasonable. How the Scalise murder fit in that thought is mysterious.

Before leaving, Bonanno met with the four other New York Bosses plus Stefano Magaddino of Buffalo. When Lucchese asked who he should contact if trouble arose, Bonanno said Magaddino.

October 25, 1957
Albert Anastasia
Anastasia was sitting in a barber chair at the Park Sheraton Hotel when two gunmen entered and filled him full of lead. In 1962, Gambino member Antonio Santantorio confidentially told the FBI that the shooters were Steve Grammauta and Joe Cahil. He added that the two were acting on orders of a group of five Gambino Capos. They had obtained the two guns from an Associate located upstairs in a room. This fact may explain why the shooters entered the barbershop from the hotel lobby.

Underboss Carlo Gambino was in on the coup. He and his allies, including Vito Genovese and Tommy Lucchese, wanted a quick confirmation of Gambino as the new Boss. How they went about that proved to be a disaster for everyone.

November 14, 1957
7TH NATIONAL MEETING OF LA COSA NOSTRA
In Apalachin, NY, at Joe Barbara's estate
After the wounding and retirement of Commission member Frank Costello, then the murder of Albert Anastasia, the other Mafia Bosses around the nation must have begun feeling uneasy. It is reasonable to assume that one of the reasons for this out of sequence National Meeting would have been to reassure the leaders that the Commission was still operating and everything was under control.

Those who plotted against Costello and Anastasia had ulterior motives. They wanted to introduce Genovese and Gambino as the new leaders, in effect, obtaining the blessing of the assembled Mafia Bosses. Bonanno wrote that he tried to avoid this scenario. Gambino was not an ally, so Bonanno hoped other Gambino powers would challenge for the throne.

This plan did not work.

On November 13, 1957, around 3 PM, two New York State Troopers observed the son of Joseph Barbara making reservations at the Parkway Motel, an area establishment. Due to Barbara's questionable reputation, the Troopers started poking around. At Barbara's estate, they observed four vehicles. Later that evening, the lawmen discover two of those cars back at the Parkway. Now they are curious and called in two Alcohol and Tobacco Agents from Albany.

Around noon on November 14, 1957, the four lawmen pulled into Barbara's driveway after seeing about five vehicles. From their unmarked car, they began jotting down license plate numbers. Suddenly a group of men came from the side of the garage and spotted them. The officers pulled out of the driveway and set up a roadblock at the hill's bottom. Due to a bridge collapse, this was the only way out of the estate by car.

During their "retreat" from Barbaras, the officers observed two other groups of vehicles near the barn and the stables. Then they saw about ten men fleeing across a field towards the woods. They called in reinforcements.

This accidental discovery of a National Meeting of La Cosa Nostra would have disastrous consequences for many.

BONANNO'S VERSION OF APALACHIN

Including my comments.

Bonanno said he took a trip to Italy in the fall of 1957, totally oblivious to the escalating cold war between Anastasia and Genovese and his allies. I believe he left because rivals were planning to kill Anastasia. He couldn't persuade them otherwise hence the trip.

Bonanno claimed he knew nothing of the October 25, 1957 Anastasia hit until he returned to New York. To believe this, you have to accept that none of Bonanno's men contacted him by phone or telegram shortly after the murder. He didn't return home due to the flu, as he stated, but to make sure he had input on the matter. The mob Boss wrote that he opposed the National Meeting for it would legitimize Albert Anastasia's successor Carlo Gambino. I believe this. Bonanno said that he never planned to attend the meeting but only was in the area to talk with Stefano Magaddino. Untrue, as will be explained below.

Bonanno claimed that the Troopers mistakenly identified him as one of the men detained near Barbara's. He said that a relative renewed his driver's license but could not give it to Bonanno before he left to meet with Magaddino. The relative gave the document to Capo Gaspar DiGregorio to turn over to Bonanno at the Magaddino meeting. Bonanno said DiGregorio forgot to do so. The fairy tale continued.

Bonanno said that DiGregorio and John Bonventre decided to hunt near the Barbara estate but had nothing to do with the meeting. Unfortunately for them, the Troopers rounded them up with the other hoods fleeing the estate. DiGregorio produced Bonanno's driver's license as identification after forgetting his own at home. Man! Below is the real story.

Note:
The Troopers found no guns in their roundup. Bonventre and DiGregorio must have been hunting with their hands.

> Starting around 2:30 PM, November 14, 1957
> NY State Trooper Sackel picked up Joe Bonanno in a cornfield on McFadden Road. Bonanno was among those who made undignified runs from Barbara's home. Trooper Mahig transported Bonanno to the police station for identification. On Bonanno, they found his driver's license, his social insurance card, and a note with the address of his uncle, Peter Bonventre. The clincher happened when they brought in John Bonventre, Bonanno's first Underboss. Trooper Sackel also found Bonventre in the cornfield with mud on his shoes. Bonventre explained he had come to Apalachin with Bonanno. They both were at the aborted meeting, and Bonanno's attempts to deny it are ludicrous.

CHAPTER EIGHT

Bonanno is Ejected

1964 would not be a good year for Bonanno. Canada deported Bonanno and put him on a plane for Chicago. Upon his arrival, the FBI served him with a subpoena for a grand jury appearance in New York. Meanwhile, the Commission was searching for him to no avail.

By September of 1964, the Commission had enough of Bonanno's disappearing ways. They voted to oust him from the Bonanno Family's leadership, which also meant he lost his Commission seat. Illegal FBI bugs and informers quickly had the news on the street. Genovese power Gerry Catena warned his crew not to do anything with Bonanno members until they selected a new leader. Los Angeles Boss Frank Desimone informed San Francisco Boss James Lanza of Bonanno's ouster. Genovese Acting Boss Tommy Eboli and Catena told the New England Boss that Bonanno was out.

Bonanno has problems with the Commission, but he was also facing a grand jury appearance. This likely would have led to a contempt sentence and time in jail. Bonanno could not afford to be off the streets if he had any hope for regaining power. He decided to pull a Houdini act.

On October 20, 1964, Bonanno dined in New York with two of his lawyers. The men then took a taxi back to lawyer Bill Maloney's home where Bonanno was to spend the night. They arrived after midnight. Two men abducted Bonanno; one fired a warning shot at Maloney's feet, then they forced Bonanno into a vehicle and took off.

JOE BONANNO'S VERSION OF HIS KIDNAPPING

Bonanno related that the two kidnappers were Stefano Magaddino's son and brother. There was also a driver but Bonanno didn't mention who he was. They took Bonanno to a farm near Buffalo. Later that day, Magaddino arrived to talk with Bonanno. According to Bonanno, the two men had off and on discussions over the next month and a half. He was then released, and he made his way back to Tucson by December 4. For some reason, Bonanno did not inform Bill of his release for two weeks.

BILL BONANNO'S VERSION OF HIS FATHERS KIDNAPPING

Not being present at the kidnapping, Bill didn't know what was going on. He spent the next number of weeks waiting to hear about his father. Then, on November 11, 1964, he remembered that he and his father has set up a secure means of communication. Bill was to go to a phone booth in Long Island each Thursday at 8 PM and wait for a call. He did this until Thursday, December 17, 1964, when the phone finally rang. A person told him his father was fine and he'd be seeing him soon. Bill was not to do anything.

The next day, Friday, December 18, 1964 Bill called Joe Bonanno's lawyer, Bill Maloney, and passed on the good news. Unfortunately, Maloney informed the press that Bonanno was alive and would appear in court on Monday. The publicity was tremendous, but Bonanno never showed. Bill stated that he then drove to Arizona, leaving early in the morning on Boxing Day.

MAFIA COMMENTS ON THE KIDNAPPING

October 21, 1964
On the day of the kidnapping, an illegal FBI bug in the office of Boss Sam Decavalcante overheard him say he had no idea what was going on.

October 22, 1964
After returning to his office after a meeting with Genovese Family Underboss Gerry Catena, Decavalcante told some of his men that Catena had no idea what is going on.

Searching for Bonanno, the FBI interviewed Philadelphia Boss Angelo Bruno. He told them he thought Bonanno kidnapped himself.

November 23, 1964

Decavalcante returned to his office after a trip to Miami, where he met Carlo Gambino, Gerry Catena, and Tampa Boss Sam Trafficante. He told his Associates that Bonanno pulled off his kidnapping using his son Bill and Vito DeFilippo as the heavies.

December 9 or 10, 1964 (approximate)

From a bugged conversation in the office of Sam Decavalcante on December 23, the FBI learned that there was a Bonanno Capos meeting on this date, give or take a day either way. Bonanno loyalists Joe Notaro and Vito DeFilippo told Sam that Bonanno had resigned at this gathering. They said Bill was present. The point is that Bill has written he did not know his father was alive until the December 17, 1964, phone call.

The Bonanno men appointed a four-person committee to represent the Family loyalist in discussions with the Commission. They picked Capo Joe Notaro to head the group.

December 23, 1964

The FBI recorded DeFilippo and Notaro talking about the Bonanno Family meeting that took place "two weeks ago," as I've outlined under December 9 or 10, 1964.

CONCLUSION

Except for Joe Bonanno's fanciful tale of his kidnapping, there is no evidence to support his version. There are significant facts that tell a different story, as I've outlined above. Around the year 2000, a son of one of Bonanno's high ranking loyalists told me he could prove Bonanno staged the entire event. Out of an abundance of caution, I suggested that he might want to think carefully before proceeding with his evidence. I never heard from him again. My boss was not at all pleased with my display of humanity. Ah well.

December 26, 1964
Very early in the morning Bill Bonanno left New York and started driving to Tucson.

December 28, 1964
An informer told the FBI that the Bonanno Capos met on this day and gave Bonanno until January 7, 1965, to clear up his legal problems and then meet with the Capos.

December 28, 1964
Bill Bonanno arrived in Tucson and checked into the Spanish Trail Motel around noon.

December 29, 1964
In the afternoon, Tucson police and FBI Agents, including Kermit Johnson, arrested Bill Bonanno in a local barbershop. They locked him up in the Prima County Jail on a material witness warrant out of New York and handed him a subpoena to appear before a federal grand jury in New York investigating his father's disappearance.

December 31, 1964
Not long after midnight, Bill Bonanno talked with FBI Agents in the Prima County Jail for about five hours.
At 9:41 AM, jail officials released Bonanno for he had obtained bail from a bonding company. They had kept him locked up for forty hours while he desperately attempted to raise money to get his freedom.
January 4, 1965
Bill Bonanno flew to New York to face a federal grand jury investigating his father's disappearance. He appeared the next day.

THE CONFUSING ERA

Tax Liens 1964

The FBI applied all different kinds of pressure to flush Bonanno out of hiding. One tactic that seemed to work was placing a tax lien on Bill Bonanno and his properties. The Feds announced that they would do the same with Joe Bonanno. This move was beneficial for the Bonanno money stream had dried up. The elder Bonanno finally decided to appear in court.

On January 12, 1965, the Commission attempted to bring an end to the Bonanno Family fiasco. They held an official installation for long time Bonanno friend and Capo Gaspar DiGregorio in Cedarhurst, Long Island. The FBI eventually identified several leading Mafia figures in attendance, including Chicago Outfit Boss Sam Giancanna, Genovese Acting Boss Tom Eboli, Genovese Underboss Gerry Catena, Capo Carmine Tramunti from the Lucchese Family and others. The trouble was Joe, and Bill Bonanno still wouldn't go away.

March 1, 1965
Bill Bonanno refused to testify before the grand jury and ended up in prison.

June 5, 1965
Officials released Bill Bonanno after he completed his grand jury contempt sentence. His freedom gave Bonanno time to plan all sorts of actions to regain power. Some of them were ridiculous.

January 28, 1966
Troutman Street Shootout

This shootout is part of Mafia lore. Bonanno claimed DiGregorio forces ambushed him and some of his men at an arranged peace meeting on Troutman Street in Brooklyn.

BILL BONANNO'S VERSION ONE

(From Honor Thy Father, 1971)

Bill's uncle and Bonanno Capo, Frank LaBruzzo, arranged a meeting with DiGregorio in the hopes of ending hostilities. Despite being, suspicious Bill agreed to the forum after they decided to meet in a Bonanno area.

The group, which included Bill, Capo Frank Labruzzo, and Capo Joe Notaro, arrived shortly after 11 PM and parked their vehicle a few blocks from the residence. As they approached the meeting spot, they saw a shotgun poking out from a doorway. All hell broke loose, with Bonanno and his three companions ducking and weaving as they fled a storm of bullets. Bill finally felt safe and called Associate Sam Perrone to pick him up.

BILL BONANNO'S VERSION TWO

(From Bound By Honor, 1999)

In this version, Capo Frank Labruzzo and Soldier Carl Simari accompanied Bill. Simari had replaced Joe Notaro from the first telling. Bonanno and his men entered the Bonventre home and waited inside for the DiGregorio negotiators to arrive. In the first version, they never made it to the house before their enemies fired upon them. Another change was that some of Bill's men were already in the place before Bill arrived. Joe Notaro was one of them.

After waiting for an hour past the agreed meeting time, Bill received a DiGregorio Capo's call. The caller said DiGregorio was ill, and his men had gotten lost on the way to the Bonventre home. They rescheduled the meeting, but the Bonanno group felt uneasy.

Bill and his men remained in the building for another two hours before deciding to leave by twos. Bill went first, closely followed by Simari. After a few strides towards the corner, Carl saw a gun and pushed Bill to the ground. The street exploded with machine gun, shotgun, and pistol fire.

Carlo and Bill dodged and weaved, firing wildly. Bill described them as like a military team. Then a machine gun opened up on Bill again with the bullets tearing past his head. Whew!

At the intersection, Bill and Carlo turned right only to see a vehicle with two men inside. Not taking any chances, they blasted the car as they ran past it. Bill thought the occupants were not hit. Finally, they reached a quiet area and called Sam Perrone to pick them up. Whew again!

Police cars raced to the neighborhood. Later the homeowner related that the police said that the combatants fired more than 200 shots! Remember, this is what Bill said happened.

Comment

Mrs. Josephine Cipponeri, of 283 Troutman Street, called police to report a man had barged through her house and out the back door. When police arrived, they found three handguns in the residence, and the rear storm door had broken glass.

After a search of the area, officers found six more hand weapons plus a shotgun. A few days later, a youth discovered the seventh gun. There were several bullet holes in three houses, including that of Mrs. Cipponeri.

A nearby brick building had some nicks in it.

Over the next few days, the police interviewed about 100 neighbors. Mrs. Cipponeri was the only one who had seen anything. Some heard noises but thought they were firecrackers. I find it difficult to believe that someone would not have recognized the massive machine gun, shotgun, and pistol fire as not being firecrackers. They didn't hear the war-like sounds, for it didn't happen. Perhaps twenty shots were fired, probably all by Bonanno and his men staging an ambush.

One might question why there wasn't a tremendous amount of damage from all the gunfire. Why weren't there a bunch of cars filled with holes? There were no reports of windows shattered. Did all these hundreds of slugs disappear except for a handful? What about all the machine gun shell casings? Where did they go? Why would a lone man, presumably running to escape death, drop three guns in the home of an elderly lady? Wouldn't he want to keep at least one to protect himself until he was out of the area? Wouldn't that also be true of the other four men who supposedly dropped their weapons in the neighborhood?

This story doesn't make sense. Over the next five decades, no serious evidence that I am aware of has identified any of the DiGregorio shooters. On the Bonanno side, the two Capos who accompanied Bill in the first version were both dead before Talese's 1971 book came out. (Frank LaBruzzo and Joe Notaro.) On May 11, 1968, hitmen killed Sam Perrone, who supposedly picked Bill up after the shootout. The newcomer, in the second version, Carl Simari, had passed away before the 1999 Bonanno book. This event sure looks like a staged incident with no Bonanno participants but Bill around telling the tale.

Frustrated by the lack of media attention, Bill took advantage of the unsuspecting author, Gay Talese, who was sporadically interviewing Bill. Bonanno told his first version to Gay, who agreed to call one of his contacts on the New York Times to report the event. A small article appeared in the paper a few days later. Now the non-event took on a life of its own.

The FBI ran around interviewing people, trying to get to the bottom of the shooting. The prosecutor formed a grand jury to investigate the Troutman Street Event. Subpoenas were flying everywhere. A pile of Mafia guys was infuriated with this outcome.

For the rest of his life, Bill Bonanno retold the story of the Troutman Street shootout. Each time his role became more heroic, as the example from his 1999 book demonstrates. Researchers who dug up the facts were crying in the wind. Bill Bonanno was a much more interesting character to interview. Others saw the opportunity to make money with his stories. There was no advantage for book agents, film producers, and the like to seriously question Bill on his stories' integrity. The events were no longer history but entertainment. That's a whole different world.

THE ACTION CONTINUES

May 17, 1966
Joe Bonanno finally appeared in court to face obstruction of justice charges for not appearing before the grand jury in October of 1964. The judge released Bonanno on bond but restricted him to the New York area.

July 7. 1966
A judge sentenced Bill Bonanno and eight other hoods to 30 days in jail plus a $250 fine for contempt before a grand jury investigating the Troutman shootout. Bonanno wouldn't go to prison until October 13, 1966.

July 13, 1966
Bonanno loyalists wounded DiGregorio Underboss Frank Mari in a drive-by shooting.

Early November 1966
Prison officials released Bill Bonanno from his contempt sentence.

WELCOME TO CANADA AGAIN

The Bonannos were broke, most of their rackets had dried up, and they were scrambling to put food on the table. At this point, Bill and his father got the idea for Bill to travel to Montreal to tap into that city's Mafia loot. Bill's visit to the Great White North was a fiasco, just like his father's trip in 1964. The Canadian government deported Bill Bonanno and his men shortly after they arrived. I will detail these events in a later chapter.

The arrest of the men created news all across the USA and Canada. Most Mafiosi avoid publicity. Bill Bonanno often stumbled into it by questionable actions. He should have known that the FBI would alert the Canadians about his presence in Montreal. As usual, the talkative Bonanno told friendly FBI Agents some of the details of his northern adventure. Most were already in the Canadian newspapers.

BACK IN THE USA

March 1967
The District Attorney charged Bill Bonanno for criminal contempt before the grand jury investigating the Troutman shooting. The judge released Bonanno on bond.

May 1967
The Bonanno's control of their Mafia Family was in its death throes during 1967-1968. But there was a brief burst in the media, which would lead many to think the Bonannos were on their way back to power. It was a mirage, perhaps cooked up by the FBI notorious for their disinformation campaigns, as we will see in a later chapter.

May 7, 1967
Charles Grutzner of the New York Times heralded the Bonanno comeback. He said he had many sources, including FBI Agents, prosecutors, police officers, lawyers, and the like. According to them, Joe Bonanno was once again on top thanks to his son Bill's efforts. Grutzner wrote that a federal official told him that the Commission had restored Bonanno to his throne because Gaspar DiGregorio couldn't do the job. The story was nonsense, as future events would show. My guess is that the leaks were part of a FBI disinformation campaign hoping to stir up trouble.

October 31, 1967
The FBI told the media that Paul Sciacca was the new Bonanno Boss. DiGregorio had stepped down due to ill health.

THE CYPRESS GARDENS MASSACRE

November 10, 1967
DiGregorio Capo Thomas DiAngelo, his brother James and Associate Frank Terelli died in the Cypress Gardens restaurant in Ridgewood, Queens.

BILL BONANNO'S VERSION

The DiGregorio faction shot and wounded two Bonanno men. Bill wrote, "We hit back-hard." He described the shooting at the Cypress Gardens as "surgically precise." Two gunmen entered; one killed a victim while the second sprayed the restaurant at a high level to make everyone dive for cover and thus see nothing. Then the first gunman finished off the other two victims. The men escaped. Bonanno was proud of his men's act of revenge.

THE REAL STORY

Thomas DiAngelo and Frank Terelli were sitting at a table in the restaurant. Just as James Terelli entered the front door and headed for the table, a gunman walked into the room from the back. He pulled a submachine gun out from under his long dark raincoat and opened up. He was 20 feet from James Terelli and 10 feet from the table. He massacred all three.

Rather than being "surgically precise," the gunfire from the machine gun not only ripped up the three men but three slugs tore holes in the front window and flew into the street. These were shots fired at James as he entered from the front door. There was no evidence of the machine gunner calmly firing high shots to distract the potential witnesses.

There were at least ten and perhaps even more patrons in the joint. Some of them described only one gunman, a 5' 4", squat, middle-aged man with glasses. No one saw a second shooter.

Sending a machine gunner into a busy restaurant indicates both desperation and callousness. Bill Bonanno boasted about the hit decades later. I find it impossible when only considering this event, to label him a man of honor. Many more deplorable actions by Bill would confirm my conclusion.

December 8, 1967
The FBI announced that Bonanno Boss Paul Sciacca had selected veteran Capo Frank Mari as his Underboss. This event was another sign that the Bonannos were not coming back to power.

THE BONANNOS RETREAT

In 1968 Joe and Bill Bonanno faced reality. Joe returned to Tucson while Bill moved Rosalie and the kids to California. I will return to their lives in a later chapter. Next, I will visit the new leaders and how they fared in the Big Apple.

CHAPTER NINE

After Bonanno

After the Commission deposed Bonanno in 1964, the Family had a succession of three leaders, each of whom served short stints on the throne. Below are brief outlines of each of these men.

GASPAR DIGREGORIO

October 4, 1905 - June 11, 1970

Born in Castellammare del Golfo, just like Bonanno, DiGregorio made his way to the United States through Niagara Falls, New York. His entry was illegal, and he never attempted to be naturalized. Each year DiGregorio would register as an alien making his presence legal.

DiGregorio spent some time in Buffalo, whose Boss had probably facilitated his border crossing. He lived at 1653 Whiting Avenue in Niagara Falls and listed his occupation as butcher.

December 4, 1924

DiGregorio married Maria Magaddino, a cousin of Boss Stefano Magaddino. He and his wife acted as witnesses at the ceremony. Sadly Maria died on August 4, 1927, in New York. The couple had one daughter named Mary Ann.

1925-1931

In 1925 DiGregorio and his brothers hooked up with Bonanno in running a small still operation. He soon became a member of Salvatore Maranzano's staff and was upfront during the Castellammarese War. Afterward, he served as best man at Bonanno's wedding, indicating their closeness.

January 7, 1934

DiGregorio married Vita Lasala.

1931-1964

Bonanno appointed DiGregorio a Capo, and he led his crew for the next 30 years without the public becoming aware of him. DiGregorio remarried, had two kids, and a partnership in the F&D Coat Company. The 1950 Kefauver Hearings ignored him, and no one connected him to the 1957 Apalachin fiasco. That is until Bonanno, in his 1983 book, falsely placed him there.

As we discussed earlier, DiGregorio was not pleased when Bill Bonanno was elected Bonanno Family Consigliere in 1964. It appears that he felt his long, loyal service to Bonanno earned him the promotion. The unhappy DiGregorio took his complaints to Magaddino of Buffalo.

After Commission investigations uncovered the Bonanno and Magliocco plot to kill Gambino and Lucchese, they deposed Bonanno and ordered a Bonanno Family election which put a reluctant DiGregorio in his place. An illegal FBI bug in Buffalo Boss Stefano Magaddino's office overheard a visiting Bonanno member telling Magaddino, "Gasparino does not want to be representative (Boss)." It would be an unhappy two years for DiGregorio.

January 12, 1965

The Commission officially confirmed DiGregorio as the Bonanno Family Boss. He probably wondered what he had gotten himself into. Besides the fear of getting a bullet in the head, DiGregorio and his men's biggest problem was legal. District Attorneys, investigating various Bonanno events, served subpoenas all over New York. It wasn't long before a host of men from both sides were facing contempt charges. Some ended up in prison. DiGregorio dodged one legal document by rushing to the hospital with heart problems.

DiGregorio appointed Capo Peter Alfano as his Underboss, and the men elected veteran Capo Angelo Caruso as Consigliere. An illegal bug heard Capo Paul Sciacca estimate the size of the Family as 170-180 members. Interestingly Bill Bonanno wrote that there were 400 inducted men at this time. Later evidence suggests Sciacca was much closer to the actual number.

February 3, 1965

The illegal FBI bug in Boss Sam Decavalcante's office captured some conversations relevant to our DiGregorio discussion. A visiting Joe Zicarelli, a Bonanno Soldier, told Decavalcante that Bonanno loyalist Joe Notaro and John Morale were ready to join DiGregorio's Family. Decavalcante confirmed this prediction two days later, relating that Morale met DiGregorio and acknowledged him as the new Boss.

February 20, 1965

Officials served DiGregorio with a subpoena to appear before a grand jury. However, on the day he was to testify, doctors admitted him to Brunswick Hospital in Amityville, LI. A doctor's examination exempted DiGregorio from a second grand jury appearance as well.

November 14, 1965

DiGregorio held a wedding reception for his daughter Catherine at the Huntington Town House in Huntington Station Long Island. The FBI and other agencies monitored the event to see who attended.

April 13, 1966
Bonanno loyalists John Morale, Rosario Morale, Frank LaBruzzo, and Joe Notaro appeared before a grand jury investigating the Bonanno Family.

Late summer 1967
It was evident to all that DiGregorio didn't have the will nor the strength to finish off the Bonanno loyalists. He stepped down, and the Commission appointed Capo Paul Sciacca as the new leader. This move didn't work out very well, either.

1999
Bonanno hated DiGregorio for his betrayal but felt he was but a puppet to Buffalo's Stefano Magaddino. In his book "Bonanno Man of Honor," old Joe took every opportunity he could to badmouth the long-dead DiGregorio. It wasn't a class act. Below are some examples from his writings.

"Deliberate and fussy soldier."
"Gaspar most deliberate in leadership."
"Slow of thought."
"Weak."
"Ineptitude as a leader."
"Boy in many ways."
"Spendthrift."
"Squandered money on clothes, entertainment, cars, and gambling."

These comments make it clear that Bonanno hadn't forgiven DiGregorio decades later.

RESIDENCES

These dates do not reflect the entire time DiGregorio lived at these addresses.

1924
1653 Whiting Avenue, Niagara Falls, New York

A two-story stone residence with an attached garage. I am unsure if this is the original home on the lot.

1935-1940
59 Rodney Place, Rockville Center, NY.
A two-story building with white siding and an attached single garage.

1946
162 North Forrest Avenue, Rockville Center, NY.
A modest two-story home on a corner lot.

1962-1970
737 Fifth Street in West Babylon, LI.
A sided bungalow with a single attached garage.

June 11, 1970
DiGregorio battled lung cancer for a long time. His body finally gave out on June 11, 1970, in St. John's Hospital in Smithtown, Long Island. The family held a wake at the James Funeral Home in Massapequa, L I. A priest conducted funeral services at Philip and James Roman Catholic Church in St James.

PAUL SCIACCA

1910-1986

Next up to the plate was veteran mobster Paul Sciacca. Below are a few comments Joe Bonanno made about him in his book.

"A nobody."
"...a half figure. These are people who only show part of themselves. When the climate changes, they show another part of themselves. You never know where they stand."

We don't know when Joe Bonanno inducted Sciacca and who sponsored him. FBI lists of that group from 1963 and 1964 don't include Sciacca. This result indicates more about the early state of FBI mob investigation of La Cosa Nostra than Sciacca's status.

Below are some of the significant highlights of Sciacca's mob career. I've included information on other members who came into importance under Sciacca.

August 17, 1957
Police arrested Frank Mari on suspicion of burglary but quickly released him with no charges. His address was 124 Forsythe Street in New York.

November 28, 1958
Frank Mari was among a group of eight men charged with vagrancy. The police investigated the murder of dope pusher Joe Demarco and used the vagrancy count to hold the men. The police quickly released Mari. At the time, his address was 20 Monroe Street in Brooklyn.

1963
Joe Valachi identified Frank Mari as a Bonanno Family member. The official transcript of the Valachi Hearings included an extensive appendix profiling hundreds of Mafia hoods, including Mari. Below is a summary:

Frank Mari
Aliases: Frankie T, Frank Russo
Description: Born September 3, 1926, Scilla, Reggio Calabria, Italy; 5' 7", 185 pounds, brown hair and eyes, medium build, sharp dresser
Schizophrenic
Family background: Wife Mildred DiPietro (sister of narcotic violator Carli DiPietro); son Matthew, brother Rocco...
Criminal associates: Carmine Galante, Tony Lisi...
Criminal history: suspect in two murder investigations...
Business: no legitimate employment
Modus operandi: Large scale underworld narcotics trafficker obtains narcotics from ... who obtain their supply from the Cotronis in Montreal.

December 3, 1964
Since the October 1964 disappearance of Joe Bonanno, the feds had been looking for Mari. The New York Daily News featured his photograph among a group of "missing" people. Finally, they

found Mari and his son in a movie theatre where the feds served him with a grand jury subpoena for the next day.

The newspaper profile of Mari included the fact that he had nine arrests, including for two murders. Most of the arrests involved narcotics, but the article added there were no convictions for the mob Soldier.

January 12, 1965
Gaspare DiGregorio was the new Bonanno Boss. Sciacca was one of his Capos.

December 1, 1965
Sciacca and four other Bonanno Family members appeared before a grand jury investigating the 1964 disappearance of Joe Bonanno. It is unclear whether he testified, but he didn't face any contempt charges afterward.

July 13, 1966
Machine gun fire wounded Frank Mari three times, but he survived. A Bonanno gunman used the same weapon later in the infamous Cypress Gardens massacre described in the previous chapter.

September 14, 1967
Sciacca's son Anthony married Florence Rando, a niece of Frank Mari. The wedding took place at Brooklyn's Regina Paces Shrine with the reception at the Woodbury Country Club on Long Island.

October 31, 1967
An FBI report stated that the Commission had approved Sciacca as the new Bonanno Boss. The Family must have elected him earlier.

December 8, 1967
An FBI report said that Sciacca had recently promoted Mari to Underboss. If the report is correct, it meant that Sciacca had either demoted his original Underboss, Peter Croatia or permitted him to step down.

1968
The FBI released a list of Sciacca Capos. They are below.

Mike Adamo
Nick Alfano
Joe DeFilippo
Giovanni Fiordilino
Patsy Gigante (acting)
John Morale
Armando Pollastrino
Phil Rastelli
Dom Sabella
Mike Sabella
Sereno Tartamella
Joseph Arthur Zicarelli

March 4, 1968
Someone filled Sciacca's former Underboss, Peter Croatia, with six slugs, but he survived. I am not sure what to make of this attempted hit, but Croatia's brother was wounded later. Someone didn't like the Croatias.

March 11, 1968
Hitmen finished off Bonanno loyalist Sam "Hank" Perrone near his Brooklyn workplace, Bingo Warehouse and Trucking Company at 141 Leonard Street. Mobster talk suggested Frank Mari was involved, and the hit was a reprisal for the Croatia shooting. The fact that a witness to the Perrone killing aftermath identified two men from photos might be behind that story. The cops never charged Mari.

Perrone and his wife were close friends with Bill and Rosalie Bonanno. She was upset by his death. Below is a summary of their relationship from her book, "Mafia Marriage."

Bill had to return to Arizona to face tax charges. According to Perrone's wife, Bill had asked Hank to accompany him. Also, she said her husband felt the war was coming to an end, and he wanted to move to Arizona with the Bonannos. She refused for various reasons. So the Perrones stayed in Brooklyn, and the Sciacca side killed Hank. Rosalie Bonanno was upset by Perrone's death, plus the fact the Bonanno Family did not come to his widow's aid.

April 1, 1968
Killers finished off veteran Bonanno member Mike Consolo as he was walking near his home. He had recently gone over to the Sciacca side, angering the Bonanno loyalists. Consolo had spent time in Montreal back in the 1960s as part of Carmine Galante's crew.

May 1968
A judge sentenced Mari to three months in jail for the illegal possession of a gun.

April 16, 1968
Shooters attempted to kill Peter Croatia's brother Francisco in a club. Like his brother, Francisco survived.

August 25, 1964
The Nassau County DA and the NYPD conducted a raid on the home of Frank Mari. The officers found a large group of men there and arrested Phil Rastelli. The address was 3 Hilldale Drive, Searingtown, LI.

October 1968
The law required Sciacca to testify before a grand jury, but he didn't show. His lawyer informed the court that Sciacca was ill and in Mid Island Hospital in Bethpage.

May 10, 1969
Charles McHarry, in his New York Daily News "Talk of the Town" gossip column, wrote that Mari was the new Boss of the Bonanno Family. He said it was unofficial and described Mari as young, ambitious, and the kind of leader who got things done with a minimum of bone-crushing.

September 1969
Something went wrong with Mari's relationship with Boss Paul Sciacca. Probably the Daily New column didn't help. He and Consigliere Mike Adamo went missing and never reappeared alive or dead. Rumors suggested the two had plotted to overthrow Sciacca, but I have no evidence to support that theory. It does seem reasonable, however. Sciacca appointed Phil Rastelli as his

new Underboss, while the membership elected veteran Sereno Tartamella as Consigliere.

November 18, 1969
Justice Hyman Barshoy ordered Sciacca to testify despite his heart problems. A doctor would be available, but Sciacca still refused.

November 20, 1969
Justice Barshoy sentenced Sciacca to 30 days and a fine of $250 for contempt after refusing to testify before the grand jury. Barshoy released Sciacca pending his appeal.

1969
The Senate Permanent Subcommittee on Investigations named Sciacca as a prominent member of organized crime in New York.

1970
Some reports suggest that Sciacca, worn out by all the court cases, and publicity stepped down. The Family then selected veteran Capo Natale Evola as their new Boss.

June 11, 1970
DA Eugene Cold arrested 35 mobsters for criminal contempt before a grand jury investigating the mob and its infiltration of business. Among those detained were Sciacca, Underboss Rastelli, and Capo Natale Evola.

October 6, 1970
At a show cause hearing, Justice Barshoy ordered Sciacca to testify for 30 minutes, but he refused. Barshoy sentenced Sciacca to 30 days and a $250 fine but released the mobster pending an appeal. Eventually, the Court of Appeals rejected Sciacca's claim, and he did the 30 days.

December 17, 1970
Sciacca was in a Massapequa barbershop when he suffered a severe heart attack. An ambulance rushed him to the Mid Island Hospital, where doctors found him in critical condition. Sciacca was to appear before a grand jury the next day.

May 14, 1971
A federal grand jury alleged Sciacca and others ran a heroin conspiracy from June 1, 1970, until September 30, 1970. The indictment said they bought and sold 512 grams of heroin on September 11, 1970, and on other occasions. Judge Jacob Mishler released Sciacca on a $10,000 bond after he pled innocent. Nothing came of these charges.

Afterward
Sciacca faded away into the woodwork before passing away in August of 1986.

NATALE EVOLA

January 22, 1907-August 28, 1973

We met Evola earlier in this book when he was part of Bonanno's wedding party. He jumped out of the background in November 1957 when New York State Troopers identified him as attending the National Meeting at Joe Barbara's estate.

June 4, 1958
The authorities arrested Evola and 16 others for a vast heroin conspiracy. Among the big-name defendants was Genovese Family Boss Vito Genovese. Evola listed his address as 972 Bay Ridge Parkway in Brooklyn. Fortunately for Evola, Federal Judge Alexander Bicks released him on a $35,000 bond. One of the fugitives on this case was Carmine Galante, whom we'll meet later.

April 4, 1959
A jury convicted Evola, Vito Genovese, and others in the heroin conspiracy case.

April 17, 1959
Judge Alexander Bicks sentenced Evola to ten years and a $20,000 fine for his heroin conviction. Bicks released Evola on $50,000 bail while he appealed. When questioned by newsmen, Evola replied, "I rely upon my conscience."

December 18, 1959
A jury convicted Evola and 19 others for conspiracy to obstruct justice in the investigations into Apalachin.

January 14, 1960
Judge Irving Kaufman sentenced Evola to five years and a $10,000 fine for his obstruction of justice conviction. Kaufman freed Evola on $50,000 bail while he appealed.

November 28, 1960
The Second Court of Appeals threw out the Apalachin obstruction of justice convictions. They said there was not enough evidence to sustain the verdict.

1963
The appendix of the Valachi Hearings transcripts included a profile of Evola. Below is a summary.

Natale Joseph Evola
Alias: Joe Diamond
Description: Born January 22, 1907, in NYC. 5' 10" 190 pounds, brown eyes, gray hair, balding.
Localities frequented: Resided 972 Bay Ridge Parkway, Brooklyn. Frequented the garment center in New York.
Family Background: Single.
Criminal Associates: Salvatore Santoro, James Plumeri...
Business: Owner of Belmont Garment Delivery and Amity Garment Delivery (both at 240 W 37th Street, NYC.)
Modus Operandi: He is a major narcotics trafficker and labor racketeer in the garment center.

January 12, 1965
The Commission confirmed Gaspar DiGregorio as Boss. Evola continued as a Capo.

March 1, 1965
The Second Court of Appeals refused the appeals for a new trial from Evola, Genovese, and others.

October 31, 1967
The Commission approved Natale Evola as the Bonanno Family Boss.

September 1969
A judge convicted Evola of contempt for refusing to testify before a Brooklyn grand jury investigating the Bonanno War.

January 2, 1970
Evola began serving his contempt of court sentence from September 1969.

January 5, 1970
Once again, a judge sentenced Evola to 30 days for contempt before a grand jury.

January 15, 1970
Evola began serving his latest 30 days contempt sentence.

January 29, 1970
The New York State Rackets Investigation organization served Evola with a subpoena while in jail on a previous contempt sentence.

February 6, 1970
Evola appeared before the Joint Legislative Committee on Crime. In their subpoena, the Committee had ordered Evola to produce the Garment Delivery Company and the Ecco Truck Company books. He did not do so, claiming they may incriminate him. The chairman called their counsel to subpoena the two businesses' executives and require them to bring the books on February 12. They directed Evola to return then as well.

Evola's refusal to answer questions angered the Committee. As a result, they ordered counsel to subpoena the records of seven other businesses connected to Evola. The mob Boss declined to respond to whether he had gained control of these companies by lending their hard-pressed owners money at loanshark rates. When they couldn't pay, he took the companies as collateral.

June 11, 1970
District Attorney Eugene Gold's men arrested Evola for criminal contempt for refusing to testify before a grand jury. It had indicted a total of 46 men for refusing to testify about mob infiltration of legitimate businesses.

October 17, 1972
DA Eugene Gold had previously bugged a construction trailer that served as Lucchese Capo Paul Vario's HQ. On this date, at a press conference, Gold announced a grand jury would begin investigating the mob's infiltration of legitimate businesses. They would start within a week, and Evola would be one of the first witnesses. Gold's men had observed Evola visiting Vario's trailer on numerous occasions.

October 25, 1972
Evola appeared before Gold's grand jury but asked for more time to prepare. Gold granted the request but indicated he wouldn't tolerate any attempt to delay.

December 1972
The New York Times carried a report that Carlo Gambino was leading a move to eliminate the Bonanno, Lucchese, and Colombo Families by rolling their members into the Gambino or Genovese Families. Eventually, Gambino wanted to end up with one Family.

There had been some discussions of such a move, but I believe it had more to do with frustration rather than seriousness. During the Bonanno War, leaders like Gambino wished for an end to the hostilities and publicity. The mess seemed to go on forever. Then the Colombo Family erupted with the return of the Gallo problem in the early 1970s. Tommy Lucchese died in 1967, and his Family struggled to regain its footing. It's no wonder bugs, and informers picked up some talk of this amalgamation plan. Nothing ever came of all this hot air.

February 6, 1973
Famous columnist Victor Riesel stirred up conversations with his national column on this date. Citing unnamed law enforcement sources, Riesel claimed that Joe Bonanno was the real Boss of the Family and that Evola was Bonanno's Acting Boss in New York.

Also, the columnist predicted that Bonanno and Evola would make a joint move on California rackets.

This report was nonsense. I will address the matter in a later chapter related to Bonanno's life after he left New York.

Evola Businesses
His level of ownership is unknown, but he had total control of each enterprise. They operated in the garment center in Manhattan.

Everready Trucking, which became Belmont Garment Trucking.
Belmont Delivery, Inc., also known as Mercury Delivery.
Felsen Rosemere Trucking
Amity Trucking
Charles Kein Corp.
Trinity Trucking Corp.
Milton Feinberg Trucking.
Henat Clothing Company.

THE EVOLA END

Evola slowly faded away in 1973 as cancer robbed him of energy. He finally died on August 28, 1973. His reign had been plagued, not by internal dissent, but by endless subpoenas and several contempt sentences. The lawyers must have made tons of money protecting his rights. Evola regularly appeared in the papers, probably making him wish for the days before Apalachin. Even before he passed, aspirants to his throne were making their moves. Phil Rastelli had a long Mafia resume to support his candidacy. I'll profile him next along with his rival, Carmine Galante.

CHAPTER TEN

Rastelli vs. Galante

In the 1970s, these two heavyweights would struggle for control of the Bonanno Family. It would end in a legendary hit that became part of the 1986 Commission Case. The profiles of these two men will run together in the hopes of avoiding too much confusion. There will be a ton of facts, but you can quickly skip over them.

February 21, 1910
Camello Galante was born in New York City.

January 31, 1918
Philip Rastelli was born in New York City.

August 1930
Police arrested Galante for attempted robbery in which officer Walter De Castillo died. They released him later.

December 24, 1930
Police wounded Galante in an attempted robbery of the Liebman Brewery. They testified that he fired four shots at a police sergeant. Later a jury found Galante guilty and sentenced him to a long term.

January 31, 1931
A doctor labeled Galante as neuropathic and psychopathic after tests in Sing Sing prison.

July 19, 1938
A doctor labeled Galante a psychopath in Clinton Prison.

May 1, 1939
Prison officials at Sing Sing released Galante. He had served eight years for the Liebman Brewery robbery attempt in 1930. The parole board required Galante to make regular appearances at their office.

1939-July 1940.
Galante claimed to work at Lubin Artificial Flowers in NYC.

July 1940-Feb 1941
Galante reported he worked part-time at Lubin Artificial Flowers.

February 3, 1941-September 15, 1941
Galante claimed to have been a longshoreman, local 856.

September 15, 1941-May 11, 1942
Galante said he worked at General Electric Plating, NYC.

THE CARLO TRESCA HIT

January 11, 1943

At approximately 8 PM, Galante reported to his parole office at 80 Center Street in NYC as scheduled. The supervisor felt the gangster was nervous and detailed two investigators to follow him for the rest of the evening. Much to their surprise, Galante jumped into a waiting car and took off. The agents took down the plate number for a person on parole was not supposed to be using a vehicle.

Around 9:40 PM that evening, a short, squat gunman killed firebrand activist Carlo Tresca as he left his office. The killer fled in a vehicle, which the police found abandoned at the 18th Street entrance to the 7th Avenue Subway. They could find no fingerprints on or in the car, which raised suspicions further.

Note:
I subscribe to Allan Block's theory that Bonanno Consigliere, John Tartamella, ordered the hit after a personal confrontation with Tresca. Tartamella was heavily involved with unions in the garment center, a pet peeve of Tresca. The writer had threatened to expose Tartamella's connections. If this theory is correct and Tartamella followed mob protocol, Joe Bonanno approved the murder.

January 11. 1943
The two parole officers read newspaper accounts of the Tresca hit and they noticed the part about the abandoned car and its plate number. It was the same as the one on the vehicle Galante drove away in the evening of the murder.

January 13, 1943
The parole officers took police to Galante's regular haunts. They found and arrested him as he exited an Elizabeth Street restaurant in lower Manhattan. The lawmen questioned Galante for many hours, but he denied getting in any car and had an alibi for later that evening. They locked him up as a parole violator.

Over the next few days, police discovered that a man, not Galante, had purchased the hit car from Cornfield Motors for $300. He put on his own plates and drove away. They also discovered a loaded .38 pistol in a garbage can opposite a second entrance from the Tresca building. Their theory was that another shooter waited there in case Tresca exited from that door.

February 5, 1943
Galante's lawyers presented Justice Philip J McCook with a writ of habeas corpus requiring jail officials to bring Galante to court and explain why they held him. McCook adjourned for about a week.

February 11, 1943
Justice Peter Schmuck dismissed Galante's habeas corpus writ. He was satisfied the parole officials had enough grounds to detain Galante.

April 29, 1943
Rastelli registered for the draft.

December 21, 1944
Officials released Galante from Clinton Prison.

February 10, 1945
Galante married Helen Marullo. Eventually, they had a son and two daughters.

September 10, 1949
Rastelli married Concette Pietrafesa in Brooklyn.

December 15, 1950
Police arrested Galante for gambling in NYC.

RASTELLI DODGES A BULLET

December 3, 1953
Police found Michael Russo wounded on 56th Road near 48th Street. He told the cops Philip Rastelli shot him. Later investigations showed that Russo had backed out of a robbery plan, which angered his partners.

December 1953
Police questioned Rastelli in the wounding of Michael Russo. Rastelli said he knew nothing.

Date unknown
Russo testified before a grand jury and identified Philip Rastelli as the man who shot him.

December 11, 1954
Mrs. Michael Russo later claimed that Connie Rastelli made her last attempt to bribe her husband not to testify about his December 3, 1953 shooting.

December 12, 1954
Shooters kill Michael Russo.

December 13, 1954
A judge released Connie Rastelli (43) on $50,000 bail after being charged with attempting to bribe Michael Russo several times since her husband wounded him in December of 1953. She lived at 59-39 58th Drive-in Maspeth, Queens.

GALANTE IN CANADA

February 26, 1954
The RCMP later related that Galante officially entered Canada on this date.

1955
Galante opened the Bonfire restaurant with Montreal Mafia leader Louis Greco and gangster Harry Ship. At the time, Galante resided at 4069 Dorchester Street in Montreal.

October 10, 1955
Police arrested Galante, and the court fined him $5 for being involved in a dice game. Corruption was rampant in Montreal during that era.

April 30, 1956
According to a much later report by the New York State Crime Commission, Canadian officials deported Galante as an undesirable.

Note:
Canada never deported Galante despite decades of accounts saying so. He left on his own accord. They did put him on a "watch list," which would have prevented his admittance. However, officials did grant Galante permission to enter Canada later to attend to business. Canadian officials took this step to allow the RCMP to monitor his activities in Montreal. They turned down a second request.

GALANTE'S DRIVING CAUSES PROBLEMS

Oct 17, 1956

The Arlington Hotel in Binghamton, NY, hosted Galante, John Bonventre, and Frank Garofalo on this day. (The latter two were former Underbosses for Bonanno.) Joe Barbara's Canada Dry Bottling company picked up the tab. Galante probably had attended the National Meeting of La Cosa Nostra at Joe Barbara's estate that Bonanno mentioned in his book.

Oct 18, 1956

New York State Trooper F W Leibe stopped a car for speeding on Route 17, near Windsor, NY. The vehicle had New Jersey plates, and Carmine Galante was driving, but he produced a license in the name of Joe DiPalermo. The Trooper quickly saw that the driver did not match the license description. He told the passengers to follow him as he drove Galante to the Vestal Trooper station. However, they took off. Galante had $1,815 in cash and a card bearing Joseph Falcone's name and address, 519 Beecker Street, Utica, NY. The Trooper locked Galante up.

October 19, 1956

Recently retired Underboss Frank Garofalo appeared at the Vestal station with lawyer Remi Aloi. Later investigations determined that the third man in the Galante car was Bonanno's first Underboss, John Bonventre.

Officials arraigned Galante before Windsor Justice of the Peace Richard Klausner, who indicated that Galante would probably do jail time for driving with a suspended license. He released Galante on $600 bail.

November 9, 1956

Galante finally gave up efforts to pressure the court and pled guilty to three charges. The judge gave him a $100 fine for speeding, 30 days for driving with a suspended license, and a $50 fine and a 15 day suspended sentence for the unauthorized use of another person's driving license.

January 1-January 8, 1958
Galante was the subject of the NJ Law Enforcement Council hearing.

Jan 9, 1958
Galante failed to appear before a special grand jury.

GALANTE AND DRUGS

July 1958
Case 1
A grand jury indicted Galante, Boss Vito Genovese, and others in a heroin case. Authorities arraigned Galante and released him on bail of $100,000. Galante then went into hiding.

June 1, 1959 (late in the evening)
Case 1
NJ State Troopers and Bureau of Narcotics agents arrested Galante in a white convertible on the Garden State Parkway. Angelo Presenzano and Anthony Macaluso were with him. Galante had been hiding out at 212 Sunset Drive in Pelican Island, NJ. Gary Muscatello owned the place and claimed to have rented it to an unknown man.

Drug agents questioned Galante all night at the Holmdel State Police barracks. They then transferred Galante to Newark Police HQ before bringing him to New York.

June 3, 1959
Case 1
Authorities arraigned Galante in a courtroom in New York. A drug agent described Galante as "The biggest dope peddler in the country." Judge Sylvester J Ryan released him on $100,000 bail.

June 4, 1959
Case 1
A picture of Galante's arraignment appeared in the New York Herald.

May 6, 1960
Case 2
Authorities released a secret narcotics indictment that included Galante and 29 others. This indictment was the second one for Galante.

May 17, 1960
Case 2
Galante turned himself into Assistant US Attorney William N Tendy. Drug Agents took him to their HQ at 90 Church Street, NY, for questioning. Finally, the US Attorney arraigned Galante before Judge F X McGohey. Galante pled not guilty, and the judge set a trial date in June. They held Galante in custody.

September 26, 1960
Case 2
A judge finally released Galante on bail after some paperwork allowed his freedom on the same $100,000 posted for his first case.

November 3, 1960
Case 2
Galante's narcotic trial started.

January 30, 1961
Case 2
The judge revoked Galante's bail after the prosecution alleged he made threats.

February 7, 1961
Case 2
Galante lost the appeal of his bail revocation.

May 15, 1961
Case 2
The judge declared a mistrial in the Galante case because the jury foreman was injured, leaving only 11 jurors. The trial had been running for about six months.

Foreman Harry Appel, 68, fell down some cellar steps in an abandoned building. Police and the court were highly suspicious that there was more to the story. Nothing came of their concerns.

June 2, 1961
Case 2
A judge released Galante on $135,000 bail.

June 19, 1961
Case 1
A judge ordered Galante to appear on July 13, 1961 for his first drug case trial.

June 30, 1961
Case 2
Defendants from Galante's drug case mistrial appeared in court to set a new trial date. Several defendants claimed they couldn't find a lawyer.

RASTELLI'S MARRIAGE PROBLEM

December 18, 1961
Concetta Rastelli shot and wounded her husband Philip in a Brooklyn bar. Both were arrested and released after police charged Philip Rastelli with possession of a gun.

January 1962.
Before this date, Rastelli spent time living in Montreal at 4120 St Catherine Street.

February 9, 1962
A judge dismissed Rastelli's gun charge from the December 18/19, 1962 shooting incident with his wife.

March 4, 1962
Concetta Rastelli was shot five times and killed in her hallway at 77 North Seventh Street, Brooklyn. Police never charged anyone, but the prime suspect behind the hit had to be Philip Rastelli.

GALANTE'S DRUG RETRIAL

April 2, 1962
Case 2
Galante's retrial finally started before Judge Lloyd F MacMahon.

June 4, 1962
Case 2
Defendant Anthony Mirra threw a chair at the Deputy District Attorney while Mirra was testifying. He later got a year in prison for this outburst. On another occasion, a defendant went into the jury box and pushed some jurors around.

June 12, 1962
Case 2
Miss Frances Kahn, Galante's lawyer, fell and injured herself, requiring hospitalization.

June 18, 1962
Case 2
Galante's second lawyer suffered a heart attack and couldn't continue. Galante eventually hired his third lawyer.

June 25, 1962
Case 2
The jury found Galante and the other twelve defendants guilty.

July 10, 1962
Case 2
Judge MacMahon sentenced Galante to 20 years and had him imprisoned immediately. There would be no bail while he appealed. The same for the others convicted. MacMahon was furious with the defendant's behavior in court, claiming they were attempting to obtain a mistrial or force mistakes they could appeal.

June 29, 1962
Case 2
The US Attorney charged Israel Schwartzberg, the secretary to Galante's first lawyer, Frances Kahn, with obstruction of justice. When Galante's third lawyer took over, he needed documents

that Schwartzberg had. But the secretary couldn't be found until the trial finished.

April 19, 1963,
An informant told the FBI that Rastelli attended a Bonanno Family meeting in the Wentworth Hotel sometime in 1963. The event was attended by Capos and other highly placed members, according to the informant. The FBI report provided no specific date for the gathering but other evidence nailed it down.

June 13, 1963
Case 2
Four defendants in the Galante trial received new trials, but not Galante.

1964
Rastelli married Canadian Irene McKee sometime this year.

February 5, 1965
An illegal bug of Boss Sam Decavalcante heard him say that Carlo Gambino complained about Bill Bonanno grabbing $150 grand from Bonanno guys in Montreal that belonged to Galante.

May 8, 1965
Rastelli was involved in a traffic accident on Woodhaven Blvd with two women passengers. One woman, Caroline Minkus (29), was thrown from the vehicle and killed. The car Rastelli was driving hit an abutment.

December 1, 1965
An informant told the FBI that Rastelli was now with the DiGregorio faction and was allied with Pollastrino, who held considerable authority.

January 5, 1970
A judge sentenced Rastelli to 30 days for contempt before a grand jury.

February 5, 1970
Rastelli began serving his 30-day contempt sentence.

February 28, 1970
The New York Times reported that the Commission had placed three men in charge of the Bonanno Family. The three were; Evola, Rastelli, and Joe DiFilippo.

June 30, 1970
Nassau District Attorney William Cahn charged Rastelli with criminal contempt for refusing to testify before a grand jury. A judge released him on $2,500 bail.

July 20, 1971
A grand jury indicted Rastelli and others on conspiracy to conduct loansharking and loansharking charges. Judge Pierre Lundberg set bail at $50,000 for Rastelli.

July 23, 1971
Rastelli's lawyer bailed him out of jail on the loansharking charges.

February 4, 1972
An informant told the FBI that Evola was Boss, Rastelli was the Underboss, and Nick Marangello was the Consigliere.

September 20, 1972
An informer told the FBI that Rastelli's former wife, Irene McKee, lived in Ottawa and had nothing to do with Rastelli.

December 18, 1972
Rastelli attended the wake of a sister-in-law.

December 29, 1972
A Suffolk County jury convicted Rastelli et al. of loansharking and loansharking conspiracy in Suffolk County. The judge continued the five men on bail while they appealed.

January 14, 1973
The New York Daily News carried a story provided by an anonymous officer in the NYPD public morals squad. It said Rastelli was the behind-the-scenes owner of the "Zoo," a popular after-hours discotheque at 305 East 60th Street.

February 5, 1973
A judge sentence Rastelli to four years in Suffolk County for his loansharking convictions, but he let Rastelli out on $85,000 bail pending an appeal result.

March 23, 1973
Rastelli pled guilty to contempt charges in Nassau County.

April 12, 1973
A judge handed Rastelli six months for criminal contempt of a Nassau County grand jury. He immediately began serving his sentence.

April 23, 1973
A District Attorney charged Rastelli with extortion concerning mobile lunch wagons.

Mid-Sept 1973
Jail officials released Rastelli from his six-month criminal contempt sentence in Nassau County.

RASTELLI IS BOSS

November 1973
After extensive lobbying of the Capos by Rastelli, they elected him as their new Boss to replace the deceased Natale Evola.

December 6, 1973
Rastelli lost his loansharking appeal. He decided to go further to the Appellate Court of NY State.

GALANTE FREE

January 24, 1974
Atlanta Prison officials released Galante on parole. He served 12 years of the 20 handed down for his heroin conspiracy conviction. With Galante free, Rastelli was suddenly under threat.

February 12, 1974
Rastelli held a lengthy meeting with Underboss Nicholas Marangello in Brooklyn at a luncheonette at 503 Grand Street.

March 7, 1974
Shooters killed Rastelli's stepson, James Fernandez (41) of Williamsburg. He ran a gambling operation for Rastelli. Many have speculated that this hit was a warning blow from Galante, but I have yet to see serious evidence to support that theory. It's reasonable, however.

March 14, 1974
Marangello met with Rastelli at 503 Grand Street at the luncheonette. Marangello later went to the Italian American Veterans Club at 45 Madison Street.

March 28, 1974
The NY Daily News carried a story predicting a war when Galante began asserting his power.

August 20, 1974
Rastelli's father died. The family held a wake for the next two days.

August 23, 1974
St Margaret's Church in Brooklyn was the site of Rastelli's father's funeral.

September 5, 1974
An FBI report speculated that Underboss Nick Marangello might take over as Acting Boss when prison officials released him in about four months and when Rastelli went to prison.

September 6, 1975
An informant told the FBI that both Rastelli and Galante were in "Humperdinks," a club owned by John Gotti. The report said Galante and Gotti knew each other from prison.

September 9, 1974
Galante appeared before a federal grand jury in the SDNY, but he refused to answer any questions.

December 9, 1975
According to an FBI report, Rastelli's second wife, Irene McKee, was deceased.

RASTELLI HAS A SERIOUS LEGAL PROBLEM

March 5, 1975
For nearly a decade, Rastelli controlled the Workmen's Mobile Lunch Association, a lucrative racket. Owners of the trucks that visited construction sites and industries dispensing food and cigarettes paid a weekly fee. In turn, the Association guaranteed them a monopoly on their stops. But the vendors would have to purchase their food from certain outlets, which also had to pay a fee or were controlled by mobsters. Any renegade lunch truck owner might find his vehicle trashed. Complaints about this type of violence led to a three-year probe by lawmen. (Similar monopolies existed in garbage collection, garment center trucking, and the like.)

On March 5, 1975, a federal grand jury indicted Rastelli, his nephew Louis Rastelli, Anthony DeStefano, and Carl Petrole in a lunch wagon extortion scam as described above.

March 6, 1975
Police arrested Rastelli in the extortion case then Federal Judge Thomas C Platt released him on a personal bond of $50,000. His current address was 473 Vandervout Ave. Rastelli claimed to make a living by renting a truck to CAI Trucking for $200 a week. Interestingly Rastelli told the court that he was divorced about ten years previously in Mexico. That must have been his second wife, Canadian Irene McKee.

March 16, 1975
Someone found Rastelli's nephew Louis Rastelli shot to death with a .357 Magnum in his lap. There was no evidence of foul play. It was probably a suicide, although I have never seen his death certificate.

March 27-April 4, 1975
Galante traveled to Florida for some reason.

March 31, 1975
An FBI report labeled Galante as the Boss of the Bonanno Family.

April 2, 1975
Police arrested Galante for failure to register as a felon in Florida. The court released him on a $500 bond. It is a good bet that the FBI provided the tip for the Florida officers.

June 6, 1975
Rastelli lost the last appeal of his loansharking conviction.

June 28, 1975
Galante's daughter Mary Lou married Craig Tobiano. The reception was at the Pierre Hotel in Manhattan.

July 8, 1975
Rastelli began serving a four-year sentence for loansharking. Reportedly his brothers Carmine, Marty, and soldier Joe Massino passed messages for him.

August 19, 1975
According to an FBI report, two informants claimed that Rastelli was still the Boss despite being in prison. Two other informants said Galante was either Boss or Acting Boss.

January 12, 1976
Jury selection began in the Rastelli lunch wagon trial.

April 23, 1976
A jury convicted Rastelli, Anthony DeStefano, and Gary Petrole in the lunch wagon racket. The latter two were to be sentenced on June 25, 1976, while Rastelli's sentence date was August 27, 1976.

August 1976
Galante bought a home for daughter Mary Lou for $60,000 at Tulip Ave and Wakeman Road in Hampton Bays, Long Island.

August 27, 1976
At his sentencing hearing, Rastelli made a desperate plea for leniency by saying, "At no time did I think I was doing anything wrong." Judge Platt sentenced the mob Boss to ten years and a

$50,000 fine. (One year for the anti-trust violation, ten years for each of three Hobbs Act violations, all the sentences are to run concurrently.

Underboss Nick Marangello took charge of IBT Local 814 in Rastelli's absence.

GALANTE EMERGES

November 4, 1976
A shooter killed veteran Capo Pietro Licata with seven shotgun slugs in Middle Village Queens after he parked his 74 Caddy. Later events strongly suggested that Galante's men were the culprits.

February 22, 1977
Three New York papers ran stories on the emerging power of Galante. Later we learned the FBI planted these to stir up trouble.

March 7, 1977
Time Magazine ran a story on how three New York papers had named Galante as the new "Boss of Bosses."

April 1977
Galante traveled to Dallas to visit someone.

July 31, 1977
Galante fell down some stairs. He visited Hampton Hospital.

August 22-August 26, 1977
Galante was in Miami for reasons unknown.

August 23, 1977
Galante appeared before a Federal Grand Jury in Miami. He asserted his Fifth Amendment rights and didn't testify.

August 24, 1977
In Miami, a judge ordered Galante to testify, but he refused. The court convicted him of civil contempt, gave a sentence of no

more than 18 months, and then freed Galante on a $50,000 bond pending appeal.

September 30, 1977: 2:20-3:30
Galante was in a social club at 1657 Bath Ave Brooklyn.

October 5, 1977
The US Parole Commission issued a warrant for Galante's arrest for associating with known criminals.

October 11, 1977
Galante's lawyers told the New York Daily News that Galante felt that "All these stories about the Mafia and the Godfather are a creation of the media..." Galante then surrendered to US Marshalls on the parole violation.

October 14, 1977
A judge held a bail hearing on Galante's parole violation but rejected his bid.

October 20, 1977
Galante won the appeal of his conviction for civil contempt before a grand jury in Miami.

Oct 30, 1977
In 2004 Capo Frank Lino became a government witness. He said a member introduced Galante as their Boss on October 30, 1977. Then Galante inducted new members Frank Lino, Baldo Amato, Cesar Bonventre, and Joey D'Amico.

December 9, 1977
Galante lost his appeal of the refusal to release him on bail back on October 14, 1977.

December 14, 1977
Galante had his final hearing on his parole revocation.

May 3, 1978
US Parole Commission rules Galante must serve the rest of his narcotic sentence that ended in 1982.

October 25, 1978
The NY Post carried an article that said someone was planning to hit Galante in prison.

November 13, 1978
Time Magazine carried a story on how someone planned to kill Galante in prison.

December 9, 1978
Galante appeared before an Eastern District of New York grand jury but refused to testify.

February 27, 1979
A Federal Judge ordered the release of Galante from the federal prison in Milan, Michigan, where he served time for his parole violation.

March 1, 1979
Galante was released from Milan prison and arrived in Newark.

March 7, 1979
Galante briefly went back to jail on some misunderstanding over his parole release.

March 23, 1979
The US Parole Commission failed to meet a new hearing deadline in the Galante matter. The judge released Galante on $50,000 bail.

June 5, 1979
Nassau County detectives arrested Cesar Bonventre and Baldo Amato at the Greenhaven Mall in Massapequa. The two had been driving Bonventre's 1974 blue Caddy when stopped. Inside the vehicle, the detectives found a loaded .38 Smith and Wesson five-shot pistol, a loaded .38 Colt, a switchblade, two woolen masks, a plastic Halloween mask, two pairs of rubber gloves, and extra bullets.

GALANE'S END

July 12, 1979

By July of 1979, the factions loyal to Boss Phil Rastelli had all their ducks in order. Rastelli had successfully petitioned the Commission for permission to whack out usurper Galante. It was only a matter of time, but Galante seemed unaware of how serious the conflict had become.

The would-be mob Boss went to Joe and Mary's little restaurant at 205 Knickerbocker Avenue in the Bushwick section of Brooklyn. After a brief talk with the owner's aged mother, Galante went out to the small back patio for lunch. The owner, Giuseppe Turano, joined him, as did Capo Leonard Coppola. A few minutes later, Galante's two bodyguards, Cesar Bonventre and Baldo Amato arrived wearing zipped up leather jackets in the 87-degree heat.

Galante was sitting at a long table facing the back of the restaurant. On his right was Bonventre with Amato to his left. Opposite Bonventre was Coppola. Owner Turano perched at the end of the table near Amato.

Around 2:45 PM, three masked men quickly entered the restaurant from Knickerbocker Avenue and headed for the patio. When one of the owner's children screamed a warning, the third gunman, Dominic "Big Trin" Trinchera, peeled off and wounded the young man in a storeroom. Russell Mauro stepped out onto the patio and unloaded his shotgun into Galante. Bruno Indelicato blasted owner Turano with his shotgun. Simultaneously Bonventre stood up and fired six shots from his semi-automatic into Coppola sitting across the table. Mauro fired another blast into Galante while Indelicato fired his shotgun into the prone Coppola's head.

The three gunmen fled out the door and towards a waiting sedan. Its driver, Santo Giordano, had been standing by the driver's door menacing any passing pedestrians with his rifle. All four jumped into the vehicle and took off. During their exit, the daughter of the owner had peaked out onto the patio, and she saw Amato crouching behind an overturned chair clutching a pistol. He and Bonventre quickly followed the three shooters out onto the street and disappeared.

There were a series of blocking vehicles in the area to ensure the hit car escaped. Among the hoods backing up the shooters were Capo Phil Giaccone, Capo Alphonse "Sonny Red" Indelicato, J P Indelicato, and others.

Not long after the hit, the NYPD filmed Bruno Indelicato as he arrived, by car, at the Ravenite Social Club in Little Italy. His father, Sonny Red, Phil

Giaccone, Consigliere Steve Cannone, and others met him on the sidewalk offering congratulations. Then Cannone went into the Ravenite to inform Gambino Underboss Aniello Dellacroce of their success. Prosecutors used this film at the famous 1986 Commission trial to help prove the Commission sanctioned the Galante killing.

At the murder scene police recovered shell casings from three guns; a .45 semi-automatic, two .38 semi-automatics, and shotgun shells. Mauro and Indelicato fired shotguns, and Trinchera shot the owner's son with a pistol. This evidence means the other shell casings were from guns fired by Bonventre and Amato. The fact that police found shell casings over a wire fence to the right of where Bonventre was sitting supports that conclusion.

Note:

A newspaper account stated that police were looking for veteran Bonanno mobster Angelo "Little Mo" Presenzano. They believed he was at the Galante lunch before the shooting. Readers may recall that NJ State Troopers arrested Presenzano with Galante and another man on June 1, 1959. At the time, Galante was on the run from an indictment. Capo Presenzano died of natural causes on July 20, 1979.

Galante's life was over, but his rival Rastelli continued to pull strings from his prison cell. The next chapter will continue that saga. Bodies will continue to drop.

CHAPTER ELEVEN

Drug Celebration

November 16, 1980
Manhattan's Hotel Pierre ballroom was the site of the wedding
reception for Sicilian Boss Giuseppe Bono. Among the hundreds
of guests were some of importance to this book. Their significance
will become apparent as the chapter develops, but it is safe to say
these guys were all familiar with drug dealing. The list is below.

Vito Rizzuto, Joe LoPresti, Gerlando Sciascia, Phil Giaccone, Dominick
Trinchera, Frank Lino, Bruno Indelicato, Joseph Indelicato, Sal Catalano,
Santo Giordano, Cesar Bonventre, and Baldo Amato.

Mid-Summer 1977

DONNIE BRASCO ENTERS

Undercover FBI Agent Joe Pistone, under the name "Donnie Brasco,"
moved his attentions from a Colombo Family crew to Bonanno Soldier
Anthony "Tony" Mirra. Gradually Brasco moved into the orbit of Soldier
Benjamin "Lefty" Ruggiero. It would be a long and dangerous ride for the

next five years. He tells the story in the book "Donnie Brasco," which I recommend for anyone interested in more detail than I provide.

RASTELLI CHALLENGED

A section of the Bonanno Family was not content with their lot after Carmine Galante's killing in 1979. With Rastelli languishing in prison, these men chafed under the direction of his surrogates. Several sit-downs took place between the two factions, but a deal remained elusive. Capo Joey Massino consulted the Commission about the long-running problem, but they initially urged more negotiations.

The core of the dissidents was composed of four Capos; Dominick "Big Trin" Trinchera, Phil "Phil Lucky" Giaccone, Anthony "Bruno" Indelicato, and the leader Alphonse "Sonny Red" Indelicato. All of these men were veterans of mob intrigue and participated in the whacking of Galante. They were also very ambitious and greedy.

In late April 1981, a member from another Family informed the Rastelli loyalists that the Indelicato group were collecting weapons. When Massino informed the Commission that it looked like the rebels were preparing to attack, they told him to defend themselves. In other words, they gave the OK to kill the insurgents.

May 4, 1981
Tony Mirra, a violent soldier and nephew of Capo Al "Al Walker" Emberatto decided to side with the Indelicato faction. He would pay dearly for this and other mess-ups later.

THE THREE CAPOS HIT

May 5, 1981
The Rastelli loyalists invited the Indelicato group for yet another peace meeting on 13th Avenue in Brooklyn. Trinchera, Giaccone, Sonny Red Indelicato, and Soldier Frank Lino went into the social club's basement room. Waiting there were; Underboss Joey Massino, Soldier Sal Vitale, Capo Gerlando Sciascia, Soldier Giovanni Ligammari, Capo Bayonne Joe Zicarelli, Soldier Santo

Giordano, Capo Nicholas "Nick the Battler" DiStefano, and a few others.

At a signal from Sciascia, three Canadians and Sal Vitale sprung from a closet. All wore masks with Vitale carrying a machine gun, Soldier Vito Rizzuto and Soldier Emanuele Ragusa with pistols, and aged Soldier Dominic Manno lugging a shotgun. The shooters killed the three Capos, but Soldier Frank Lino made a miraculous escape.

Associate Duane "Goldie" Leisenheimer pulled up in a van and drove Zicarelli and DiStefano away. The Dominick "Sonny Black" Napolitano crew, including James Tartaglione, Anthony Rabito, and John Cerasani, wrapped the three corpses in blankets and dumped them in a second van. Years later, Tartaglione testified he followed the van containing the three to Woodward Street. A John Gotti crew met the vehicle, and they buried the bodies. Massino et al. had wiped out the opposition to Rastelli's rule in one stroke.

A wayward shot struck conspirator Santo Giordano in the side, and his buddies had to haul him away. They first went to a Giordano uncle's apartment, where a doctor came over to take care of the wounded man. However, his injuries were too severe, and they took him to Wyckoff Heights Hospital. Giordano ended up paralyzed from the waist down.

May 6, 1981
The day after the hits, the FBI set up surveillance on the Capri Motel at 555 Hutchinson River Parkway in the Bronx. They were able to snap pictures of Massino, Sciascia, Rizzuto, and Ligammari leaving the building. The four hoods had been resting up after their successful murder plot the evening before. An informant certainly tipped the agents to the gathering spot. These photos would come in handy more than twenty years later.

May 11, 1981
Mrs. Phil Giaccone reported her husband missing to the police.

May 14, 1981
Capo Dominick "Sonny Black," Napolitano told undercover agent Donnie Brasco about the three hits. He also ordered Brasco to

find and kill Capo Anthony "Bruno" Indelicato. The latter's father had prevented Bruno from attending the May 5 meeting just in case it was a setup. Lucky!

OOPS!

May 24, 1981
Children playing in an empty lot at the corner of Ruby and Blake Street in East Brooklyn found an arm sticking out of the ground. The arm had a tattoo of two hearts and a dagger and another that said, Holland 1945, Dad.

The police dug out the body covered in a rough blanket tied with a rope. The victim wore an orange t-shirt, brown pants, and cowboy boots. Three days later, the coroner identified the body as the missing Alphonse "Sonny Red" Indelicato. There was one bullet in the head and two in the body.

THE CAT'S OUT OF THE BAG

July 24, 1981
Three FBI Agents visited Capo Dominick "Sonny Black" Napolitano at his Motion Lounge in Brooklyn. They showed him a picture of the three of them with Joe "Donnie Brasco" Pistone, the undercover agent who had successfully penetrated the Bonanno Family. Napolitano played dumb.

When the Agents left, Napolitano called in his crew, and they began trying to find Brasco to no avail. Napolitano finally told Boss Santo Trafficante of Tampa because he had met Brasco. Then Napolitano passed on the bad news to Boss Rastelli and Boss Paul Castellano of the Gambino Family. It must have been a shock to all of them. Rumors began floating around that the Mafia had put a price on Pistone's head. Visits by FBI Agents to the Bosses quickly put an end to that supposed plan.

Despite the extreme jeopardy Napolitano was in; he didn't run. It is impossible to tell what he was thinking. Perhaps he had delusions that he could talk his way out of the mess of allowing an undercover agent to get so close to him. The Romantics believe Napolitano knew he was doomed but soldiered on regardless.

SONNY BLACK IS FINISHED

August 14, 1981

Capo Frank Lino drove Napolitano and Consigliere Steve "Stevie Beef" Cannone to Associate Ron Filocommo's father's Staten Island home. Capo Frank Copa opened the door to what was supposed to be a Bonanno Family meeting. Cannone turned and walked away. Lino showed Napolitano to the basement steps, then shoved him down the stairs. Filocommo and Richard Riccardi killed him with pistol shots to the head. Years later, Lino testified that Napolitano said, "One more time and make it good" after being shot once." He didn't want to continue to suffer from the pain. There was no begging for his life.

While the killers placed Napolitano's body in a Bellevue Hospital mortuary bag, Lino took the dead man's keys to Massino, who was waiting in a van with Sal Vitale. A group of unknown men took the corpse to a lot at South Avenue and Bridge Street in Staten Island and buried it in a shallow grave. They couldn't find the full depth grave dug earlier.

It would be a year before Napolitano's body was found.

August 29, 1981

After hearing from informants that Napolitano was missing, the FBI scooped up Lefty Ruggiero before the bad guys killed him too. Pistone's street smarts and FBI money disguised as illegal loot had conned the compulsive gambler. Lefty wouldn't get out from behind bars for quite some time.

BIG TRIALS

November 23, 1981
Three Capos Trial
A federal grand jury dropped an indictment based mostly on Joe Pistone's intelligence gathering while undercover as Donnie Brasco. The good guys arrested Soldiers John "Boobie" Cerasani, Nicky Santora, Jimmy "Jimmy Legs" Episcopia, and Antonio Tomasulo. Also named were Lefty Ruggiero, who was already behind bars, and Sonny Black Napolitano resting in a grave.

Among the counts were conspiracy to murder the three Capos, plotting to kill Anthony "Bruno" Indelicato, distributing narcotics, and gambling. Not all accused faced every charge. These men were members of Sonny Black's crew.

February 18, 1982
The chickens finally came to roost for violent mobster Tony Mirra. For Capo Joe Massino and his men, Mirra was a wild card whose temper made him unpredictable. The other two strikes against him resulted from his introduction of FBI Agent Joe Pistone into their milieu. Then, to top matters off, Mirra sided with the losing Capos in their attempt to take over the Family. He knew there was a target on his back and laid low.

Massino ordered Capo Al Emberatto to take care of his nephew Mirra. Emberatto passed the order on to Richard Cantarella, then down to Joe D'Amico. The latter two were also relatives of Mirra, and he suspected nothing. On February 12, Mirra attempted to enter the underground parking garage at Independence Plaza; D'Amico, his passenger, fired a shot into his head, killing him instantly. Cantarella drove D'Amico away. Not many mourned his passing.

March 25, 1982
Three Capos Trial
The feds announced a superseding indictment that added five more defendants to the original November 23, 1981 account. The judge issued a warrant for Capo Joey Massino, but he went into hiding for the next two years.

August 12, 1982

A man walking his dog discovered Dominick "Sonny Black" Napolitano's body in a wooded area. It would take the medical examiner until November 10, 1982, to formally identify the remains of Napolitano.

August 27, 1983

Three Capos Trial

After a month-long trial in the US Courthouse in Foley Square, a jury found Benjamin "Lefty" Ruggiero, Nicholas "Nicky" Santora, Antonio "Mr. Fish" Rabito, and Antonio "Boots" Tomasulo guilty of RICO conspiracy. The predicate acts needed to prove a RICO conspiracy were the murder of the three capos, gambling, narcotics trafficking, etc. The jury found John "Boobie" Cerasani not guilty. Joe Pistone was a marvelous witness whose testimony kept the room mesmerized.

November 15, 1982

Three Capos Trial

For their RICO conspiracy convictions, Judge Robert Swift sentenced Ruggiero and Santora to 15 years each. He gave Rabito 13 years and Tomasulo five. Two years later, an appeals court reversed the convictions of Santora and Tomasulo.

April 21, 1983

Parole officials released Boss Philip Rastelli from Lewisburg prison.

1983

Boss Phil Rastelli inducted Associates James Tartaglione and Salvatore "Good Looking Sal" Vitale into the Bonanno Family. Vitale was Joey Massino's brother-in-law.

July 1983

During the three Capos hit back on May 5, 1981, a wayward shot paralyzed Soldier Santo Giordano from the waist down. Despite this handicap, he continued to follow his passion of flying using a co-pilot. Something went south in July. Giordano's plane crashed and burned near Edwards Airport in Bayport, LI, killing both him and his companion.

CESAR BONVENTRE

April 1984
Joey Massino was unhappy with Cesar Bonventre for not sending him money or visiting while running from the Three Capos trial. According to Sal Vitale, Massino was also put off by Bonventre's arrogant attitude and swagger. He probably feared Bonventre's growing power as well. Whatever the case, Massino held a meeting with Vitale, Duane Leisenheimer, and Louis "Ha Ha" Attanasio. Massino explained that Bonventre had to go, and they would sucker him by saying there was to be a meeting with Boss Phil Rastelli.

Vitale picked up Bonventre and Attanasio in a rented Dodge K Car. They understood that the use of a stolen vehicle would put Bonventre on guard. As they drove down a street leading to Leisenheimer's garage, Attanasio fired a shot into Bonventre's head from the back seat. The victim put up a violent struggle, so Attanasio fired a second shot. When the car stopped in the garage and the passenger door opened, Bonventre's body rolled out, and his head took another few slugs. He was now dead. Vitale drove the car, with the body in the trunk, to the Clinton Dinner. Capo Gabriel Infanti took over at that point.

THE PIZZA CONNECTION

April 9, 1984
Pizza Connection
Federal officials announced charges for 40 defendants in what became to be known as the Pizza Connection. Bonanno Capo Sal Catalano, Capo Cesar Bonventre, Soldier Baldo Amato, and Soldier Giovanni Ligammari were among them. It was an international heroin smuggling ring with the dope entering the United States, and the money went to Europe.

April 9, 1984
A Milwaukee jury found former Bonanno Capo Mike Sabella not guilty of extorting a vending machine company run by an undercover FBI Agent.

Lefty Ruggiero had pled guilty to this charge in November of 1983, and the judge sentenced him to 11 years.

April 16, 1984
Pizza Connection
Working on a tip and with a warrant, New Jersey State Police found Bonventre's dismembered body in two 55 gallon drums in the fourth-floor office of T&J Trading Company in Garfield, NJ. They found some personal items in a third drum. The glue on Bonventre's body led the FBI to the Industrial Latex Co. in Wallington. They discovered traces of Bonventre's hair, blood, and one of his shoes in an industrial vat.

May 1984
Parole officials send Rastelli back to prison for associating with known criminals.

July 21, 1984
Three Capos Trial
Capo Joey Massino turned himself in to face charges in the three Capos murders.

October 1984
Pizza Connection
Police found Cosmo "Gus" Aiello lying dead in a Clifton, New Jersey parking lot. Previously when he pled guilty to a federal conspiracy to make and sell counterfeit designer shirts, the prosecutor said he was "A major suspect" in the Cesar Bonventre hit.

February 20, 1985
Pizza Connection
A superseding indictment in the Pizza Connection Case added the murder of Carmine Galante and lunch companions as an additional charge. On the hook for those murders were Capo Sal Catalano, Giuseppe Ganci, and Soldier Baldo Amato.

THE COMMISSION CASE

February 26, 1985
Commission Case
The feds announced the 23 count Commission indictment that included 23 racketeering acts. They hoped to decimate the ruling body of La Cosa Nostra in one trial. Bonanno Boss Phil Rastelli was among the leaders named in the indictment, and they had him locked up on a parole violation.

February 28, 1985
Commission Case
Rastelli collapsed during his arraignment in the Commission Case, and an ambulance took him to Beekman Downtown Hospital. The doctors released Rastelli after finding nothing wrong. He went back to jail.

June 13, 1985
Bonanno Family Case
US Attorney Raymond Dearie announced the indictment of many Bonanno members, including Rastelli. I will refer to these matters as "The Bonanno Family Case," which involved labor racketeering in the moving and storage business. Rastelli and his friends controlled Teamster Local 1814, which helped them extort payoffs, rig bids, and fix prices. Also named in the indictment were former Underboss Nick Marangello, Capo Joey Massino, Soldier Carmine Rastelli and others. While in court facing arraignment Rastelli keeled over and was hauled off to the hospital.

June 26, 1985
Commission Case
A superseding Commission indictment added Bonanno Consigliere Steve "Stevie Beef" Cannone to those accused of ordering Carmine Galante's killing. The FBI arrested Cannone at his home around 8:30 AM.

October 21, 1985
In Tampa, Lefty Ruggiero pled guilty to one count of conspiracy in the King's Court affair. This event was an undercover sting operation run by FBI Agent Joe Pistone and others. They lured

many Mafia characters to the bottle club in the hopes of catching them committing crimes. Lefty and others fell for the sting.

November 12, 1985
Commission Case
A second superseding Commission indictment added Anthony "Bruno" Indelicato and charged him with the 1979 murders of Carmine Galante and two others in the same incident.

November 15, 1985
Bonanno Family Case and the Commission Case
A judge ordered Rastelli's release from prison, stating that the parole commission hadn't treated him fairly when they put him back in jail in 1984. Rastelli entered the hospital for serious internal surgery.

December 1985
Commission Case
Former Bonanno Consigliere Steve "Stevie Beef" Cannone removed himself from the Commission case by dying of natural causes.

January 10, 1986
Bonanno Family Case and the Commission Case
Judge Charles Sifton released Rastelli on a $2 million bond in the Commission Case and $2.5 million in the Bonanno Family indictment. Rastelli had been in Beekman Downtown Hospital for a gallbladder operation before they freed him.

February 1986
Bonanno Family Case
Rastelli lay on a stretcher during his arraignment in the Bonanno Family trial.

April 16, 1986
Bonanno Family Case
During the Bonanno Family trial jury selection, Rastelli collapsed again, and an ambulance took him to Long Island College Hospital. After treatment for an unknown problem, they released him the same day.

May 9, 1986
According to turncoat testimony years later, Associate Joe Platia drove Associate Robert Capasio to a rendezvous with Soldiers Joey D'Amico and Frank Lino. The two men killed Capasio on Rastelli's orders but immediately worried if Platia would rat on them.

May 10, 1986
Joseph Platia was sitting in his new Lincoln in a parking lot near West 55th Street near 10th Avenue when someone put three bullets in his head from the passenger seat. A passing cabby saw the action, and a man exiting the vehicle and walking away. He hailed some cops who arrested Steven Locurto, who was carrying the murder weapon. The District Attorney later charged Locurto with second-degree murder. We'll hear more from Locurto later.

May 15, 1986
Bonanno Family Case
During the Bonanno Family trial, prosecutor Laura Brevetti suggested that Rastelli should either be in jail so officials could monitor his medicine input or that an FBI Agent went to Rastelli's home each morning before trial. For her, Rastelli was deliberately not taking his meds in the hopes of gaining a mistrial.

May 23, 1986
Bonanno Family Case
Rastelli fell on a few steps leading to the lobby of the Brooklyn Federal Court House. After a quick fix at Long Island College Hospital, Rastelli was good to go.

August 18, 1986
Commission Case
Judge Richard Owen severed Rastelli from the Commission Trial after the prosecutor said it was a cost-saving matter since Rastelli was already on trial in the Bonanno Family case.

August 27, 1986
Commission Case
Officials denied Bruno Indelicato bail in the Commission Case. They were supposed to release him the next day from another matter.

September 5, 1986
Massino Case
A judge ordered Joe Massino to trial to face RICO Conspiracy charges, including the three Capos hit back in May of 1981. The court continued Massino's $500,000 bail.

September 8, 1986-November 19, 1986
The Commission trial started and finished on these dates.

October 15, 1986
Bonanno Family Case
A jury found Rastelli, Joe Massino, Nick Marangello, Carmine Rastelli, and others guilty of labor racketeering. Interestingly some newspaper accounts speculated whether Capo Gabriel Infante might become the next Boss. This theory didn't do him any good, as will become apparent. Judge Charles Sifton tentatively permitted Rastelli and Massino to continue on bail while they appealed their case.

November 19, 1986
Commission Case
The Commission Case jury came in with a boatload of guilty verdicts. Among those going down were Bonanno Capo Sal Catalano and soldier Bruno Indelicato.

January 13, 1987
Commission Case
Among the sentences handed out by Judge Owens in the Commission Case was a 40-year stretch for Soldier Bruno Indelicato for the murder of Galante and his two companions. The judge gave him 20 years for the RICO conspiracy (The planning of the murders) and 20 years for the RICO conviction. (The carrying out of the murders.) Later an appeals court threw out the RICO conspiracy count, leaving him 20 years instead of 40. That decision was a big win for Indelicato.

January 16, 1987
Bonanno Family Case
Judge Sifton gave out the following sentences and forfeitures in the Bonanno Family case; Rastelli -12 years, $29,000, Massino-10 years, $3,000, Marangello-eight years, $9,000. The rest of the

defendants received a variety of penalties. Judge Sifton tentatively allowed Rastelli and Massino to continue on bail. That mercy didn't last long.

January 21, 1987
Bonanno Family Case
Judge Charles Sifton revoked the bails of Rastelli and Massino and ordered them to prison immediately.

March 2, 1987
Pizza Connection
The lengthy Pizza Connection trial finally came to an end with guilty verdicts for most defendants. Bonanno Capo Salvatore Catalano, Soldier Giovanni Ligammari, and Soldier Bruno Amato were among those convicted.

June 3, 1987
Massino Case
A jury found Massino not guilty of the three Capos murder and acquitted him of conspiring to kill Joseph Pastore and Bruno Indelicato. They decided that Massino and Vitale were guilty of possessing some stolen fish and a hijacking conviction for Massino. However, the jury ruled the racketeering conspiracy (The fish and hijacking) didn't continue beyond 1979. This decision meant the judge had to throw out the convictions, and the two went free.

June 22, 1987
Pizza Connection
In the Pizza Connection sentencing, Judge Pierre Leval handed Sal Catalano 45 years, a $1.15 million fine, and $1 million in restitution to go to a drug rehabilitation program. The judge sentenced three others as well.

June 23, 1987
Pizza Connection
Judge Leval sentenced Giovanni Ligammari to 15 years, a $50,000 fine, and a $200,000 payment into a drug rehabilitation program. The judge also penalized others the same day. Due to an appeal, Baldo Amato's sentencing didn't happen until May 3, 1988.

October 8, 1987
The feds signed a consent agreement with Teamster Local 814 to put it under trusteeship. Rastelli et al. used to extort the trucking business by controlling this local. This legal move ended a gold mine for the Bonannos.

December 1987
Boss Joe Massino ordered a hit on Capo Gabriel Infante because he messed up the disposal of Capo Cesar Bonventre's body. No one ever found Infante's remains. Authorities would charge Massino and Louis Restivo for this hit in 2004.

May 3, 1988
Pizza Connection
Department of Justice Lawyer Robert Stewart's opening remarks outlined the Carmine Galante hit. Later, Judge Leval ruled the proceedings should not include the Galante murder. Baldo Amato's lawyer, Paul Bergman, contented the initial inclusion of the Galante matter prejudiced the jury against his client. Bergman demanded a mistrial. It was a game of chicken, and Bergman won for Amato. The feds agreed to drop the heroin conspiracy conviction if Amato would plead guilty to the lesser RICO charge. Judge Leval then sentence Amato to a mere five years. He had won the jackpot thanks to excellent lawyering by Bergman.

THE GUS FARACE FIASCO

February 28, 1989
Gus Farace Matter
Bonanno Associate Gus Farace killed undercover DEA Agent Everett Hatcher at a secluded overpass in Staten Island. Why he did so remains elusive. From a van, Farace fired four shots into Hatcher, who was sitting in his idling car. It was an arranged meeting meant to discuss a drug deal. Unfortunately, Hatcher's backup team got separated from him, although the murder probably would still have happened. Law enforcement put an all-out press on contacts of Hatcher but was unable to find the killer. Due to the pressure, the mob guys were also soon looking for Farace.

Note:

Farace's father was a brother-in-law of infamous Colombo Soldier and informer Greg Scarpa. That connection made Farace a cousin of equally notorious Colombo Soldier Greg Scarpa Jr.

March 4, 1989

Gus Farace Matter

A newspaper account of the Hatcher funeral in Parsippany, NJ, stated that the 4,000 in attendance included FBI head William Sessions and NY Mayor Ed Koch.

May 24, 1989

Gus Farace Matter

Police and FBI Agents arrested Margaret Scarpa, a daughter of Bonanno Soldier Gerard Chilli, for lying to the FBI about her contacts with Gus Farace. The criminal complaint alleged that she had met with Farace, in her parent's apartment, immediately after the Hatcher killing. An informer was present at the time. Scarpa told the informant that she had hidden Gus in a neighbor's home. The complaint said phone records backed up these allegations. Someone using Scarpa's home phone called Gus Farace's beeper around 9:30 PM, which was about the time of the Hatcher murder. Then at 2:06 AM, the informer dialed Farace's beeper. Someone using the neighbor's phone returned the call. These revelations were mysterious, but a fuller story would soon come out.

May 26, 1989

Gus Farace Matter

WNBC TV released a report that said Domenic Farace, Gus' cousin, told the FBI that he was in the van when Gus Farace shot Hatcher. He also revealed that Gus had thrown the gun into Fresh Kills Creek near West Shore Parkway. (NYPD scuba divers eventually found the .357 Rugar murder weapon.) Later information revealed that Domenic was in the Scarpa apartment with Gus Farace and Margaret Scarpa immediately after the murder. It was he who beeped Farace at the neighbor's home.

September 13, 1989

Gus Farace Matter

After learning that Associate John "Johnny Boy" Petrucelli was hiding Farace, Lucchese Boss Vic Amuso ordered that he kill the fugitive. Petrucelli refused, and this was his death sentence. Joseph Consentino, a lifelong friend of Petrucelli and another man, killed "Johnny Boy" and left him on the lawn outside a White Plains apartment.

October 6, 1989
Law authorities filed a criminal complaint in Brooklyn Federal Court that accused Gus Farace's wife and her brother of conspiracy to distribute marijuana. The scheme ran from 1987 until February 1989 and involved bringing in marijuana from Texas. Most of this information came from Domenic Farace and was a pressure tactic to get someone to reveal Gus Farace's whereabouts.

October 11, 1989
Pizza Connection
The US Second Circuit Court of Appeals removed all the restitution penalties imposed by Judge Leval at sentencing. That saved Catalano $1 million and Ligammari $200,000. The bad news was that the court turned down the conviction appeals of Catalano, Ligammari, and others.

October 14, 1989
Gus Farace Matter
The feds, acting on the October 6 complaint, arrested Antoinette Farace, Gus' wife, and her brother Henry Acierno for conspiracy to distribute marijuana.

November 17, 1989
Gus Farace Matter
Fugitive Gus Farace and his buddy Joseph Sclafani drove to a rendezvous in the Bensonhurst area of Brooklyn around 11 PM. They double-parked in front of Louis Tuzzio's parent's home. Louis Tuzzio and James Galione, both Bonanno Associates, fired upon them from a blue van. They killed Farace and severely wounded Sclafani. Mario Gallo, another Associate, acted as a lookout. Gambino Boss John Gotti was infuriated by the wounding, for Sclafani was one of his Associates.

January 30, 1990
Gus Farace Matter
Bonanno Associate Louis Tuzzio was uncertain what awaited him at a Bonanno Family meeting. He told his mother that he was either going to be inducted into the Family or killed. It was the latter. Cops found his body, still behind the wheel of a stolen car in an isolated area in Brooklyn. Soldier Robert Lino shot the Bonanno Associate in the head with Daniel "DeDe" Mongelli also present. It would take years before these men and others faced trial in the Farace killing.

May 1990
Gus Farace Matter
Joseph Sclafani pled guilty to hiding Gus Farace.

June 4, 1991
A judge ordered Bonanno Boss Philip Rastelli's release from the federal prison hospital at Springfield, Illinois. He had just undergone cancer surgery and was permitted to go home to die.

RASTELLI DIES

June 24, 1991
Bonanno Boss Philip Rastelli died in Booth Memorial Hospital in Queens of liver cancer. He had led the Bonanno Family since 1973, although he spent a great deal of that time behind bars. Shortly after that, the Capos elected Underboss Joey Massino as their new leader even though he was in prison.

November 24, 1991
Gus Farace Matter
ABC television ran the movie, "Dead or Alive: The Race for Gus Farace" at 8 PM. Tony Danza starred as Farace.

CHAPTER TWELVE

The Massino Basciano Era

1995
A grand jury indicted Capo Vincent Asaro for providing mob protection for a large stolen car ring. However, a judge dismissed the charges, but an appeal court overturned his decision. The indictment also named about eight other hoods, most of whom eventually pled guilty.

October 9, 1996
Two gunmen whacked out car thief John "Johnny Boy" Borello in his white Pontiac on 75th Street in Brooklyn. One hood fired from the vehicle's back with a shotgun while the other killer blasted away with his semi-automatic pistol from the passenger side. Incredibly the female passenger was not hurt. Court papers linked Borello to Asaro's stolen car ring.

January 21, 1998
Capo Frank Lino pled guilty to stock fraud along with others. It was a massive pump and dump scheme where crooked brokers would hard-sell a penny stock until the price rose significantly. Then the insiders would sell, making big profits. Lino was involved in settling the countless disputes that always arose in affairs like this. Soldier John "Boobie" Cerasani also pled guilty.

January 29, 1998
The FBI arrested Acting Consigliere James Tartaglione, Acting Capo Generoso Barbieri, and Soldier Paul Spina for running a loansharking operation.

June 1998
A judge ruled a mistrial in Vincent Asaro's stolen car ring case.

January 1998
A jury convicted Capo Vincent Asaro for forgery for putting a fake birthday and address on his driving license application. The court had suspended his driving permit for drunk driving.

February 19, 1998
Justice Arthur Cooperman sentenced Asaro to six months for his driver's license forgery. Appellate Judge William Friedman released Asaro until the following Monday when another judge made a bail decision.

November 19, 1998
A NY Supreme Court jury convicted Capo Vincent Asaro for controlling a sizeable stolen-car ring. He protected a group that stole cars then sold the parts between 1994 and 1995. Defense Attorney Stephen Mahler argued that Asaro only lent money to one of the thieves, but this strategy didn't work.

CAPO GERLANDO SCIASCIA KILLED

March 18, 1999
Allegedly Capo Pat DiFilippo killed Capo Gerlando Sciascia on orders from Massino. Sciascia was in the back seat of a vehicle driven by Jimmy Spirito. He believed they were going to a meeting. DiFilippo, according to later testimony by Spirito, turned around and shot Sciascia. They dumped his body in the street to make it look like a drug deal gone wrong. Boss Joey Massino told his close confidants to pretend that they didn't know who killed Sciascia. Massino feared Sciascia's growing power and independence.

May 27, 1999
Family members found the bodies of Giovanni Ligammari and his son Pietro hanging in the basement of their home. Officials released Giovanni from prison on September 20, 1995, after eight years of a fifteen-year sentence from the Pizza Connection trial. Despite talk of the deaths being murders, the evidence indicated suicide. Father and son simultaneous suicides are extremely rare. Both were Bonanno Soldiers.

August 10, 2000
Prison officials released Louis "Ha Ha" Attanasio.

2000
The prison doors opened for Anthony "Bruno" Indelicato after 13 of his 20 year Commission sentence.

July 19, 2000
Police arrested New Jersey Capo Joseph Taormina near his Fairfield home. After searching the house, his vacation place, and a warehouse, the authorities charged him with racketeering, gambling, purchasing illegal cigarettes, and loansharking.

THE FRANK SANTORO HIT

February 15, 2001
Someone told Capo Vince "Vinny Gorgeous" Basciano that Associate Frank Santoro had threatened to kidnap Basciano's son. In response, the Capo gathered a hit team to hunt Santoro down. They found Santoro walking his dog near his Throggs Neck home in the Bronx. Dominic Cicale jumped out of the hit car and opened up with a pistol. Basciano fired a shotgun blasting the victim four times. Whether he had threatened the kidnapping or not, it didn't matter. He was dead. Also on the hit crew were Soldiers Anthony "Bruno" Indelicato and Anthony Donato. The autopsy showed that Cicale missed with all five pistol shots.

July 2001
A judge sentenced Soldier Anthony "Bruno" Indelicato to eight months for a parole violation.

July 2, 2001
A grand jury indicted Soldier James "Big Louis" Tartaglione and James Pastore for extortion of an auto tinting store.

October 17, 2001
A New Jersey grand jury indicted Capo Joseph Taormina and two Bonanno soldiers on various charges stemming from the July 19, 2000 raids.

October 26, 2001
Consigliere Anthony Graziano's son-in-law, John Zancocchio, pled guilty to loansharking and conspiracy to defraud the IRS. A judge would sentence the Bonanno Soldier on March 6, 2002. Back in 1990, Zancocchio spent six months in prison for another run-in with the IRS.

November 6, 2001
Authorities arrested Sal Vitale, Joseph Cuccio (bank manager), Thomas Driscoll, George Fillipone, Lawrence Neder, Daniel Talia, and Vincent DeCongilio for a money-laundering scam involving the European American Bank in Melville, Long Island.

2002
Future Acting Boss Salvatore Montagna appeared before a grand jury. Later, he pled guilty to criminal contempt for refusing to testify. This admission would cost him dearly later.

March 6, 2002
A judge sentenced Bonanno Soldier John Zancocchio to 70 months in prison and six years of probation for loansharking and conspiracy to defraud the IRS. He also assessed $350,000 in restitution to the IRS, plus a $75,000 fine.

CONSIGLIERE GRAZIANO CHARGED

March 19, 2002
A New York grand jury indictment named 15 Bonanno members, including Consigliere Anthony Graziano, Acting Capo Robert Lino, Capo Frank Porco, with various counts. They charged

Graziano with conspiring to murder Colombo guys John Pappa and Calvin Hennigar for shooting up a Graziano controlled nightclub called Hipps. The indictment also claimed Capo Frank Lino helped murder Louis Tuzzio in January 1990.

Graziano did not kill Pappa and Hennigar but settled the problem with a sit-down with Colombo Family heavyweights.

March 19, 2002
Florida authorities charged Consigliere Anthony Graziano with participation in massive stock fraud in Florida. The crooks used telemarketing to entice unsuspecting people to invest in overpriced stocks. The indictment had 63 criminal counts and 29 defendants.

May 2, 2002
US Magistrate Linnea Johnson refused to grant Bonanno Consigliere Anthony Graziano bail in the Florida stock fraud case.

2002
Based in NJ, Capo Joe Taormina died, thus avoiding a lengthy prison time from his July 19, 2000 indictment. Boss Joe Massino replaced him with Joe Sammartino.

October 2, 2002
The feds announced a 24 count superseding indictment against Consigliere Anthony Graziano, Capo Richard Cantarella, and others. This document was an upgrade on the March 19, 2002 indictment.

December 10, 2002
A 36 count, grand jury indictment, named Bonanno Capo Vincent Badalamenti, Soldier Simone Esposito, and a bunch of Lucchese guys.

Another grand jury indicted Ron Filocomo Sr for loansharking. It was in his house that Capo Dominick "Sonny Black" Napolitano died.

December 17, 2002
Soldiers James Tartaglione and James Pastore pled guilty to extortion of an auto tinting shop. The indictment first came down on July 2, 2001.

December 23, 2002
Consigliere Anthony Graziano pled guilty to RICO charges in Brooklyn federal court. These events started with a March 19, 2002 indictment described above.

2003
Soldier Salvatore Montagna, a member of Patrick DeFilippo's Bronx crew, pled guilty to criminal contempt before a 2002 grand jury. A judge sentenced him to five months' probation. Later the feds used this to deport him to Canada.

MASSINO GOES DOWN

January 9, 2002
FBI Agents arrested Boss Joseph Massino for the killings of Sonny Black and newspaper delivery superintendent Robert Perrino. They also arrested Underboss Sal Vitale, Capo Frank Lino, and Acting Capo Daniel Mongelli. It was a 19 count superseding indictment. Previously indicted were Anthony Graziano, Richard Cantarella, and Frank Coppa.

March 2003
Rumors begin flying that Underboss Salvatore Vitale had become a federal witness. He was the brother-in-law of Boss Joseph Massino.

April 2003
Before a judge, turncoat, Underboss Salvatore Vitale pled guilty secretly and admitted to eleven hits.

May 30, 2003
The feds released a second superseding indictment in the Massino case. It included the murders of Anthony Mirra, Louis Tuzzio, and Dominick "Sonny Black" Napolitano. They laid the killing of Tuzzio at Capo Frank Lino's feet and the execution of Capo Napolitano they blamed on Soldier Ron Filocomo.

July 18, 2003
A judge sentenced Consigliere Anthony Graziano to eleven years for illegal gambling, loansharking, and an investment scam. He also ordered Graziano to repay $1.6 million.

August 20, 2003
Another superseding indictment with 13 counts included charges that Massino ordered Cesare Bonventre and Lindy Infante's killings.

Another indictment charged Massino, Pat DeFilippo, and Joseph Spirito with conspiracy to murder and the murder of Capo Gerlando Sciascia on March 18, 1999.

September 9, 2003
Capo William "Willie Glasses" Riviello pled guilty to racketeering.

September 12, 2003
A judge sentenced Capo Frank Porco to two years for racketeering, loansharking, and gambling.

September 30, 2003
Feds moved to forfeit $11 million of Massino's assets.

December 12, 2003
The feds dug up the body of newspaper guy Robert Perrino.

MASSIVE BONANNO INDICTMENT

January 20, 2004
The feds announced a 20-count indictment that devastated the leadership of the Bonanno Family. Among the more than 27 persons named were Acting Boss Anthony "Tony Green" Urso and Acting Underboss Joseph Cammarano. Brooklyn US Attorney Roslynn Mauskopf revealed that an Acting Capo had taped some of his colleagues. The press quickly speculated that this person was Acting Capo James "Louis" Tartaglione.
For Canadians, the big name was that of Soldier Vito Rizzuto, labeled as "The Godfather of the Italian Mafia in Canada."

February 5, 2004
Officials caught Soldier Anthony "Bruno" Indelicato for a parole violation.

March 2004
Boss Joe Massino promoted Soldier Dominick Cicale to Acting Capo to replace Vincent Basciano, who became the new Acting Boss because Anthony Urso was locked up.

March 4, 2004
Before a judge, Capo Daniel Mongelli pled guilty to taking part in the murder of Associate Louis Tuzzio. The latter wounded Joseph Sclafani, a Gambino Associate, during the murder of Gus Farace back in 1999.

March 15, 2004
Soldier Ron "Monkey Man" Filocomo pled guilty to the murder of Dominick "Sonny Black" Napolitano in August of 1981 and the 1980 murder of Colombo Associate Michael Aiello. Bonanno leaders had lured Napolitano to Filocomo's father's home, then Filocomo and Soldier Ricard Richards killed him.

March 18, 2004
Capo Robert "Little Robert" Lino pled guilty to the murder of Robert Perrino and the 1990 killing of Louis Tuzzio and gambling charges. Later he got 27 years. After Bonanno guys lured Perrino to a social club, Lino shot him in the head.

May 25, 2004
The Massino trial opened. Expert witness Ken McCabe revealed that Vincent "Vinny Gorgeous" Basciano was now the Acting Boss of the Massino Family. Former Capo Frank Lino testified that Joe Massino was present when shooters killed the three Capos on May 5, 1981.

May 26, 2004
At the Massino trial, government witness Capo Frank Lino testified about the murders of the three Capos and that of Sonny Black, all in 1981. He testified that Massino was involved in the planning of all four murders. The Bonanno's intended to kill Lino at the three Capos hit, but he quickly fled. In the Napolitano murder,

Lino shoved him down the basement stairs where two men shot the Capo.

June 2, 2004
A judge sentenced Acting Capo Daniel Mongelli to 24 years for his role in the Luis Tuzzio murder. He had pled guilty on March 4, 2004.

MASSINO GUILTY

July 30, 2004
The jury found Boss Joe Massino guilty of all twenty-two counts in the indictment. In mini-trial immediately after the guilty verdict, the jury ruled that Massino should forfeit $10 million. Later that same day, Massino asked to see the judge and thus began his turning.

November 19, 2004
An 18 count superseding indictment charged Acting Boss Vinny Basciano and Soldier Anthony Donato with the murder of Frank Santoro on February 15, 2001. The FBI arrested the two men and took them to Cadman Plaza for arraignment before Judge Nicholas Garaufis. The judge also arraigned Boss Joe Massino, Capo Pat DeFilippo, and Soldier Joe Spirito for the murder of Capo Gerlando Sciascia.

November 30, 2004
Before his November arrest, Vincent Basciano ordered the murder of Randy Pizzolo. Mike Mancuso took over as Acting Capo and ordered Soldier Dom Cicale to carry out the contract. Soldier Anthony "Ace" Aiello lured Pizzolo to a Monitor Street meeting in the northern area of the Greenwood section of Brooklyn. When Pizzolo got out of his vehicle to greet Aiello, the latter shot him seven times with his 9 mm Luger.

According to later testimony, Pizzolo had angered Acting Boss Vince Basciano with his wild behavior and less than perfect construction work. When Pizzolo ignored a suggestion to move to Florida, he was a walking dead man.

December 29, 2004
Police arrested Capo Louie "Ha Ha" Attanasio on the island of St Maarten and ordered him deported to the US, where he was facing charges for the murder of Capo Cesar Bonventre.

January 3, 2005
While they were both in the Metropolitan Correctional Center, Joe Massino secretly taped Acting Boss Vince Basciano, admitting he ordered the murder of Randy Pizzolo (November 30, 2004.)

February 11, 2005
Soldier Louie Restivo pled guilty to the murder of Anthony Tomasulo in May of 1990. Tomasulo was the son of Soldier Anthony "Boots" Tomasulo, who was in the Dominick "Sonny Black" Napolitano crew infiltrated by FBI Agent Joe "Donnie Brasco" Pistone. The son tried to retain ownership of his father's extensive joker poker racket, but Underboss Sal Vitale said the operation now belonged to the Family. Tomasulo was furious, which led Consigliere Anthony Spero and Vitale to order his death. When Vitale became a government witness, he revealed the details of this murder.

Former Acting Boss Anthony "Tony Green" Urso pled guilty to gambling, loansharking, extortion, and racketeering murder. He admitted to luring Associate Anthony Tomasulo to a club where Restivo killed him.

Former Acting Underboss Joe Cammarano admitted taking part in the murder of Anthony Tomasulo back in 1990.

May 26, 2005
A judge sentenced Soldier Louis Restivo to ten years for the murder of Anthony Tomasulo. For years Restivo was a partner with Joe Massino in his popular CasaBella restaurant.

BASCIANO INDICTED

June 24, 2005
The feds released a grand jury indictment that named Acting Boss Vincent Basciano and former Massino lawyer Thomas Lee. It charged Lee with racketeering, conspiracy to murder, and obstruction of justice.

While acting as Massino's lawyer, Lee passed messages back and forth from the jailed Massino to his Acting Boss Basciano, who was still on the street. He informed Massino of inductions plus passed on a Basciano request to kill Capo Pat DeFilippo and two mob turncoats' sons. When Massino became a government informant, he revealed Lee's role and even taped some of their conversations.

The indictment accused Basciano of conspiracy to murder Pat DeFilippo and soliciting the murder of federal prosecutor Greg Andres.

August 31, 2005
Restivo went to prison a few months after being sentenced. Prison officials released him on May 7, 2014.

THE END FOR ACTING BOSS ANTHONY URSO

September 15, 2005
A judge sentenced former Acting Boss Anthony "Tony Green" Urso to 20 years and former Acting Underboss Joseph "Joe Sanders" Cammarano to 15 years.

September 27, 2005
Soldier Joe Spirito admitted to being in the car when Pat DeFilippo allegedly killed Capo Gerlando Sciascia at Boss Joe Massino's request.

January 2006
Soldier Dominick Cicale decided his best interests lay with the government. He would later testify against Vincent Basciano.

February 16, 2006
The feds announced an indictment naming Anthony "Bruno" Indelicato as involved in the December 2001 Frank Santoro murder. (Indelicato drove the hit car while Anthony Aiello shot gunned the victim.) The document accused Acting Boss Mike Mancuso of murder and racketeering, including the Pizzolo hit from 2004.

THE END FOR ACTING BOSS VINCENT BASCIANO

February 27, 2006
The trial of Basciano and DeFilippo began with Judge Nicolas Garaufis presiding. Barry Levin, Basciano's lawyer, admitted that his client was in the Mafia.

The government used former Acting Capo Dominick Cicale as their main witness. In his testimony, he provided the reason behind the Santoro hit order (Santoro threatened to kidnap Basciano's son), the efforts made to find Santoro, and the details of the actual murder and who participated.

May 9, 2006
A jury convicted Pat DeFilippo and Vincent Basciano of racketeering. The jury couldn't come to a unanimous conclusion as to DeFilippo killing Gerlando Sciascia or Basciano murdering Frank Santoro. The judge declared a mistrial on those counts.

July 12, 2006
A jury convicted Soldier Baldo Amato of racketeering charges, including involvement in the murder of Robert Perrino of the New York Post and the killing of Sebastiano DiFalco. They found Bonanno Soldier Stephen Locurto responsible for participation in the 1986 murder of Joseph Pliata.

July 28, 2006
Prison officials moved Basciano to solitary after another inmate told them Basciano had a hit list for five people, including Judge Garaufis, prosecutor Greg Andres and turncoats Thomas Lee,

Dominick Cicale, and James Tartaglione. An intense investigation followed.

September 20, 2006
A judge sentenced Capo Louis "Ha Ha" Attanasio and Soldier Peter Calabrese to 15 years each for the 1984 murder of Capo Cesar Bonventre. Attanasio shot Bonventre while Calabrese took part in the disposal of the body.

September 21, 2006
Prosecutors announced that the Attorney General had authorized super isolation for Basciano. They locked him up for 23 hours a day, reduced his visits to once every two weeks, and placed restrictions on his lawyers.

October 27, 2006
Judge Nicholas Garaufis sentenced Baldo Amato to life for the murders of Sebastiano DiFalco and Robert Perrino.

SALVATORE "THE IRONWORKER" MONTAGNA

November 2006
Various media outlets reported that Salvatore "Sal the Ironworker" Montagna was the new Acting Boss of the Bonanno Family.

March 14, 2007
Judge Nicholas Garaufis sentenced Capo Pat DeFilippo to 40 years on racketeering charges. In his sentencing, the judge said the evidence proved DeFilippo killed Capo Gerlando Sciascia. Hence, it was a factor in his decision on DeFilippo's length of prison time.

July 31, 2007
In a retrial of the Santoro murder case, the jury found Basciano guilty. The government effectively used turncoats Sal Vitale, Dominick Cicale, James Tartaglione, and disgraced lawyer Thomas Lee. The jury also found Basciano guilty of conspiracy to murder Dominick Martino, soliciting the murder of Sal Vitale, conspiracy to distribute marijuana, and some gambling charges.

2007
A judge sentenced Soldier Joe Cammarano Jr to 27 months on an extortion charge. His father was once the Acting Underboss of the Bonanno Family.

March 31, 2008
Judge Nicholas Garaufis sentenced Basciano to life for the Frank Santoro killing and a variety of other charges. He also leveled a restitution order of $5 million.

August 6, 2008
Former Acting Boss Michael Mancuso took a guilty plea for killing Randy Pizzolo on November 30, 2002. Soldier Anthony "Bruno" Indelicato also admitted to being the wheelman in the Santoro murder, and Soldier Anthony Donato admitted his guilt in the same crime.

December 16, 2008
Judge Nicolas Garaufis handed down the following sentences.
Anthony "Bruno" Indelicato - 20 years for the December 14, 2001, Santoro murder.
Michael Mancuso - 15 years for the 2004 Pizzolo murder.
Anthony Aiello - 30 years for being the shooter in the 2004 Pizzolo murder.
Anthony Donato - 25 years for the Santoro hit.

THE END FOR ACTING BOSS SALVATORE MONTAGNA

April 2009
FBI and US Immigration officials arrested Acting Boss Salvatore "The Iron Worker" Montagna for being an undesirable alien. He had pled guilty to criminal contempt back in 2002. They deported him to Canada.

July 2, 2009
Someone killed Soldier Anthony "Little Anthony" Seccafico. Later, Capo Peter Lovaglio turned informer and detailed this hit.

July 2009
Officials released Anthony Rabito from prison.

November 16, 2009
Former Capo and Pizza Connection defendant Sal Catalano finished his drug sentence. He reportedly moved back to Sicily.

June 21, 2010
Capo Joseph Sammartino Sr pled guilty to loansharking.

July 02, 2010
Hector Pagan shot James Donovan in the leg in an attempted robbery of his Gravenhurst body shop. Donovan bled to death in the hospital. A jury convicted Soldiers Ricard Riccardi and Luigi Grasso of this murder in 2014.

August 2, 2010
Acting Capo Anthony Pipitone, Vito Pipitone, Frank Terzo, and Joe Spatola were all sentenced to short terms for an assault on some kids they thought vandalized a mob-connected restaurant. They picked on the wrong kids.

October 15, 2010
Judge Nicholas Sammartino sentenced Capo Joe Sammartino, the Bonanno NJ leader, to 18 months and a $50,000 fine for extortion. According to the feds, Sammartino was part of the Bonanno ruling panel.

2011
The Bonanno Capos demoted Consigliere Anthony Graziano due to the publicity from his daughter's reality TV show "Mafia Wives."

2011
US Attorney General Eric Holder ruled that Basciano would face the death penalty if the jury convicted him in his upcoming trial. Judge Nicholas Garaufis had written to Holder citing the mounting public expense of defending Basciano, saying a death sentence appeal would cost even more.

2011
Officials released former Acting Capo Peter Lovaglio from prison.

VINCENT BASCIANO AVOIDS DEATH

May 16, 2010
A jury convicted Vince Basciano of capital murder in the Randy Pizzolo killing from 2004. Six turncoat witnesses testified against Basciano, including former Boss Joe Massino, former Underboss Sal Vitale and Capos James Tartaglione and Dominick Cicale. The most damaging evidence was a January 3, 2005 tape of Basciano admitting to Massino that he had ordered the hit.

June 1, 2011
The jury, in the penalty phase, did not vote for the death penalty for Basciano. Ten jurors wrote a letter saying that if someone like Massino didn't get the ultimate punishment, they would not impose it on Basciano.

Judge Nicholas Garaufis had some things to say about Basciano. "No words are strong enough to convey the depravity with which he has lived his free life."
"...bleak pathetic and ignorant life."

Basciano spoke as well. As usual, he claimed not to have had a fair trial, that he was broke and had no money.

Court officials revealed that the government had spent over $5 million defending Basciano.

July 20, 2011
In a formality, Judge Nicholas Garaufis sentenced Basciano to life plus ten years for the 2004 Pizzolo murder. The judge ruled that Basciano still owed $5 million in restitution from his 2008 conviction in the Frank Santoro murder.

January 20, 2012
Judge Nicholas Garaufis sentenced mob turncoat Dom Cicale to ten years, but he had already served seven and would be out soon due to having 18 months taken off for good behavior. Cicale said, "I am so sorry, there is not a day when I do not pray for the souls of my victims."

CHAPTER THIRTEEN

The Mancuso Era

December 16, 2008

Former Acting Boss Mikey Mancuso took a guilty plea for killing Associate Randy Pizzolo on November 30, 2002. Soldier Anthony "Bruno" Indelicato admitted to being the wheelman in the Santoro murder, while Soldier Anthony Donato admitted his guilt in the same crime.

Judge Nicholas Garaufis handed down the following sentences:

Mikey Mancuso got 15 years for the 2004 Pizzolo murder.

Anthony "Bruno" Indelicato received 20 years for the 2001 Santoro hit.

Anthony Aiello took 30 years in the 2004 Santoro murder.

Anthony Donato got 25 years for the 2004 Santoro killing.

August 19, 2011

Prison officials taped Mikey Mancuso talking about the beat down two of his men gave to Lucchese Associate Michael Meldish. It took place in front of the famous Rao's restaurant on Pleasant Avenue in front of witnesses. Mancuso excitedly said, "They beat him, kicked him, and everything." Meldish had the nerve to date a former girlfriend of Mancuso.

December 7, 2012

Judge Carol Amon sentenced Capo Nick Santora to 20 months for extortion and four months for associating with bad guys while on probation. Santora had pled guilty previously. He admitted attending a mob sit-down where he represented Bonanno Associate Joseph Galante Jr in a dispute over $30,000 Galante owed to Rocky Napoli. Santora agreed that his presence was to enforce any decision that the disputing parties made.

December 29, 2012

Good guys monitored a Staten Island meeting of Acting Boss Thomas DiFiori, Florida Capo Gerry Chilli, Acting Capo Peter Lovaglio, and others. The feds later arrested some of these guys for parole violations.

March 31, 2013

Judge Nicholas Garaufis sentenced former Capo Generoso "Jimmy the General" Barbieri to six years for conspiracy to commit murders and other charges. Since Barbieri had already been behind bars for that length of time, officials freed him. Garaufis praised Barbieri for his courage in becoming a witness for the government.

While in prison, Barbieri learned that Acting Boss Vincent Basciano planned to murder Assistant US Attorney Greg Andres. He contacted the FBI and became a government witness. During Basciano's two trials, Barbieri was a key witness against him. The former Capo entered the Witness Protection Program.

May 29, 2013

Lucchese Associate Terrence Caldwell shot and wounded Bonanno Soldier Enzo Stagno in his car. It later emerged that another Lucchese Associate, Michael Meldish was behind the hit attempt. He used Lucchese Soldier Christopher Londonio to hire Caldwell. On November 15, 2019, a jury convicted Caldwell, Londonio, and two Lucchese Family leaders on various charges. Among these, the jury found Caldwell guilty of attempted murder in aid of racketeering and using a weapon to aid racketeering in the Stagno wounding.

MICHAEL MANCUSON WON THE ELECTION

June 2013
Bonanno Capos elected Mikey Mancuso the new Bonanno Boss even though he was in prison. He was doing 15 years for his involvement in the 2004 murder of Randy Pizzolo.

July 9, 2013
The FBI arrested the crew of Capo Nicky Santora on various charges.

July 8, 2013
After petitions from the government, Judge Nicholas Garaufis agreed to reduce former Boss Joe Massino two life sentences to time served. Massino had been in prison or Witness Protection jail for ten and a half years. Massino testified in a Vincent Basciano trial and one for Genovese Family Capo Anthony Romanello. In the future, Massino would get by with a monthly federal stipend, social security payments, and income from some rental properties the government allowed him to keep.

Judge Garaufis said, "In helping the government, he (Massino) has also helped himself, and his co-operation in no way excuses or justifies his life of crime.

Massino stated, "I pray every night for forgiveness for all the people I hurt, especially the victim's families."

September 2013
Former Underboss Joe Cammarano Sr died in prison. He was serving time for murder.

November 15, 2013
Lucchese Associate Terrence Caldwell killed Michael Meldish in his vehicle. The Lucchese Family leadership had ordered the murder for various reasons, including that Meldish was dating a girlfriend of incarcerated Bonanno Boss Michael Mancuso. In 2019 this crew of Lucchese members and Associates would be convicted of this hit and many other crimes.

January 23, 2014
The FBI arrested Soldier Vinny Asaro, Capo Jerome Asaro, Acting Boss Thomas Di Fiore, Acting Capo Jack Bonventre, and Soldier John Ragano on various charges. They accused Vinny Asaro of being involved in the 1978 Lufthansa heist made famous in the movie "Goodfellas" and the murder of a suspected informant. DiFiore faced extortion counts.

August 1, 2014
Judge John Gleeson sentenced Soldier Luigi Grasso to 38 years and Soldier Richard Riccardi to 36 years of being involved in the July 2, 2010 murder of James Donovan. The shooter, Hector Pagan, testified against them.

October 9, 2014
Capo Jerome Asaro pled guilty to disinterring the body of murder victim Paul Katz. In 2012, Informant Gaspare Valenti told the feds he had been present, in 1999, when Lucchese Associate Jimmy Burke and Bonanno Soldier Vinny Asaro strangled Katz, believing he was an informant. Valenti knew where the body was because he helped bury it in the basement of a home owned by legendary hijacker Jimmy Burke.

Vinny Asaro told his son Jerome to move the corpse in the mid-1980s. Informer Valenti did not know this when he directed the feds to the basement graveyard. However, federal officials still found pieces of the body when they dug up the cellar and used DNA to identify small pieces of the remains.

November 23, 2014
Infamous Joe "Bayonne Joe" Zicarelli Associate Harold Konigsberg died. He had become an informant in the 1970s but was not involved in LCN for many decades.

March 23, 2015
Judge Nicholas Garaufis sentenced Underboss Tom DiFiore to 21 months for an extortion conviction from 2014. Di Fiore was also Acting Boss since 2012.

March 26, 2015
Judge Allyne Ross sentenced Capo Jerome Asaro to seven and a half years for being involved in the 1969 Paul Katz murder. In the mid-eighties, Asaro moved the corpse and pled guilty to accessory to murder after the fact in October 2004.

March 26, 2015
The feds arrested Capo Joe Palazzolo on a parole violation for meeting with Consigliere Anthony Rabito.
This arrest ruined Boss Mikey Mancuso's plans to name Palazzolo as his new Acting Boss replacing the jailed Thomas Di Fiore.

JOE CAMMARANO JR IS THE NEW ACTING BOSS

March 2015
Bonanno Boss Mikey Mancuso reluctantly selected Joe Cammarano Jr Acting Boss. Mancuso needed a frontman so he could avoid a parole violation for associating with bad guys. The Bonanno Capos dutifully elected Cammarano Jr.

July 28, 2015
Judge Nicholas Garaufis sentenced Associate Anthony Basile, a turncoat, to 12 years despite the prosecution's pleas that he deserved life. In 2006 a jury convicted Basile of participating in the murder of Robert Perrino. After the verdict, Basile attempted to become a government informer but lied to the FBI and acted up in prison. At that point, the feds dropped the plea agreement. With time served and good behavior Basile would have 13 months left to do.

August 4, 2015
Prison officials released former Acting Boss and Underboss Thomas Di Fiore from his extortion sentence handed down on March 24, 2015. They credited him with time served waiting for his trial and sentencing, plus good behavior.

November 13, 2015
A jury found former Capo Vinny Asaro not guilty of participation in the famous 1978 Lufthansa robbery and the 1969 murder of

Paul Katz. The verdict was a stunning defeat for the prosecutors who used an Asaro cousin, Gaspare Valenti, as their chief witness. Former Underboss Salvatore Vitale also testified about Asaro passing along jewels from the

Lufthansa heist. Defense lawyers blunted his testimony somewhat when Vitale admitted the government gave him $250,000 for his co-operation.

February 16, 2016
Testifying in the Nicky Santora crew trial, former Capo James "Louie" Tartaglione publicly admitted to luring his friend Russell Mauro to his death in 1991. Mauro had been one of the killers of Carmine Galante back in 1979.

May 10, 2016
Justice Mark Dwyer declared a mistrial for Capo Nicky Santora, Soldier Vito Badamo, Soldier Ernest Aiello, and Associate Anthony Santora. The Justice ordered that all the defendants remain behind bars. They took Santora back to the prison ward of Bellevue Hospital. The DA would decide later whether to retry the men.

June 21, 2016
Capo Anthony Pipitone was given two years in prison for attending a party with other mobsters while out on parole.

March 29, 2017
The feds arrested Acting Capo Ronald Giallanzo and nine others on a variety of charges, including loansharking.

June 2017
Vinny Asaro pled guilty to ordering the arson of a car in a road rage incident.

December 28, 2017
Judge Allyne Ross sentenced Vinny Asaro to eight years for ordering the arson of a car. Asaro believed a motorist had cut him off, so he gave chase. Later he had two mutts find and torch the offending vehicle. It wasn't long before he was caught and convicted. Judge Ross said she was adding time to the average sentence based on her belief he dodged the bullet many times in the past.

January 12, 2018
The feds arrested Acting Boss Joe Cammarano Jr, Acting Consigliere John Zanocchio, Capos Simone Esposito, Joseph Sabella, George Tropiano, and Soldier Albert Armetta.

2018
Former Consigliere Nicky Santora died of natural causes.

August 2018
Boss Mikey Mancuso was in a halfway house finishing up his 15-year sentence.

March 12, 2019
Prison officials officially released Bonanno Boss Mikey Mancuso from his 15-year sentence that included the 2004 murder of Randy Pizzolo. He had been in a halfway house since August 2018.

ACTING BOSS JOE CAMMARANO JR WINS

March 13, 2019
A jury acquitted Acting Boss Joe Cammarano Jr and Acting Consigliere John Zanocchio of various RICO conspiracy charges. They found Zanocchio not guilty of beating Associate Steven Sabella in their Pulse Gentlemen's Club's back room. The government failed to prove that the two men were involved in loansharking and extortion in aid of racketeering.

After his beating, Sabella claimed the two men pushed him out of his lucrative rackets, causing financial ruin. He became an informer in 2018. Former Capo Peter Lovaglio also testified for the prosecution and said he was present in 2015 when the Bonanno Capos elected Cammarano as their new Acting Boss.

ACTING BOSS JOE CAMMARANO JR LOSES

March 2019
Recently freed Bonanno Boss Mikey Mancuso made significant changes in his Family. He demoted Acting Boss Joe Cammarano Jr, Acting Consigliere John Zanocchio and Capos Vito Grimaldi, and Joseph Grimaldi. Street talk suggested that Mancuso was furious with the Cammarano/Zanocchio defense strategy in their trial. A defense lawyer, John Meringolo, mocked the many changes in the Consigliere position during Mancuso's reign, trying to show that just because Zanocchio was Acting Consigliere, it didn't mean anything. Mancuso felt his men should have prevented this insult to him.

May 2019
Former Consigliere Anthony Graziano died.

July 22, 2019
Judge Alvin Hellerstein sentenced Bonanno Capo Joe Sabella to 87 months for various charges. Previously Sabella admitted to extorting a demolition company, fraud, and assault of a strip club owner. From the owner, he and others took over the club plus loansharking and gambling rackets. The feds had arrested Sabella on January 12, 2018, along with Acting Boss Joe Cammarano Jr and Acting Underboss John Zanocchio.

October 2019
Soldier Vinny Asaro suffered a massive stroke in the Federal Medical Prison in Springfield, Illinois.

April 17, 2020
Judge Allyne Ross granted Vinny Asaro an early release due to the Covid 19 virus's dangers to his fragile health.

CHAPTER FOURTEEN

Bonannos in the Wastelands

After a few futile years attempting to regain control of their Mafia Family, in 1968, Joe and Bill Bonanno retreated out west, forever exiled in disgrace from La Cosa Nostra. They would spend the rest of their lives unsuccessfully trying to rewrite mob history.

As far as La Cosa Nostra was concerned, Bonanno was a non-entity to be avoided at all cost. However, for ambitious good guys, Bonanno remained a big prize. He and his son Bill had brought this continued attention on themselves by publishing books, doing TV and magazine interviews, and the like. The result was many years of tension and costs for old Joe and even time in prison. Below is a summary of some of the known events.

October 1961
Bill Bonanno had been managing the Celebrity Lounge located inside the Romulus Steak House in Phoenix. In October, the joint closed, and Phoenix police arrested Bill for passing a $1,930 bogus check. After his conviction, a judge sentenced Bonanno to three years' probation and restitution.

October 21, 1964
Two men kidnapped Joe Bonanno on this date. The event started a massive federal, state, and local effort to find him.

Eventually, the good guys concluded that Bonanno had arranged the kidnapping himself to avoid appearing before a New York grand jury.

December 21, 1964
An Arizona Republic investigation showed that there were six liens against Bill Bonanno's Tucson area properties. One went back to 1954.

December 23, 1964
US Attorney Robert Morgenthau told the press that the IRS was placing liens on Bonanno's Tucson home and other properties. This IRS move was another effort to smoke Bonanno out of hiding.

December 26, 1964
Very early in the morning Bill Bonanno left New York and started driving to Tucson.

December 28, 1964
Bill Bonanno arrived in Tucson and checked into the Spanish Trail Motel around noon.

December 29, 1964
In the afternoon, Tucson police and FBI Agents, including Kermit Johnson, arrested Bill Bonanno in a local barbershop. They locked him up in the Prima County Jail on a material witness warrant out of New York and handed him a subpoena to appear before a federal grand jury in New York investigating his father's disappearance.

December 31, 1964
Not long after midnight, Bill Bonanno talked with FBI Agents in the Prima County Jail for about five hours. At 9:41 AM, jail officials released Bonanno for he had obtained bail from a bonding company. They had kept him locked up for forty hours while he desperately attempted to raise money to get his freedom.

January 4, 1965
Bill Bonanno flew to New York to appear before a federal grand jury investigating his father's disappearance. He appeared the next day.

July 10-25, 1967

Bill Bonanno was in Europe visiting his former mistress. They took a side trip to Spain to watch the bullfights.

December 16, 1967

Joe Bonanno returned to Tucson from New York.

BILL BONANNO HAS MONEY PROBLEMS

February 25, 1968

A special federal tax court hearing in Tucson named Bill Bonanno as a respondent. He owed the feds a pile of money.

February 1968

Bill Bonanno asked a Tucson lawyer whether it was legal to use someone else's credit card. Joseph H Soble told him it wasn't. A little later, Soble discovered that Bill Bonanno had charged $500 worth of plane tickets to his account at Gulliver's Travel Agency. Soble told the firm not to provide the vouchers to Bonanno, but they did. Bill and Joe Bonanno Jr had ordered two round trip tickets to New York and used them. Soble refused to pay the travel agency, but someone else did. Soble would testify about this at a later Bill Bonanno trial despite being threatened.

March 1968

Joe Bonanno returned to Tucson. He had a heart attack soon after.

March 1968

Helga Reynolds had returned to Tucson after five years of living in Germany. She had been the mistress of Bill Bonanno and bore a son with him. The FBI noticed her living at the Tidelands Motor Inn.

March 14, 1968

Aldo Vineri, an investigative Judge in Palermo, Sicily, put Joe Bonanno, Carmine Galante, and others on trial for a narcotics conspiracy. None of the American defendants were there, so this was a trial in absentia. Nothing much came of this endeavor.

March 30, 1968
Police arrested Joe Bonanno Jr and another man for armed robbery and auto theft. The police dropped the charges on April 3, 1968.

April 1, 1968
Public records at a federal tax hearing in Tucson showed that Bill Bonanno owed about $61,000 in unpaid taxes from 1959, 1960, and 1961.

April 11, 1968
Joe Bonanno arrived at the SF airport, and Bill and Rosalie Bonanno picked him up. He had been visiting his daughter, who lived in the area.

April 16, 1968
Joe Bonanno was driven to the SF airport by Bill. Joe flew home to Tucson. The FBI was watching.

May 17, 1968
Officials subpoenaed Joe Bonanno to appear before a grand jury in New York. They released him on $150,000 bail after he pled innocent.

June 5, 1968
An ambulance rushed Joe Bonanno to St Joseph's Hospital after he complained about heart pains. He was supposed to testify the next day in New York before a grand jury.

June 12, 1968
Doctors released Joe Bonanno from the hospital, where they found he didn't have a heart attack but had heart problems. While waiting for his father's release Bill Bonanno chatted with the press.

BOMBS AWAY

July 21, 1968
A bomb went off in a garage at the Grace Ranch owned by Detroit mobster Peter Licavoli.

July 22, 1968
Bill Bonanno wounded a man lurking around Joe Bonanno's back fence. Two bombs went off immediately afterward, tearing a big hole in the brick fence and destroying the brick BBQ.

August 6, 1968
Joe Bonanno failed to testify before a New York grand jury about his 1964 obstruction of justice case. His lawyer claimed Bonanno was too ill.

August 8, 1968
Judge John Cannella of New York ordered that a heart specialist in Tucson examine Joe Bonanno's heart.

August 7, 1968
Peter Notaro, a Bonanno loyalist, purchased a home at 1331 N Rosemont Avenue in Tucson.

August 15, 1968
Peter Notaro and his family moved into their new home.

August 16, 1968
Two blasts, spaced about 30 seconds apart, wrecked the rear patio gate at Notaro's new residence shortly before 10:15 PM.

August 21, 1968
A New York auto leasing firm repossessed Bill Bonanno's 1967 Caddy in Tucson. They towed it away from the Tidewater Motor Inn at 919 N Stone Street. Bonanno had made no payments on the lease since he left New York in February 1968.

September 1968
Bill Bonanno's lawyers met with the IRS in Tucson in the hopes of reaching a deal on Bill's tax problem from February 25.

September 23, 1968
Peter Notaro told Bill Bonanno that there was a strange man parked outside his home. With all the bombings, Bonanno was extraordinarily concerned and went to Notaros. He pointed a rifle at the man only to discover he was an undercover police officer. He arrested Bonanno on charges of possession of a deadly weapon

with the intent to assault and drawing a deadly weapon other than for self-defence.

September 16, 1968
A bomb went off behind the Wig Beauty Salon at 2739 East Speedway. The former wife of Bonanno Soldier Charles Battaglia worked there. At a later hearing, she would testify that a man identifying himself as David, an FBI Agent, called and said she should quit her job.

September 27, 1968
Before Judge William Netherton, Bill Bonanno pled not guilty to the weapons charges from September 23.

CREDIT CARD FRAUD

October 15, 1968
A federal grand jury in New York indicted Bill Bonanno, Joe Bonanno Jr, and Peter Notaro on credit card fraud charges.

October 17, 1968
Greg Genovese, a son-in-law of Joe Bonanno, testified in a deposition in the Cerrito libel case against Look Magazine.
His parents lived in Endicott, NY, when he was young, then moved to Arizona. While in Endicott, they would socialize with Boss Joe Barbara. At some earlier date, the San Jose Boss, Joe Cerrito, inducted Genovese into his Family as a favor to Joe Bonanno. He was a dentist.

Note:
San Jose Boss Joe Cerrito sued Life Magazine after it named him as a Mafia Boss.

October 29, 1968
Joe Bonanno's lawyer, Albert Krieger, obtained a delay in Bonanno's appearance before a New York grand jury.

November 1968
Joe Bonanno's lawyer, Albert Krieger, appeared before the NY Supreme Court to explain why the judge should not hold Bonanno in contempt for not appearing before a New York grand jury in June 1968.

December 3, 1968
A federal grand jury in New York indicted Bill Bonanno and Peter Notaro for conspiring to use a stolen credit card to buy airline tickets, motel accommodations, and meals. They also charged Notaro for lying before a grand jury about this matter. Judge Edward Weinfeld issued bench warrants for their arrests.

December 15, 1968
A judge allowed Bill Bonanno the second continuance (delay) in his credit card case. He was now living in San Jose.

March 11, 1969
Life Magazine won their lawsuit with San Jose Boss Joe Cerrito. An informant told the FBI earlier that Cerrito regretted initiating the suit.

April 17, 1969
Bill Bonanno paid a $150 fine for pulling a gun on an undercover police officer parked outside Peter Notaro's home on September 23, 1968. The prosecutor dropped the charge of possession of a deadly weapon with intent to assault.

May 4, 1969
Two bombs went off on E Speedway Blvd, damaging the Salon de Paris beauty shop and a building next to the Italian Bakery and Delicatessen. The owner of the bakery was Peter Sciortino, a former business associate of Joe Bonanno.

June 1969
Joe Bonanno's lawyer Albert Krieger asked the New York Judge Edmond Palmiere to ease Bonanno's bail restrictions. He said Bonanno wanted to move to the Woodside-Atherton area of California. Bonanno's daughter Catherine lived in Atherton, and her husband, a dentist, ran a dental clinic in the area. The judge

refused to lower the $150,000 bail but said he'd consider easing Bonanno's movements so he could explore moving to California.

July 1969
In California, the Atherton Civic Interest League petition their city council to discourage or, if possible, prevent Joe Bonanno from moving to their community.

July 21, 1969
Tucson police arrested Paul M Stevens in connection with the bombing of Joe Bonanno's home.

July 22, 1969
Acting Tucson Police Chief William Glikinson interviewed Joe Bonanno at his home for about an hour. Bonanno assured the Chief that he would not interfere in the investigation.

BOMBERS REVEALED

July 23, 1969
Tucson police arrested William J Dunbar in connection with the bombing of the Bonanno and Notaro homes. He was hiding out in a trailer camp on San Carlos Lake in Gila County. Judge Jack Marks kept his bond at $10,000.

August 12, 1969
David Hale resigned from the FBI. The same day suspected bombers Dunbar and Stevens were in court in Tucson for their preliminary hearing on bombing charges. Witness Jane Hitchcock testified that both Dunbar and Stevens told her they bombed Joe Bonanno's home. She added that Dunbar claimed that an FBI friend wanted to start a Mafia war.

September 6, 1969
Tucson police announced they were investigating former FBI Agent David Hale's involvement in the rash of Tucson bombings.

September 11, 1969

William Dunbar told the Arizona Republic that he was the victim of female vindictiveness. He said that Jane Hitchcock made up the story accusing him of being involved in the Bonanno bombing because she blamed him for her vehicle's repossession.

September 16, 1969
Judge John Collins set February 3, 1970, for Paul M Stevens and William J Dunbar's trial date. He continued the two on $10,000 bail each.

September 17, 1969
A federal grand jury indicted Bill Bonanno on tax charges for concealing assets.

JOE BONANNO IN TROUBLE

October 4, 1969
The feds arrested Joe Bonanno and Peter Notaro for conspiracy and extortion in an attempt to free Soldier Charles Battaglia from prison. US Commissioner Raymond Terlizzi had Notaro locked up on a $15,000 bond while Bonanno remained under detention in his home due to medical problems. This story made the front page in the Tucson Daily Citizen.

October 10, 1969
A Tucson federal grand jury indicted Joe Bonanno and Peter Notaro for conspiracy and extortion in the Battaglia case.

October 28, 1969
Peter Notaro finally posted his $15,000 bail and was released from jail.

November 3, 1969
Joe Bonanno and Peter Notaro pled not guilty to the Battaglia conspiracy to obstruct justice case.

CREDIT CARD TRIAL

November 11, 1969

In the Bill Bonanno credit card trial Don Torrillo, the card owner, testified that he gave up the card to Hank Perrone out of fear. He said that he was too afraid to report the false charges until Perrone died by gunfire.

As described in the February 1968 entry, a Tucson lawyer testified that he told Bill Bonanno that it wasn't legal to use someone else's credit card.

Jean Sands, a hostess at Pancho's Mexican Restaurant in Tucson, testified that Bill Bonanno used the Torrillo card to pay for six guests' dinners.

Allan Bloom, son of the Bloom Clothing store owner, testified that Bill tried to purchase clothes using Don Torrillo Diner's Club credit card.

When the cashier at the clothing store tried to verify the credit card with Diner's Club, they asked to speak with the customer. Bill said he was Torrillo but made a mistake when he confirmed a fake address. It was a trick question used by the Diner's Club to ferret out fraud. The cashier confiscated the card from Bonanno.

November 4, 1969

US Attorney Ann Bowen signed an affidavit that David Hill, a guest at the Joe Bonanno home, was planning on leaving the country. The police arrested Hill and served him with a subpoena to appear before a Tucson grand jury.

November 14, 1969

The jury convicted Bill and Peter Notaro of mail fraud conspiracy in the Torrillo credit card.

JOE BONANNO WINS

March 4, 1970

A Tucson jury found Joe Bonanno, Peter Notaro, and Charles Battaglia not guilty of three counts related to an attempt to free Battaglia from an extortion sentence. The prosecution tried to show that the three were working to obtain false testimony that the feds used illegal wiretaps in Battaglia's 1967 conviction. Defense lawyers destroyed William Reinke, the chief prosecution witness, which led to the not guilty verdicts.

Bonanno told the press, "I don't hold no grudge against nobody." Notaro told the press, "Justice was done right."

March 9, 1970

New York Judge Walter Mansfield sentenced Bill Bonanno to four years and a $10,000 fine for 55 counts of mail fraud in the Don Torrillo credit card matter. He gave Peter Notaro one year and a $1,000 fine for 53 counts of mail fraud. Mansfeld continued Bonanno on $15,000 bail and Notaro with $10,000.

May 2, 1970

The Arizona Republic ran an interesting story on the Bonannos and a profile done by True Magazine. The Bonannos opened a casino in Haiti in 1963, operating under a license granted by dictator Francois "Papa Doc" Duvalier. Bill Bonanno confirmed this to the newspaper and claimed to have been in Haiti many times. After Bill left Haiti, Bonanno member Vito DeFilippo took over the casino.

The newspaper stated that the Bonannos played a significant role in keeping Duvalier in power after President Kennedy wanted him removed. The Mafia helped Duvalier obtain weapons after the USA had cut him off. The CIA wasn't happy.
I have been unable to authenticate this claim.

The True Magazine article included the story that Duvalier hosted Joe Bonanno in his palace when Bonanno went into hiding in 1964. The Arizona Republic stated that its sources discounted this theory. So do I.

BOMBERS PLEAD

July 14, 1970
Bombers William Dunbar and Paul Stevens pled guilty to reduced charges before Judge William Frey.

July 24, 1970
During their sentencing hearing, Judge William Frey gave both Dunbar and Stevens, $286 fines. Dunbar pled to an accessory to bombing count while Stevens admitted to possession of explosives.

The men testified that Tucson businessman Walter Prideaux was an accomplice while FBI Agent David Hale was the planner. Dunbar stated that Hale recruited him at the Complete Auto Supply owned by Prideaux. In turn, Dunbar recruited Stevens, who was an electrical engineer at Hughes Aircraft. Prideaux drove the men to Peter Licavoli's Grace Ranch (July 21, 1968) plus took the injured Stevens to hospital after Bill Bonanno wounded him (July 22, 1968.) Both men refused to testify, claiming their 5th amendment rights.

HONOR THY FATHER

1971
"Honor Thy Father," an account of the Bonanno Family focusing on Bill Bonanno, was published. The author was Gay Talese, who became friends with the family over six years. It was an invaluable book for Mafia fans and historians, but the author was incredibly naive. He believed nearly everything Bill Bonanno told him. The book was a great success, and a TV network made a movie based on Talese's account.

January 8, 1971
A San Francisco federal grand jury indicted Joe Bonanno Jr and two associates for extorting an area pilot who borrowed money from one of the associates and did not pay it back.

January 9, 1971
The FBI announced the arrest of Joe Bonanno Jr and two associates on a federal grand jury extortion indictment.

January 23, 1971
Before Judge Robert Peckham, Joe Bonanno Jr and two associates pled not guilty to extortion of the pilot.

MORE BILL BONANNO TROUBLE

January 18, 1971
Bill Bonanno turned himself into US Marshall in Los Angeles. They would send him to Terminal Island to begin his four-year credit card fraud sentence. Peter Notaro surrendered to US Marshalls in Tucson the same day.

February 16, 1971
Bill Bonanno pled guilty to concealing his ownership in his Long Island home by transferring it to two Associates. Bonanno was attempting to avoid having the house seized for the $50,000 he owed the federal government. Judge George Rosling remanded Bonanno to prison to await sentencing. The feds had flown Bonanno in from his prison cell on Terminal Island, California.

February 25, 1971
A San Francisco grand jury indicted Bill Bonanno for extortion involving an area pilot and a loan of about $2,500.

February 26, 1971
Judge George Rosling sentenced Bill Bonanno to one year and a fine of $1,500 in his fraud case involving his Long Island home.

August 1971
Esquire Magazine carried the first of a three-part summary of Gay Talese's book Honor Thy Father.

September 29, 1971
A Tucson grand jury indicted many people, including Joe Bonanno Jr, in a complicated plot that involved an attempt to recoup $32,000.

Allegedly Bonanno Jr and a friend plotted to kill a man so he couldn't talk to the police about other crimes.

December 17, 1971
A federal jury found Bill and Joe Bonanno Jr guilty of running a collection racket in San Jose and San Francisco. They convicted Bill on one extortion count and one conspiracy charge while they found Joe Jr guilty on three counts of extortion and one of conspiracy. This proceeding was their second trial, for the first one ended in a mistrial when a prosecution witness took the Fifth Amendment.

At trial, pilot Robert Piper explained that he had borrowed $2,900 from Alfred Salciccia to finance a heroin deal. However, when he was flying the heroin from Mexico to California, the heroin disappeared. Salciccia wanted his money back and enlisted the services of the Bonannos to help.

January 23, 1972
The Arizona Republic ran a very critical review of Gay Talese's book Honor Thy Father. Author Joe Flaherty felt Talese was too lenient on the Bonannos criminal affairs.

February 15, 1972
Judge Robert Peckham sentenced Bill Bonanno to three years and Joe Bonanno to five years for their conspiracy and extortion convictions involving the San Jose pilot.

February 16, 1972
Judge Thomas Murphy issued an arrest warrant for Joe Bonanno Jr in a Phoenix extortion and murder plot.

February 18, 1972
Joe Bonanno Jr surrendered to FBI Agents in San Jose to face charges in the Phoenix extortion and murder plot.

June 19, 1972
Judge Walter Craig set aside the jury's guilty verdict for Joe Bonanno Jr in the vast Phoenix conspiracy case involving extortion, arson, and a witness's planned murder. He said the evidence produced at trial for the government did not support Bonanno Jr's indictment charges. It appeared that Bonanno Jr

and a buddy conned a desperate defendant into paying them to kill a witness against him. They took the money and did nothing.

July 1972
The Tucson police force put together a 20-minute information film for Tucson business people. It was titled "The Mafia: How it Operates and How it has infected Tucson.? The film named Joe Bonanno as a significant Mafia figure.

SUPREME COURT RULING

October 30, 1972
The US Supreme Court upheld Bill Bonanno's three-year sentence for extortion of the San Jose pilot and Joe Bonanno Jr's conviction and five-year term in the same case. They took Bill back to his Terminal Island prison while Joe Jr remained free on bond.

February 5, 1973
Various newspapers carried a ridiculous article by veteran reporter Victor Riesel. He claimed Bonanno was the most substantial Mafia figure in the US and planned a move on California.

February 16, 1973 (Date approximate)
Veteran Mafia expert Ralph Salerno reported that Joe Bonanno envoys were in New York planning his return to power. This report was way off base, for Bonanno had zero chance of even being reinstated in La Cosa Nostra, let alone returning to power. Time would prove Salerno's prediction wrong.

HONOR THY FATHER MOVIE

February 29, 1973
CBS ran a film titled Honor Thy Father based on Gay Talese's book of the same name. It starred Joseph Bologna as Bill Bonanno, Brenda Vaccaro as Rosalie Bonanno, and Raf Vallone as Joe Bonanno.

In an interview, Talese said he saw Bill as a tragic figure and a very intelligent man who had little chance of dishonoring his father. The author noted that the book had sold 2.5 million copies plus an additional 200,000 hardcover. That put a lot of money in the hands of the talented Talese.

August 1973
Joe Bonanno Jr began his extortion conviction sentence.

November 17, 1973
Tucson city council announced that they would have to demolish Joe Bonanno's home and others to make room for a road widening. Bonanno's doomed residence address was 1847 Elm Street. His new home address was 255 N Sierra Vista.

Note:
Around 2010 my boss was touring in Arizona and figured it would be fun to visit Bonanno's home that some mutts had bombed. I innocently provided the 1847 Elm location, not knowing the building was long gone. The boss wasted an hour or so looking for the address before giving up. Luckily he didn't fire me for the blunder.

March 8, 1974
Prison officials released Bill Bonanno from Terminal Island Prison on parole from his two convictions.

JOE BONANNO WANTS BACK IN

September 4, 1974
Bonanno called Los Angeles Soldier Frank "Bomp" Bompensiero in San Diego. Bonanno was in LA visiting his son Joe Jr. who was in prison at Terminal Island. Bonanno told Bompensiero that he asked Joe Salardino to lobby new Buffalo leaders for his reinstatement in LCN. Unknown to Bonanno, Bompensiero was an FBI informant and reported the call. In my opinion, there wasn't a snowball's chance that this reinstatement would ever happen.

Later, a Buffalo informant reported that a discussion took place in which someone stated that there was no chance the Commission would ever reinstate Bill Bonanno.

February 12, 1975
A group at Arizona State University paid Bill Bonanno $1500 to speak about prison life.

February 13, 1975
A group at Northern Arizona University paid Bill Bonanno $1500 to speak about prison life.

October 22, 1975
Judge Robert Peckham vacated Joe Bonanno Jr's extortion sentence. The judge ruled that the parole board didn't give Bonanno Jr consideration as he ordered. Peckham resentenced Bonanno Jr to five years' probation.

TRASH COVER BEGINS

December 1975
The Narcotics Strike force began its trash cover of Joe Bonanno. Each week they would replace his garbage bags in the container. Then they went through the trash and tried to piece together Bonanno's documents. This operation ran until April 1979.

May 18, 1977
The Narcotics Strike Force obtained legal authority to place a beeper on Joe Bonanno's vehicle. Years later, Bonanno claimed they placed the beeper then got permission to do so.

NARCOTIC STRIKE FORCE TROUBLES

July 1977
A Pima County Sheriff's deputy reported to his superiors that some Narcotics Strike Force officers were eavesdropping on of

Bonanno's phone conversations when they were only supposed to note the phone numbers involved.

October 5, 1977
Edwin Richards of the Narcotics Strike Force resigned. He pled no contest to the charge of illegal wiretapping and eavesdropping. The authorities fired James Liddiard for insubordination and neglect of duty. They alleged he knew about the unlawful eavesdropping but never reported it to his superiors.

June 12, 1978
A judge gave Bill Bonanno 30 months for the parole violation of inaccurate reporting of income.

June 21, 1978
A judge ordered Bill and Joe Bonanno returned to prison for parole violations concerning their 1971 extortion convictions. Bill was in violation for associating with convicts on July 10/11, 1974, in North Hollywood. He was also in trouble for not correctly reporting his income. Joe Jr was also in violation for not accurately reporting his income.

PENTHOUSE NONSENSE

June 1978
Penthouse Magazine carried a story that Joe Bonanno was the real Godfather. The article was ridiculous and based on incomplete information coming from Bonanno's home's trash cover. Except for false analysis of Bonanno's notes, there was no evidence in New York or other mob cities that Bonanno was a power. At the time, the FBI had most mob Families under surveillance, electronic surveillance, and informers' information. To date, I have yet to see anything remotely supporting the Penthouse story claim of Bonanno being the top dog.

August 9, 1978
Bill Bonanno turned himself in to begin a 30-month probation violation sentence.

August 31, 1978
Joe Bonanno Jr surrendered to begin a 34-month probation violation sentence.

MORE JOE BONANNO TROUBLE

September 1978
The US Organized Crime Strike Force, based in San Francisco, served Joe Bonanno with a grand jury subpoena in Tucson. They wanted him to testify in San Francisco about the business records of Bill and Joe Jr.

October 1978
The Narcotics Task Force obtained legal permission to install a wiretap on Joe Bonanno's home phone. It operated from October 6 until October 31, 1978.

Early 1979
Lou Peter's, a California Cadillac dealer, acting for the FBI, told Joe Bonanno that the court had subpoenaed him about his dealings with Bill Bonanno. Joe Bonanno ordered Peters to get rid of records that showed Bill Bonanno had sold a Cadillac through Peter's agency for cash. Jack DeFilippi, a Bonanno relative, helped Peter's hide the documents. Later Bonanno told Peters to lie to a grand jury about the Bill Bonanno deal.

March 1, 1979
Carmine Galante was released from jail and arrived in Newark.

Joe Bonanno appeared before a Tucson grand jury investigating Bill Bonanno's business dealings. Authorities had subpoenaed Bonanno back in September of 1978.

JOE BONANNO'S HOME IS RAIDED

March 16, 1979
A judge signed a warrant allowing a search of Joe Bonanno's home.

March 17, 1979
Law enforcement agents raid Bonanno's home with media in hand. They confiscated lots of documents, including his autobiography manuscript.

March 18, 1979
The Narcotic Strike Force finds a windfall in Joe Bonanno's trash as he cleaned house after the raid.

April 26, 1979
A San Francisco grand jury indicted Joe Bonanno and relative Jack DiFilippi for conspiracy to obstruct justice. The authorities believed Bonanno and DeFilippi played a role in hiding Bill and Joe Jr's business records.

April 27, 1979
Joe Bonanno surrendered in Tucson on his San Francisco obstruction of justice case. The judge released him on bond.

November 16, 1979
A judge ordered Bonanno to stand trial next year for his conspiracy to obstruct justice case in San Francisco.

June 79
Time Magazine did a story on how the FBI seized Bonanno's memoirs.

December 1979
Authorities released Joe Bonanno Jr from his parole violation.

April 1980
The conspiracy to obstruct justice case of Joe Bonanno and Jack DiFilippi began in San Francisco. There would be no jury.

April 21, 1980
Judge Ingram delayed Joe Bonanno's trial to let him complete medical exams.

May 1980
Officials released Bill Bonanno from prison.

May 7, 1980
Judge Ingram delayed Joe Bonanno's trial due to Bonanno's illness.

July 1980
The Bonanno trial ended. Judge William Ingram would rule on guilt in September.

JOE BONANNO GUILTY

September 2, 1980
Judge William Ingram found Joe Bonanno and nephew Jack DeFilippi guilty of obstruction of justice. Bonanno had told auto dealer Lou Peters to hide records that showed Bill Bonanno had sold a Caddy through Peter's dealership for cash. Later Bonanno told Peters to lie to a grand jury about the matter. The feds recorded Bonanno giving these instructions.

September 8, 1980
Fay Bonanno died after a long illness.

October 1980
Doctors at St Mary's Hospital in Tucson removed a cancerous tumor on Joe Bonanno's bladder.

November 8, 1980
St Mary's hospital released Joe Bonanno after he recovered from his cancer operation.

December 19, 1980
The IRS sued Bill Bonanno for $22,449 in back taxes, penalties, and interest.

January 13, 1981
Judge William Ingram sentenced Joe Bonanno to five years and a fine of $10,000 for obstruction in the matter of his sons' business records.

BILL BONANNO HITS A NEW LOW

January 15, 1981
A grand jury indicted Bill Bonanno, Joe Bonanno Jr, Anthony Bressi, and Raymond J Tedesco in a home improvement scam. There were twenty-one counts of grand theft and one count of conspiracy to commit grand theft. Three Bonanno-connected companies were involved; Los Gatos Construction and Development Company, Olympic Construction Company, and Kachina Enterprises.

January 22, 1981
Joe Bonanno Jr and Ray Tedesco surrendered after being indicted in a home improvement fraud scheme.

January 23, 1981
Bill Bonanno did not surrender in the home improvement scam but fled to Mexico. The FBI issued a complaint charging him with unlawful flight to avoid prosecution.

February 1981
Bill Bonanno won $6000 in a civil suit against two former Tucson cops who illegally tapped his phone.

March 1981
A newspaper claimed that Rosalie Bonanno filed for divorce in March of 1981 but dropped the complaint a month later.

November 23, 1981
Mexican police arrested Bill Bonanno on the home improvement fraud indictment. The FBI had tipped them off that Bonanno's wife would be visiting Bill. The cops followed her right to her husband. They took him to the US border and turned him over to the FBI.

November 26, 1981
Bill Bonanno pled not guilty to grand theft and conspiracy to defraud in a home remodeling enterprise. He and others allegedly defrauded elderly customers in a home repair scam using Los Gatos companies. Judge Alan Lindsay set Bonanno's bond at $1 million.

May 19, 1982
US Magistrate Raymond Terlizzi reduced Bill Bonanno's bond to $50,000 cash in the home fraud case.

May 20, 1982
Officials released Bill Bonanno as he awaited trial in the home fraud case.

June 2, 1982
Bill, Joe Bonanno Jr, Anthony Bressi, and Raymond J Tedesco pled not guilty in the home repair scam indictment.

1983
Simon and Schuster published Joe Bonanno's autobiography "Man of Honor." It was a smashing success and a tremendous boon to mob historians, even though the account was entirely self-serving.

JOE BONANNO TV STAR

April 1983
Mike Wallace of CBS TV's 60 Minutes show interviewed Joe Bonanno and his three children at Bonanno's Tucson home. Bonanno glossed over Mafia violence and drugs and tried to keep the conversation on how he was an honorable man with a tradition. It is an interesting watch for mob fans and historians and is available on YouTube.

April 30, 1983
The Supreme Court refused to hear Joe Bonanno's appeal of his obstruction of justice sentence.

September 1983
Joseph Bonanno underwent a 57-day evaluation of his health.

November 22, 1983
Judge William Ingram reduced Joe Bonanno's sentence for obstruction of justice from five years to a year and a day due to his poor health.

December 5, 1983
Bonanno began his one year sentence for obstruction of justice. Prison officials assigned him to the Terminal Island hospital unit.

May 1984
Judge Raul Ramirez dismissed the Bonanno home fraud case because the prosecution used evidence obtained from the defendant's trash. The Ninth Circuit Court of Appeals reversed Ramirez's decision and ordered a new trial.

July 29, 1984
Terminal Island officials released Joe Bonanno from his obstruction of justice sentence. He did almost eight months of the year and a day term.

JOE BONANNO AND THE COMMISSION CASE

November 20, 1984
Prosecutor Rudy Giuliani questioned Joe Bonanno for three hours. He said Bonanno gave information about 40 years of organized crime. Giuliani helped develop the Commission Case in New York and wanted Bonanno to testify about what he had written in his autobiography.

November 28, 1984
Court officials arraigned Joe Bonanno Jr and his wife on cocaine conspiracy charges. The indictment alleged he tried to sell five oz. of cocaine on April 15, 1983.

September 4, 1985
In Tuscon's St Mary's Hospital, Rudy Giuliani gave Joe Bonanno immunity from self-incrimination, but he refused to testify. Judge Owen then ordered Bonanno to testify the next day.

September 5, 1985
When Joe Bonanno refused to testify, Judge Owen found him in civil contempt. He also threatened to keep Bonanno in jail for 18 months or the end of the Commission trial. Judge Owen ordered officials to take Bonanno to Tucson's Metropolitan Correctional

Center. Once there, Bonanno complained of chest pains, and an ambulance took him back to St Mary's Hospital.

Sept. 6, 1985
Federal Marshalls flew Bonanno from Tucson to the Springfield, Illinois Prison Hospital.

November 19, 1985
A jury found Bill Bonanno guilty of conspiracy and eight counts of grand theft in a home improvement scam involving elderly Alameda County residents. He cheated nine older adults out of $110,000. The jury found him not guilty of some other counts.

Bill Bonanno took the stand during the trial and described what he felt was years of unfair persecution by authorities. He then listed some of his accomplishments. Judging by the verdict, his plea did not go over too well.

February 2, 1986
A judge sentenced Joe Bonanno Jr to four months for lying about a San Diego cocaine case.

March 27, 1986
Judge Joseph Karesh sentenced Bill Bonanno to four years in California State Prison on the home fraud scheme. He released Bonanno on a $100,000 appeal bond.

May 1986
A jury found Bill not guilty of fraud, but they convicted his brother Joe Jr of eight counts involving a $240,000 investment involving the marketing of Presidential posters.

October 31, 1986
The feds dropped Bonanno's Commission subpoena because the trial was over except for the verdict. Judge Owens ended Bonanno's civil contempt sentence and ordered Bonanno's immediate release from Springfield Prison Hospital.

November 1, 1986
Officials released Bill Bonanno from Springfield Prison Hospital.

November 13, 1986
A judge sentenced Joe Bonanno Jr to four years in a fraudulent investment scam involving Presidential posters. A jury convicted him in May 1986 of eight counts of fraud and conspiracy to defraud investors of $250,000.

November 25, 1986
A federal grand jury indicted Joe Bonanno for criminal contempt for refusing to testify at a Tucson deposition. Rudy Giuliani wanted to question Bonanno about his autobiography, in which Bonanno told the history of the Commission.

JOE BONANNO RULED INCOMPETENT

July 2, 1989
A judge dropped the criminal contempt of court charge from Joe Bonanno's refusal to testify about the Commission at a Tucson deposition. Doctors ruled Bonanno was incompetent to stand trial.

August 18, 1989
Bill Bonanno began serving his home fraud sentence in May 1986.

MAFIA MARRIAGE

The following tale is from "Honor Thy Father" by Gay Talese. Bill Bonanno must have told him the story. Why I don't know.

In the early 1960s Bill Bonanno began having an affair with a bar waitress. It went on for quite some time. At some point Bill's wife confronted the other woman at her apartment. The girlfriend called Bill who went over and took his wife home. Both women told Bill he would have to decide which one he wanted. Bill procrastinated.

One day Bill went to his girlfriend's apartment and the babysitter told him she had gone out for the evening. Bill sent the young sitter home and waited in the darkened apartment. He then saw his girlfriend exit a car driven by a man and walk to her front door. Then...

"He grabbed her dress by the top, ripped it off, and began to tear it into several pieces. As she screamed he charged into her bedroom closet and began to rip other dresses. When she fought to stop him, he hit her, knocking her across the room. After the floor was littered with shredded clothing he left."

For some reason the couple continued to see each other. It was a mess and remained so for quite some time according to Talese.

1990

The William Morrow Company published Rosalie Bonanno's autobiography titled, "Mafia Marriage." It was a heartbreaking book from a mentally and sometimes physically abused woman. Below are a few summaries of events she wrote about:

He bought his mistress the same color and model car he purchased for her.

Bill said, "You're so fat."

Bill said, "You're so skinny."

When she wanted to leave his hideout in Mexico to return home, he prevented her.

Once when finding Rosalie in a bar, he physically took her to a hotel room, stripped off her clothes, took everything she had, and left her naked in the room for a day.

He slapped me across the face.

He dominated me.

On at least two occasions, Rosalie mentioned that Bill gave her bruises on the arm.

She said her marriage made her unhappy, but Bill would never allow divorce.

They had no check books, no savings, no life, health, or car insurance.

She had no money of her own for many years.

In March of 1981, Rosalie went to the Santa Clara County Courthouse and filed for divorce. Three days later, Bill called and threatened and cajoled her into withdrawing the papers.

Most of the time, Bill picked out the family home without consulting her.

One day she found a lipstick stain on his underwear.

When she would confront Bill about his affair, she would only get denials and sometimes a slap on the face.

Once when Bill hit her, Rosalie called her mom in New York for money to fly home. Her mother said the problem was between her and her husband.

Rosalie confronted Bill's pregnant mistress in her residence. Bill came and furiously took her home.

One day Bill made Rosalie promise to do something, and after that, his relationship with the pregnant girlfriend would be over. A desperate Rosalie agreed. Bill took her to a home where the beaten up girlfriend was staying.

Rosalie lied to the girl and said she was divorcing Bill. It is pretty clear Bill had beaten his girlfriend and was frantically trying to appease her so she wouldn't call the police.

Soon after the above incident, Rose took a sleeping pill. When that didn't give her instant relief, she took another, then a third. Bill found her unresponsive and rushed her to the hospital. The papers called it an attempted suicide.

"I twisted myself like a pretzel to please him."

MAFIA MARRIAGE TV MINI SERIES

May 20, 1993
CBS ran a mini-series titled "Love, Honor, and Obey: The Last Mafia Marriage." Ben Gazzara played Joe Bonanno; Nancy McKeon was Rosalie with Eric Roberts as Bill Bonanno.
The book and the TV series were the products of lengthy work by Rosalie, Bill, and TV producer Bob Dellinger. The latter told reporters that Rosalie and Bill were technical consultants for the film and made over $500,000 for the book and TV deal.

Dellinger met Bill Bonanno while they were both in prison on Terminal Island. After Rosalie initially refused to write the book, the two partners pitched a series called "Mafia Mistress" based on Bill's girlfriend. No network would touch it. In my opinion, if that program would have made the air, it would have been yet another insult to the long-suffering Rosalie. Bill, as always, was desperate for money and fame, so Rosalie's feelings were insignificant.

In an interview, Rosalie described the movie as follows, "It's the story of a woman who lived within the constraints of her life and found contentment there."

April 29, 1991
Officials released Joseph Bonanno Jr from prison after he completed his fraud sentence.

Jan 14, 1995

Joe Bonanno celebrated his 90th birthday a few days early at a party of some 300 guests in Tucson. As always, Bill Bonanno invited the press.

BOUND BY HONOR?

1999

St Martin's Press released Bill Bonanno's book "Bound by Honor." In an earlier chapter, I pointed out where Bill's stories often conflicted with his previous ones, his father's account, and the facts. Below are some other questionable claims of Bill Bonanno.

Joe Bonanno put together a guerilla force to help the Allies in their Sicilian invasion during World War Two. No evidence of such an effort exists.

After being killed by Gambino shooters in October of 1957, Boss Albert Anastasia's body hung from the barber's chair. During the shooting, Anastasia stood up then crashed to the floor. This error is a trivial matter.

Bill mistakenly places Richie "The Boot" Boiardo in the Gambino Family when he was a Genovese member. Again, this is a trivial matter.

Bonanno wrote that he participated in negotiations between Boss Tommy Lucchese and John F Kennedy's father in the lead up to the 1960 Democratic convention. There is no way to prove this matter's truth, but I find it highly unlikely that the Mafia Bosses would have included Bonanno on this mission. Secondly, whether this meeting even took place is up for debate.

When writing about his father's ill-fated trip to Canada in 1964, Bill stated that Joe never intended to take up Canadian citizenship. Joe Bonanno's immigration papers contradict that claim.

Bill Bonanno and some Soldiers visited Montreal in November of 1966 in the hopes of rounding up some money for their depleted bank accounts. As described earlier, they were arrested and ultimately deported. In his new book, Bill covered these events by saying, "One day there were erroneous stories in the papers about my being arrested in Canada..."

After the phony Troutman Street shootout in 1968, Bonanno claimed the NYPD invited him to examine some of the scene's weapons. Bonanno wrote that he recognized it as belonging to Phil Rastelli, a Gregorio loyalist, because of a spot of rust on one pistol. That account is ridiculous. Why would any Mafioso hold on to a gun so easily recognizable? Bonanno was trying to prove his account of an ambush was correct. This attempt failed like all the others.

The most incredible story Bonanno told was when Mafioso John Roselli supposedly related how he had assassinated JFK from a sewer on Elm Street. Chicago Boss Sam Giancanna was supposed to pick up Roselli afterward but didn't do so. An examination of that sewer opening proved that it would be impossible to fire a rifle from that spot and hit JFK. The gun wouldn't have room to elevate enough. Furthermore, no scientific evidence even hinted at a shot from that spot. Bonanno expanded on the possibilities of what connections Roselli must have had to gain access to the sewer. Including this JFK tale served to promote interest in the book. It belonged in the sewer where Roselli never was.

Bonanno wrote that the Mafia killed Teamster leader Jimmy Hoffa with an exotic poison shoved down his throat. The result would be a feigned heart attack. They disposed of Hoffa's body by putting it in a car that was then crushed and melted.

I guess this story is as good as others on the Hoffa mystery, but why did the loquacious Bonanno wait so long to tell it?

BONANNOS TV MOVIE

July 25, 1999
Cable TV showed "A Godfather's Story" based on the Joe and Bill Bonanno books. Martin Landau played the old Bonanno, Tony Nardi acted as Joe Bonanno between the ages of 35-61, while Bruce Ramsey portrayed Bonanno as a young adult.

JOE BONANNO EXITS

May 11, 2002
Joe Bonanno passed away from heart trouble in Tucson's St Mary's Hospital with his three children and others by his side.

May 20, 2002
The family held Joe Bonanno's funeral in Tucson at St Peter and Paul Church.

February 4, 2004
Rogue FBI Agent David Hale gave his side of the story to the Arizona Daily Star. Hale claimed they framed him, and it was a vigilante group that did the bombings in Arizona back in 1968.

July 2004
Rosalie Bonanno arranged the sale of some of Joe Bonanno's possessions on eBay.

January 2005
Joe Bonanno's Tucson home was for sale on eBay.

January 24, 2005
Tucson based Commanche Properties Inc. announced a partnership with Bill Bonanno to produce three films.

January 31, 2005
The Securities and Exchange Commission announced it was suspending trading in Commanche Properties shares for ten days. After Commanche publicized its opening, it sold 2,200 over the counter stock until the SEC halted trading. The concern was that Commanche launched a "spam campaign" looking for investors. Under SEC rules, over the counter shares must only be peddled to experienced investors like institutions. After ten days, the SEC lifted its suspension but cautioned potential investors to do their due diligence with over the counter stocks.

In a later announcement, Commanche president Anthony Tarantola denied his company had anything to do with the spam selling. He included Bill Bonanno in that category along with advisor Michale Paloma. Newspaper accounts claimed that Paloma had problems with the SEC in the past.

November 2, 2005
Joe Bonanno Jr died of a heart attack.

January 1, 2008
Bill Bonanno died of a heart attack in Tucson.

Comment

From afar, I respect and admire Rosalie Bonanno. She endured being the wife of an extremely flawed man who dominated her with physical and mental abuse. Despite being thrown into decades of chaos, not of her own making, she survived and raised four respectable children. She is the Bonanno who deserves admiration.

CHAPTER FIFTEEN

Montreal Timeline Part One

INTRODUCTION TO MONTREAL'S MAFIA MILIEU

In the early 1950s Bonanno Capo Carmine Galante established a formal crew in Montreal. That bilingual city in the Province of Quebec was wide open at the time with gambling, prostitution, protection rackets, bank robberies, drug smuggling, and the like. Corrupt politicians and police afforded the hoods significant protection but had to periodically fight off the efforts of "reform movements." Galante's powerful personality and the aura of the Mafia helped him "organize" crime in Montreal.

Galante formed alliances with the two most powerful Italian criminals, Vic Cotroni, a Calabrian, and Luigi Greco, a Sicilian. At some unknown point Galante inducted both men into the Bonanno Family. Each leader was already surrounded by their own trusted crews so Galante gradually inducted some of them until there were approximately 20 "made men" in Montreal. When Galante faced legal problems in the US around 1959, Boss Joe Bonanno appointed Cotroni and perhaps Luigi Greco as Capos. The evidence is still unclear whether Greco held that formal title but he was a power in any case.

Cotroni ruled into the 1970s but age, health, a Crime Inquiry, legal problems, and exhaustion took their toll. Greco had died accidentally in a fire thus removing the leader of the Sicilian faction. They were not pleased when Cotroni moved another Calabrian, Paolo Violi, into the second in command position.

Things worked against Violi, especially when Bonanno Boss Phil Rastelli appointed him Acting Capo when Cotroni was briefly in prison on a contempt sentence. For decades Corsican gangsters refined heroin in France. But by the 1970s Sicilian Mafia figures were producing heroin on their own. Suddenly, the Sicilian members of the Montreal crew had the connections to extreme wealth. Violi didn't and he was against dealing in drugs. When renegade Carmine Galante forced his way into leadership of the Bonanno Family, Violi's time was up.

Galante wanted the riches from the drug trade and the Sicilians in Montreal were the key. He quickly approved Soldier Nicolo Rizzuto's plea for permission to kill Violi. A gunman shot gunned Violi in January 1978 ending the leadership of the Calabrian faction in Montreal. The Sicilians were now on top and would remain unchallenged for thirty years.

The main power in Montreal was Nicolo Rizzuto. Although only a Soldier in the Bonanno Family he actually wielded as much power as any American Mafia Boss and perhaps more. I don't mean he had any influence with the Commission but in his own area. But by "area' I mean that he had great influence in South America, Sicily, and other locations. The wealth of him and his blood family and close Associates dwarfed the income of Bosses like Paul Castellano and John Gotti.

The Rizzuto clan forged alliances with other criminals in Montreal. Despite the killing of the Calabrian Violi, most Calabrians fell in line behind the Rizzutos and gained economically. They allied with the loosely structured West End gang which had excellent contacts at the airports and port which facilitated the movement of drugs. Over time they established working relationships with the extremely powerful Hells Angels who were anxious to peddle the Mafia's cocaine.

As always, there were endless disputes, minor and major and most everyone in the criminal milieu looked to the Rizzutos to arbitrate these matters. Due in part to their formal connection to the Bonanno Family but more to their wealth and the vast number of men they could order to do their will, most everyone accepted, sometimes unhappily, the Rizzutos' decisions. But the sharks are always waiting for a sign of weakness.

The long-time inner circle of the Rizzuto clan were: Nicolo Rizzuto, his son Vito, Nicolo's son-in-law Paulo Renda, Rocco Sollecito and Francesco Arcadi. Three of these men would be killed but another generation was ready to step in.

In January of 2003 a combined police force places bugs and cameras in the Consenza Social Club, the headquarters of the Rizzuto group. The intelligence gathered would result in the arrest of all the top leaders of the family in 2004. That same year the US government came calling for they wanted Vito Rizzuto to face trial for his part in the famous 1981 Three Capos Hit. Although Rizzuto fought extradition for some time he was no longer able to arbitrate disputes nor could his fellow leaders. The bad guys who used to look to the Rizzutos to settle conflicts began to take matters into their own hands. It was chaos.

For a time it looked like the Rizzutos were finished. Old Nick Rizzuto, his grandson Nick Jr, his son-in-law Paulo Renda, and other top aides and friends died during this violent period. Mafia experts in Canada announced their demise and I agreed with them. We were all wrong.

Vito Rizzuto returned from a US prison after completing his plea deal sentence in the Three Capos Hit. Suddenly his enemies started turning up dead all over the world. Meanwhile a shaky alliance of those against the Rizzutos self-imploded. A younger generation of Rizzutos and allies began to assert themselves. They didn't have the prestige of their fathers so it wasn't surprising some did not want to follow their lead. A few older Rizzuto leaders were killed by a Calabrian faction but as a result their two top guys ended up dead.

Meanwhile the two new Rizzuto leaders dodged a huge legal bullet. A combined police force operation succeeded in bugging them and taped incriminating conversations. For a time it appeared these young hoods were off to the slammer for a long time. Nope! The cops didn't conduct their surveillances properly so the new leaders walked free. How long they will be able to stay on top is unclear but it does appear most everyone has had enough of the violence and want to get back to making huge amounts of money in the drug dealing business.

The timeline that follows is lengthy and contains hundreds of names. It might be best for readers to look for these important people as you skim through the material. Perhaps you could write them down on a piece of paper you could refer to as you read.

Carmine Galante
Vic Cotroni
Paolo Violi
Nicolo Rizzuto
Vito Rizzuto
Joe DiMaulo
Raynald Desjardins
Lorenzo Rizzuto
Stefano Sollecito

Montreal: The Early Years

March 9, 1923
Vito Rizzuto Sr married Maria Renda.

February 18, 1924
Nicolo Rizzuto was born in Cattolica Eraclea in Sicily.

1933
A jury convicted Luigi Greco of armed robbery. The judge sentenced him to 15 years.

August 1933
Police found Vito Rizzuto Sr's body in a swamp in the United States.

1942
Vic Cotroni opened Le Cafe Royal, which operated as a gambling den.

1944
Prison officials released Luigi Greco from his armed robbery sentence. He served 11 of the 15 years.

1945
Vic Cotroni opened the Faison Dore club. It was an instant hit featuring entertainment popular in France.

March 20, 1945
Nicolo Rizzuto married Libertina Manno. She is the daughter of Cattolica Eraclea Mafia Boss Antonio Manno.

April 22, 1946
Vito Rizzuto parents, Nicolo and Libertina Rizzuto, baptized him in Cattolica Eraclea.

1951
Paulo Violi arrived in Canada from Calabria, Italy.

February 21, 1954
Vito Rizzuto arrived in Halifax on his eighth birthday accompanied by his parents and sister.

Galante Takes Montreal

February 26, 1954
Capo Carmine Galante visited the Montreal office of Immigration Canada seeking permanent admission. He stated that he would open a restaurant, and he had $5,000 on him. As a step in his entry, officials told Galante to visit a specific doctor for a physical.

March 1, 1954
After visiting the doctor, Galante returned to the Montreal Immigration office and began filling out "Form 1000". When he came to question #17, he stated that the legal system had convicted him of an offense in the USA. After Galante completed the form, the Immigration officer asked Galante about his crime. Galante responded that in 1926 he had received a suspended sentence for an assault when he was 16. The Immigration officer told Galante that they would conduct further investigations and contact him later about his application.

March 5, 1954
Through his lawyer, Paul Fontaine, Galante wrote to Immigration officer J M Langois explaining that he has decided not to proceed with his permanent residence permit application. Galante stated that he was returning to the US and his lawyer Fontaine presented his ticket to the Immigration officer to prove Galante had left Canada.

May 6, 1954
Moreno Gallo, his sister, and his mother arrived in Canada to join his father, who immigrated two years earlier.

October 8, 1954
Judge Francois Caron released a report of his 30 month long inquiry into the behavior of Montreal police in the 1940s. It was clear from the document that some police allowed illegal activities to exist.

December 10, 1954
The Montreal Police asked Immigration Canada if they had immigration records for a Camillo or Carmine Galante employed at the Bonfire Restaurant.

December 15, 1954
The Montreal Immigration office requested Camillo or Carmine Galante's records from 1948 to November 30, 1954, from Ottawa head office.

December 28, 1954
The Central Records section of Immigration Canada informed their Montreal office that they had no record of a Carmine or Camillo Galante entering Canada between 1948 and 1953. Furthermore, they had no record of entering Canada between January 1, 1954, through November 30, 1954. These records mean Galante entered Canada unnoticed in February 1954.

January 5, 1955
In Montreal, the Immigration office asked their Ottawa HQ if they had any record of Galante entering Canada since March 1954.

January 7, 1955
Central Records of Immigration Canada informed their Montreal office that they had no record of Galante entering Canada until the end of November 1954. They also searched what December 1954 records they had and didn't find a Galante entry.

January 20, 1955
The Chief of Records of Immigration Canada informed the Montreal office that even with the additional information sent to them, they do not have any record of and entry by Galante through to the end of November and some December 1954 records.

February 22, 1955
There were stories in various Montreal and Toronto newspapers about the influx of American gamblers to Montreal. Most mob historians believe the American gamblers moved to Canada to avoid the heat created by the US's Kefauver Hearings.

February 24, 1955
Laval Fortier, the Deputy Minister of Immigration Canada, informed the RCMP Commissioner that Immigration's Montreal office was investigating Carmine Galante and wanted HQ to request Galante's US rap sheet. Fortier explained that he did not give his permission for fear of interfering in RCMP investigations.

April 6, 1955
L H Nicholson, the RCMP Commissioner, explained to Laval Fortier, the Deputy Minister of Immigration Canada, why a group of American gamblers had been in Montreal the last three years. He then asked Fortier for his Departments to prevent the entry of a list of American gamblers, including Galante.

April 15, 1955
Immigration Canada issued a "Lookout" notice for Carmine Galante, who frequently visited Montreal and stayed with Michel Consolo. Immigration officers were to prevent Galante from entering Canada. The order included other Americans as well.

April 21, 1955
Val Fortier, Deputy Minister of Immigration Canada, sent out a memorandum to all his offices informing them that they could not hold a Board of Inquiry if they detained American racketeers. Fortier ordered his men to issue an Order of Deportation instead.

April 27, 1955
Superiors at Montreal's Immigration office ordered their men to make discrete inquiries from time to time to see if Galante was in Montreal. If he was, they were to inform the Eastern District Superintendent.

May 16, 1955
A shooter fired on local gangster Kenneth "China Boy" Winfred but missed.

May 17, 1955
A shooter wounded gangster Benjamin "Baby Yack" Yubacovitz in the thigh. Hamilton gangster John Papalia was with Yubacovitz but was not hit. Police took Winfred, Yubacovitz, and Papalia into protective custody but soon released them.

May 24, 1955
Paolo Violi shot and killed fellow Calabrian Natale Brigante on a Toronto street. Violi fled, although he had a knife wound. Police eventually captured Violi and brought him to trial. The jury found him not guilty of manslaughter.

July 18-22, 1955
A series of violent brawls broke out in several Montreal nightclubs this week. Places hit were the All American Cafe, the Montmarte Cafe, the Savoy Club, the El Morocco, and the Down Beat Club. These acts were efforts by the Mafia to bring the owners into their protection racket.

July 21, 1955
A judge issued arrest warrants for Luigi Greco and Frank Petrulla. Both were powers in the local underworld and were with the Mafia.

July 22, 1955
Montreal Police arrested Luigi Greco at his home at 4069 Dorchester Street West. They confiscated several weapons and $4,000. Judge Henri Masson arraigned Greco on weapons charges and denied bail after Greco pled not guilty.

July 28, 1955
Judge Henri Masson Loranger arraigned Frank Petrulla on a gun possession charge. Police alleged that Petrulla threatened club owner Ned Roberts with a gun. After Petrulla pled not guilty, the judge released him on $2,000 cash bail.

July 30, 1955
Judge Masson Loranger dismissed the charge of possession of a gun dangerous to the public against Luigi Greco. He still faced possession of unregistered weapons charges.

September 30, 1955
Judge Gerald Almont fined Luigi Greco $50 and costs for each of three charges of possessing an unregistered gun. The judge also ordered Greco to keep the peace for a year and post a $950 peace bond.

April 10, 1956
The Superintendent of the Eastern District of Immigration Canada informed his superiors that neither his officers nor the RCMP had found any evidence of Galante being in Canada the last year.

June 22, 1956
The City of Montreal refused to grant Vic Cotroni an operating permit for one of his clubs. Cotroni appealed to the Quebec Court of Appeals but lost.

October 26, 1956
Paul E Fontaine, Galante's Montreal lawyer, wrote to the Superintendent of the Eastern District of Immigration Canada and requested a brief visit to Montreal for Carmine Galante. Lafontaine stated that Galante wanted to deal with business problems at the Bonfire Restaurant, where he was a part-owner. Galante wanted to visit between November 14, 1956, and November 29, 1956, arriving by train.

November 7, 1956
At the RCMP and Canada's Income Tax Investigation Division's request, the Minister of Immigration Canada issued a permit for Galante to visit Canada between November 15, 1956, and November 29, 1956. The two agencies wanted to conduct surveillance on Galante. Immigration Canada decided that if Galante didn't show up on those specific dates, he would still be let in for two weeks to help the RCMP and the Tax Investigation officers conduct their investigations.

December 13, 1956
Galante entered Canada by way of the port of Lacole and was officially permitted entry until December 22, 1956.

Note:
The port of Lacole refers to the main entry point into Canada on the highway between New York and Montreal. Locally it is sometimes called Blackpool, the old name of the American border post.

December 21, 1956
Galante departed Canada by way of the port of Lacole.

January 1, 1957
The Minister of Citizenship and Immigration canceled Galante's entry permit that he used in December.

January 14, 1957
Thieves broke into the Outremont branch of the Bank of Montreal and rifled 132 safety deposit boxes.

April 10, 1957
Lawyer Paul Fontaine asked Immigration Canada to allow Galante to enter Canada from May 1, 1957, until May 14, 1957. He said Galante needed to deal with business matters surrounding Alpha Investments and the Bonfire Restaurant.

April 23, 1957
Lawyer Paul Fontaine provided Immigration Canada with more information behind Galante's desire to visit Montreal. Galante wanted to talk with his partners Harry Ship and Luigi Greco about the failing Bonfire Restaurant.

April 25, 1957
Immigration Canada informed Galante's lawyer that he would not be permitted to visit Canada as he requested.

January 12/13, 1958
Hoods looted many safety deposit boxes in the Caisse National Economic at 1554 Van Horne Street. Employees did not discover the heist until Monday morning. An investigation showed that the criminals hadn't forced the bank vault door. This discovery strongly suggested the bad guys had an inside accomplice.

May 3, 1958
Criminals robbed the Brockville Trust Company of many bonds, securities, cash, and jewelry. They cut a hole in the roof of the adjoining building then lowered themselves into an office. From there, they cut sideways through brick and steel into the bank vault. The crew then broke into hundreds of safety deposit boxes.

Unfortunately for them, Rene Robert dropped his bank book and a receipt that gave his vehicle's license plate, model, and color.

May 5, 1958
Bank employees discovered the break-in at the Brockville Trust Company. Police quickly found Rene Robert's information and traveled to Montreal to apprehend him. The Montreal Police arrested Robert after a short chase. In the vehicle, they found a key to a locker at the Central Railway Station. The locker contained two bags stuffed with bonds and securities from the Brockville robbery.

May 6, 1958
A Brockville trust employee estimated the take as $500,000 in bearer bonds, $600,000 in registered bonds, and a big haul of security stocks. Later they put the total as $3,350,000.

May 21, 1958
An unknown man tried to cash a $1,000 bond stolen from the Brockville heist. When questioned by the bank employee, the man grabbed the bond and fled.

July 4, 1958
Immigration Canada issued a warrant for the arrest of Carmine Galante. They wanted to force him to appear before a hearing on his presence in Canada because he was on a list of prohibited people. The RCMP had informed Immigration Canada that Galante was in Canada at Montreal's Sheraton Hotel. A few days later, the RCMP discovered Galante wasn't there.

A staff member of a New York District Attorney was following Galante to serve him with a warrant for his arrest in a drug conspiracy. He couldn't serve the warrant until Galante returned to the US.

August 14, 1958
The Montreal office of Immigration Canada informed their HQ that it appeared that Galante had returned to the US.

CHAPTER SIXTEEN

Montreal Timeline Part Two

VIC COTRONI BECOMES THE
TOP DOG IN MONTREAL

1959
Twins Rocco and Giuseppe "Joe" Violi arrived in Canada from
Calabria, Italy.

July 9, 1959
After a long sting operation, RCMP officers arrested Giuseppe
"Pep" Cotroni and Rene Robert for conspiracy, possession of and
trafficking in heroin.

October 21, 1959
Three days into his heroin trial Pep Cotroni told Judge Wilfrid
Lazure that he wanted to plead guilty. It was evident to everyone
that the prosecution case was powerful. Cotroni admitted to
trafficking 13 pounds of heroin.

November 9, 1959
Judge Wilfrid Lazure sentenced Pep Cotroni to ten years in prison for his heroin guilty plea. The judge ordered Cotroni to pay a $60,000 fine plus restitution of $28,000, which the undercover agents had paid Cotroni for the heroin.

April 2, 1960
A jury found Pep Cotroni guilty of possession of $9,700 worth of bonds. He had stupidly paid a contractor for a job with bonds from the Dominion of Canada, Canadian National Railway, and Ontario Hydro, all stolen from Brockville. When the contractor tried to cash the bonds, the police arrested him, and he quickly explained how they came to be in his possession.

May 6, 1960
In New York, the feds announced a massive heroin conspiracy indictment involving 29 men. Included in the list were Canadians Pep Cotroni, Luigi Greco, Rene Robert, and Peter Stepanoff. Among the Americans were Carmine Galante and Sal Giglio, who operated in Montreal in the 1950s.

May 18, 1960
Judge Wilfrid Lazure sentenced Pep Cotroni to seven years for the illegal possession of the Brockville bonds. The judge ordered that Cotroni serve this sentence after the ten-year term he received for his heroin conviction.

THE VIOLIS HAVE IMMIGRATION PROBLEMS

July 20, 1960
A jury convicted Rocco Violi of doing bodily harm with a knife, and the judge sentenced him to six months. This conviction would cause Violi trouble in the future.

November 3, 1960
Goons including Frank Cotroni smashed up the Chez Paree club. It was part of an attempt to force the owner to pay protection to the local Mafia.
A judge issued warrants for eight men, including Cotroni.

November 4, 1960
A judge released Frank Cotroni on bail after police charged him with carrying an offensive weapon. Eventually, a judge sentenced Cotroni to three months.

November 25, 1960
Judge Omer Legrand sent Frank Cotroni to trial for the November 4, 1959 trashing of the Chez Paree nightclub. The club owner, Solomon Schnapps, told the judge that he and Cotroni were friends. No club employee saw anything but an off duty police officer, and a reporter testified to Frank Cotroni's involvement. The judge refused Cotroni's plea for bail.

February 1, 1961
A special officer of Immigration Canada ordered the deportation of Rocco Violi due to his criminal record.

February 20, 1961
At an Immigration Appeal Board hearing, officials confirmed the deportation order for Rocco Violi.

February 24, 1961
Immigration Canada deferred Rocco Violi's deportation as long as he met certain conditions.

December 22, 1961
A jury convicted Rocco Violi of a hit and run accident. The judge gave him a small fine.

February 1962
A jury found Pittsburgh Capo Sam Mannarino and George Rosden not guilty in a trial involving stolen bonds from the 1958 Brockville Trust heist. They declared William Rabin guilty while the judge threw out the charges against Norman Rothman at the end of the trial.

October 16, 1962
Immigration Canada ordered the deportation of Joe Violi due to his criminal record.

November 19, 1962
An Immigration Appeal board confirmed Joe Violi's deportation order.

December 10, 1962
Immigration Canada deferred the deportation of Joe Violi as long as he met certain conditions.

April 1963
The RCMP arrested local gangster Armond Duhamel for possessing stolen bonds after he returned from a world trip.

August 24, 1963
McLean's Magazine, Canada's equivalent to Time Magazine, published a story on the Mafia which included labelling Vic Cotroni as the head of the Montreal Mafia.

December 24, 1963
Prison officials found the body of Armond Duhamel. He was awaiting trial for possessing stolen bonds.

April 1, 1964
Immigration officials informed Rocco and Joe Violi of their pending deportation due to their criminal records. They then arrested the two men and put them in jail. Their case became a cause celeb when the public and politicians learned Immigration Canada had held them for eight months. Later the Supreme Court overturned this ruling saying Immigration illegally detained the brothers. Rocco and Francesco Violi also had rap sheets, but Canada had granted them citizenship, thus eliminating deportation as a possibility.

April 1964
Domenico Violi, the father of the four Violi brothers, traveled from Italy to visit his sons. Immigration Canada deported him due to his criminal record. Domenico eventually settled in Ohio.

JOE BONANNO VISITS

May 14, 1964
Joe Bonanno and his wife legally entered Canada at the Blackpool Quebec crossing.

May 20, 1964
Joe Bonanno met with Giuseppe Saputo and his son Lino at the Saputo Cheese Company offices. Giuseppe agreed to sell Bonanno 20% interest in G Saputo and Sons, Cremerie Cosenza, and Cremerie Stella in exchange for $8,000. Giuseppe Saputo put this information down on a sheet with the Saputo letterhead. He also added, "You have been very helpful to us over the years advising us, and we are happy to have you take an active interest in our companies." Giuseppe Saputo signed the paper. This document would cause the Saputos' embarrassment to this day.

Note:
Lino Saputo has consistently denied any connection between his companies and Joe Bonanno after the May 20, 1964 meeting. He has testified that once they learned of Bonanno notoriety in a May 1964 edition of the Montreal Matin newspaper, he and his father never completed the agreement.

May 24, 1964
Bonanno went to the Immigration Canada offices in Montreal and filled out papers requesting landed immigration status. To support his desire to create jobs for Canadians, Bonanno presented the Saputo letter. The officer asked Bonanno to come back later with a medical certificate.

May 27, 1964
Senior Immigration Officer Jean-Marc Bonneau dealt with Bonanno when he returned to their offices. Bonneau served Bonanno with deportation papers, which Bonanno signed, plus a waiver promising not to appeal. These decisions would have permitted Bonanno to return to the US immediately. However, the RCMP arrested Bonanno for making a false statement on his landed immigration form on May 24. Bonanno had denied having

a criminal record. Immigration had discovered an old wage and hour violation for one of Bonanno's companies back in the 1940s.

May 28, 1964

In Ottawa, the Immigration Department rejected Bonanno's lawyers' request for immediate deportation and the dropping of the false statement charge. They also denied a request for bail.

June 3, 1964

Immigration HQ changed their mind and ordered the immediate deportation of Bonanno. Judge T A Fontaine set bail of $2,000 for Bonanno, but Immigration officials took him into custody anyway.

July 4, 1964

Immigration officials went to Montreal Police HQ to deport Bonanno. However, one of his lawyers presented documents detailing a Habeas Corpus hearing that afternoon before Justice Roger Ouimet.

Bonanno's lawyers presented a Habeas Corpus writ to Justice Quimet and a supporting Bonanno affidavit. The Justice didn't have time to deal with it, so he put off the matter until a later date.

June 9, 1964

Justice Quimet ruled there were grounds to have a formal Habeas Corpus hearing, which he would hold later. He would hold a bail hearing on this matter on June 12.

June 10, 1964

Officials hauled Joe Bonanno before Judge Paul Hurteau for arraignment on three perjury charges. They claimed Bonanno lied on his affidavit accompanying his Habeas Corpus writ to Justice Quimet. His three lies were:

The Immigration officer did not serve him with a deportation order.

The deportation order was subject to appeal.

Immigration illegally held him for deportation on June 3, 1964.

Judge Hurteau ruled that he would hold a bail hearing for Bonanno on this matter on June 12.

June 12, 1964
Bonanno's lawyers presented a petition for bail that included
some declarations by the mob Boss. All four of Bonanno's lawyers
signed the document.

Below are a few of them:
Bonanno loves this country and desires to set up permanent
residence here.
He entered Canada legally with his wife, and his detention is illegal.
He has acquired a 20% interest in a local creamery, and negotiations
are underway to purchase similar holdings in two other creameries.

Justice Quimet rejected Bonanno's request for bail while he waited
for a Habeas Corpus hearing. This ruling made Bonanno's plea
for bail on the perjury charges mute. Bonanno stayed locked up.

Note::
In their books, both Joe and Bill Bonanno denied that Joe had any intention
of taking up permanent residence in Canada. The documents prove they lied.

June 29, 1964
Judge Emile Trottier dismissed the three perjury charges facing
Bonanno, but he remained detained.

June 31, 1964
Justice Roger Quimet rejected Bonanno's Habeas Corpus writ.
He also turned down Bonanno's plea for bail. However, before
Immigration officers could take Bonanno off for deportation, his
lawyers announced that they would be going to an appeal court.
Immigration had to stand down, but Bonanno remained locked up.

July 3, 1964
Bonanno's lawyers appeared before Chief Justice Lucien Tremblay
of the Court of Appeals. They hoped he would grant a petition for
bail without having to go before the full court. He rejected that
idea, which meant Bonanno would remain locked up until the full
Court of Appeals met in the fall. This decision wasn't a pleasant
alternative for the frustrated Bonanno.

CANADA BOOTS BONANNO OUT

July 30, 1964
Immigration officers deported Bonanno by plane to Chicago.

July 31, 1964
Immigration Canada announced the deportation of Bonanno on July 30. The release said Bonanno did not leave voluntarily and that he had promised to stop legal proceedings to gain legal admittance to Canada as a landed immigrant.

September 11, 1964
Antonio Manno, the Mafia Boss of Cattolica Eraclea in Sicily, arrived in Canada without problems. He was the father-in-law of Nicolo Rizzuto.

February 5, 1965
An illegal FBI bug in the New Jersey office of Boss Sam Decavalcante overheard him telling an underling that Boss Carlo Gambino was angry because Bill Bonanno had taken $150,000 from Bonanno guys in Montreal that belonged to the imprisoned Carmine Galante.

June 15, 1966
Bonanno Soldier Vincenzo Asaro illegally entered Canada under an assumed name. The RCMP and FBI Agents began following him in hopes of capturing his son, who had been on the run from justice in the US for years.

June 21, 1966
A swarm of RCMP and FBI Agents raided a home and arrested Vincenzo Asaro and his fugitive son Joseph. Also present were Frank and Vito Cotroni. Vic Cotroni allegedly offered to pay RCMP Sergeant Gerald Barbeau $25,000 to make the arrest elsewhere. Cotroni didn't want his wife to know he was at the home of his mistress.

June 22, 1966
Immigration Canada quickly deported Vincenzo Asaro. His son would soon follow.

July 7, 1966
The RCMP raided Vic Cotroni's Repentigny cottage and arrested him for RCMP Sergeant Gerald Barbeau's attempted bribery on June 21, 1966.

September 1966
After arresting a minor criminal, the cops became curious about a set of keys he had. Eventually, they discovered one of them fit the door of a duplex at 5146 Trans Island Avenue. Teams of cops watched the residence from September 1966 until March 1967. The cops made a significant discovery in April.

THE BONANNOS RETURN

November 28, 1966
In court testimony years later Montreal Capo Vic Cotroni admitted that he met with Bill Bonanno, Vito DeFilippo, Pat DeFilippo, Carl Simari, Peter Magaddino, Peter Notaro and Giuseppe Saputo in Saputo's Montreal home.

On this date, police observed Peter Notaro entering a residence in Ville St Michel. Not long afterward, Vic Cotroni went into the home. At that time, the law did not know whose home it was. Police watched as nine men gathered at a shopping center and used two payphones. They witnessed Bill Bonanno, Giuseppe Saputo, Paulo Violi, and Vic Cotroni take turns talking. The most reasonable explanation for the calls is that the men spoke with Joe Bonanno in New York.

Around midnight Montreal Police arrested the six Americans and Montreal gangster Luigi Greco. They found three pistols in one of the two cars the men were using. Interestingly Bill Bonanno was driving a vehicle owned by Giuseppe Monticello, Saputo's son-in-law. His passengers were Vito DeFilippo and Greco. Carl Simari, Peter Magaddino, Peter Notaro, and Pat DeFilippo occupied the second vehicle that contained the guns.

Police hauled the six men to their headquarters, where a police photographer took a picture of the group of sullen men. They charged Bill Bonanno with driving without proper registration. When the police asked Bonanno why he was in Montreal, he replied that he was looking after his father's interest in the Saputo Cheese Company. Magaddino, Simari, and Pat DeFilippo faced three counts of possession of dangerous weapons.

Note:

At a later immigration hearing for a relative, Immigration authorities asked Giuseppe Monticello why he lent his vehicle to Bill Bonanno. He replied, "Because he has a stake in the Saputo Company."

November 30, 1966

Peter Notaro, Peter Magaddino, Carl Simari, and Pat DeFilippo pled guilty to possessing dangerous weapons. Judge Jean Tellier sentenced them to two days in jail to give Immigration Canada time to organize their deportations. Bill Bonanno pled not guilty to his driving charge and released him on a $100 bond. Later that day, Immigration Canada ordered his removal.

CANADA KICKS THE BONANNOS OUT AGAIN

December 1, 1966

Immigration Canada officials and RCMP officers escorted Vito DeFilippo to Montreal Airport. They put him on Air Canada flight 564 to New York on a one-way ticket.

December 2, 1966

Immigration officials and RCMP officers escorted Bill Bonanno to the US border to complete his deportation.

December 3, 1966

Immigration officials and RCMP officers escorted Carl Simari, Peter Magaddino, Peter Notaro, and Pat DeFilippo to the US border to complete their deportation.

The arrest and deportation of these six Americans created news all across Canada and the US. Many wondered why the men were in Montreal during the Bonanno War. Few noticed that Giuseppe Saputo hosted these men and accompanied the group to a shopping center where they made a call to Joe Bonanno. Fewer still were aware that Bill Bonanno was using Giuseppe Saputo's son-in-law's vehicle.

THE BANK TUNNEL CAPER

March 28, 1967
Montreal Detective-Sergeant Francois Fortin made entry into a duplex at 5146 Trans Island Avenue and discovered fresh cement in a basement section.

March 29, 1967
A squad of police with equipment returned to the Trans Island Avenue duplex and started digging. They eventually found an entrance to a tunnel filled with dirt and construction equipment. After clearing that mess, the police found a 53-foot tunnel leading to the City and District Savings Bank basement wall directly behind the duplex. Someone had drilled some holes in the wall.

April 1967
A judge issued warrants for Frank Cotroni and 11 other men in the bank tunnel conspiracy.

April 4, 1967
Judge Gerald Laganiere rejected bail requests from Frank Cotroni and his father-in-law Paul Desormiers.

April 10, 1967
At a preliminary hearing on the bank tunnel case, witness Ernest Bildeau said last August he heard Frank Cotroni ask Paul Desormiers for $25,000 to help dig the tunnel. Bildeau went on to say that Desormiers agreed to give $5,000 plus $100 a week to the tunnel diggers.

April 11, 1967
Witness Ernest Bildeau testified that Paul Desormiers told him a cave in stopped the tunnel project.

April 12, 1967
A salesman from Windsor, Ontario, testified that defendant Francesco Fuoco purchased concrete drilling equipment from him on two occasions and returned some drills later. He readily identified Francesco Fuoco in court.

April 13, 1967
Judge Laganiere refused bail for Frank Cotroni.

April 14, 1967
During the preliminary hearing, Judge Laganiere took the jury, the defendants, the prosecutors, and plenty of police guards to the City and District Bank, as well as the duplex behind it where the tunnel started.

April 18, 1967
During the preliminary hearing for the bank tunnel case, the Crown presented testimony about the bank alarm and how the hoods had bypassed it. Detective Sergeant Francois Fortin testified about entering the duplex where the tunnel began.

April 20, 1967
Judge Laganiere ruled that the Crown had presented sufficient evidence to send some of the accused to trial. He permitted Frank Cotroni to give a voluntary statement, which is a step to avoid further proceedings. It didn't work for Frank.

April 21, 1967
A representative of Frank Cotroni paid $100,000 in cash to free him. Paul Desormiers also paid his lower bail. Judge Laganiere freed the two men.

Summer 1967
Nicolo Rizzuto was a partner in four construction-related firms and works at Expo 67, Montreal's World Fair.

April 11, 1969
Quebec's Attorney General halted the Cotroni bank tunnel trial. Technically all the defendants were free, but Montreal police arrested them on a new warrant. Judge Mark-Andre Blain arraigned the defendants on the new indictment.

May 2, 1969
Justice Paul Shorteno refused a defense motion to end the bank tunnel trial on a writ of prohibition.

June 17, 1969
Judge Maurice Rousseau rejected six defense motions to stop the judicial process in the bank tunnel case. However, he put off the preliminary hearing for the nine men until the fall.

January 1970
Judge Maurice Rousseau sent the nine defendants to trial after the preliminary hearing concluded. There was no media coverage of the hearing, for the defendants asserted their rights to no publicity.

January 1970
Judge Maurice Rousseau sent the nine defendants in the bank tunnel case to trial after the preliminary hearing. There was no media coverage of the proceedings, for the defendants asserted their rights to no publicity.

1970
A jury convicted Vincent DiMaulo, brother of Joe DiMaulo, of the murder of "Ti-Cul" Allard. The Judge gave him a life sentence.

CONSULTING MYER LANSKY

February 1970
Vic Cotroni, Paolo Violi, John Papalia, and others gathered in Acapulco to meet with Myer Lansky, the gambling expert. They were seeking his advice on casinos, for, in November 1969, the National Assembly in Quebec had created an agency to operate casinos.

Due to extensive law enforcement bugging operations in Montreal, the RCMP knew about the Mexican meeting. They passed this information to the FBI, who contacted Mexican police. The latter questioned Cotroni et al. but laid no charges. Over the years, everyone involved in the gathering would deny it or fudge their answers.

April 1970
Immigration Canada permitted Domenico Violi to enter Canada to attend the funeral of his son Joe. The son died in a traffic accident. Domenico had to post a $15,000 bond to ensure he left Canada.

August 10, 1970
Judge Jacques Antil heard Theodore Aboud plead guilty to four counts of fraud involving a total of $1,558,000. Aboud stated that he had to confess to save his family from death. Detective Captain Paul Beaudry testified that Aboud was a front for powerful gangster Conrad Bouchard who worked with Frank Cotroni. The crime was a very sophisticated operation involving loans and fake securities, and the like.

BUGGING PAOLO

December 1970
The Montreal Police began a bugging operation of Paolo Violi's Reggio Bar on Jean-Talon Street. An undercover officer named Bob Menard rented an apartment above the place and succeeded in winning the friendship of Violi. It was a massive mistake on Violi's part.

FRANK COTRONI VACATIONS IN MEXICO

January 14, 1971
Frank Cotroni, his wife, and his in-laws flew to Mexico City on vacation.

January 15, 1971
The Frank Cotroni group drove to Acapulco.

February 1, 1971
Mexican police arrested Frank Cotroni and another man for using a stolen credit card to purchase $2,080 worth of jewelry.

February 6, 1971

Before a judge, Frank Cotroni pled not guilty to the credit card fraud charge. Authorities held him without bail.

February 13, 1971
A judge released Cotroni from his credit card charge. The jewelry store owner refused to press charges after someone paid the bill in full. Before he could leave the courthouse, Mexican police arrested Cotroni on a complaint from American Express claiming Cotroni defrauded them of $5,200 in February of 1970.

February 18, 1971
Frank Cotroni hosted a lavish press conference to declare his innocence in the Mexican matter. He said, "It was just a case of mistaken identity."

Present at the news conference was Montreal man Robert Corbeil. He described how he lent his Caddy to a friend in Acapulco, who in turn lent it to Cotroni to take his family out to dinner. At this point, the Mexican police arrested Cotroni. The jewelry store owner recognized the vehicle and everyone assumed the driver, Cotroni, was the man who fraudulently purchased the jewels. Corbeil said he bought the jewels before Cotroni arrived in Mexico, and there was no fraud involved.

Cotroni was attempting to deflect some of the negative publicity he received from the Montreal media about the Mexican affair. At the press conference, he was free on $5,000 bail from an attempted bank robbery conspiracy.

April 1971
Domenico Violi and his wife visited Canada to visit their sons. Immigration Canada deported them to the United States. There Domenico obtained landed immigrant status for himself, his wife, and three other sons.

July 1971
A judge fined Frank Cotroni a total of $1,000 for ignoring turning over documents to Revenue Canada. The papers concerned Cotroni's 1965-1970 tax returns.

July 18, 1971

Moreno Gallo and Enzo Porco bombed the home of Aimee Irish after being hired to do so.

THE BANK TUNNEL CASE ENDS FOR FRANK COTRONI

August 24, 1971
Judge Jacques Trahan dismissed the bank tunnel charges against Frank Cotroni, Paul Desormiers, and his two sons. In their first trial then Judge Trottier said the Crown's main witness was not trustworthy. When Judge Trahan admitted this comment into evidence, the Crown conceded they had no new evidence. The defense then argued that the Crown had not made a case. Judge Trahan agreed and dismissed all charges against the defendants. The bank tunnel case had been running off and on since April of 1967. In the end, only two lower-level gangsters were found guilty.

November 26, 1971
A jury convicted Joe DiMaulo, Joe Tozzi, and Julio Ciamarro of killing Jean Claude Rioux in the Casa Loma bar on March 12, 1970. Rioux's drinking companion allegedly shot the bartender and a customer after an argument. The gunman fled, but Rioux stayed behind. His girlfriend and a club watchman testified to seeing the three accused with Rioux before being told to leave. A policeman investigated the club after finding the front door glass shattered. He found the three dead men.

Judge Maurice Cousineau sentenced each defendant to life in prison, which was the mandatory sentence for first-degree murder. Famous defense lawyers Leo-Rene Maranda, Sidney Leithman, and Raymond Daoust announced that they would appeal.

Two separate juries found the man accused of killing the other two victims in the club not guilty.

December 13, 1971
A judge fined Frank Cotroni a total of $6,000 for ignoring an order to turn over documents to Revenue Canada. This incident was a

repeat of the July 1971 matter. Cotroni continued to ignore the order, so the judge increased the fine

SAPUTO CHEESE IS RAIDED

May 18, 1972
Using a warrant, five Montreal Police Sergeants, ten uniformed officers, a police photographer, and a microbiologist raided the Saputo cheese plant. While purported to be a raid concerning health conditions, the real purpose seemed to be a fishing expedition by the good guys. What follows is a summary of some of the trials and hearings that followed. They are not necessarily in chronological order.

The day after the raid, Montreal Police Constable Antoine Carocchia penned a press release that Justice James Hugessen later ruled as prejudicial. Part of the document said," Important US Mafia figures met owners of the Saputo firm on several occasions in the past." While true, this statement had nothing to do with the stated purpose of the raid. It would have been alright if the press had dug up this information independently, but the police had no business doing so. Acting on Lino Saputo's complaint, the Justice fined Constable Carocchio $200 for contempt of court. (November 1, 1972.)

The government charged the Saputo firm with 14 health violations but decided to proceed with only one. They claimed that Saputo did not provide adequate soap and towels for their employees. The prosecution had testimony from the microbiologist and pictures that showed dirty towels and lack of soap. The defense brought forth two members of Montreal's health inspection unit. Dr. Lefebre testified he had inspected the Saputo plant the day before the police raid and found no problem with the soap and towels. City inspector Charron backed up Lefebre by explaining that he accompanied Lefebre on the May 17, 1971, and found similar results.

During their cross-examinations, the defense lawyers hammered away at their theory that there was more behind the raid than concerns health. At the end of the trial, on November 1, 1972, Judge Bernard Tellier stated that he found the police deployment (so many men) and the publicity unusual and even excessive. He posed the question if motives for the raid had nothing to do with health. Despite his concerns, Judge Tellier found the Saputo firm guilty for not supplying adequate soap and towels for their employees. He leveled a fine of $50 and $50 in costs.

During their May 18, 1972 raid on the Saputo plant, police photographed documents in Lino Saputo's briefcase. The papers would cause Saputo a great deal of trouble up to the present day.

In September of 1971, the Quebec Municipal Commission began an inquiry into the administration of St Leonard. There had been many complaints from citizens and local politicians. Lino Saputo and some of his relatives became tangled up in the investigation, much to their displeasure. A summary of the complicated matter follows.

The Commission investigated the purchase and sale of three corner lots in St Leonard. Some of their evidence came from Lino Saputo's documents in the May 18, 1972 raid on his cheese plant. There would be battles over the correct interpretation of the information on these papers.

Before the Commission, the allegation was that the St Leonard planning committee approved zoning changes on the three lots in question, having turned down similar requests from previous owners. The problem was whether payoffs were involved and did front men secretly own the properties.

The Gerlando Tutino lot:

Gerlando Tutino
Tutino, Lino Saputo, and Giuseppe Borsellino are related by marriage.
Tutino applied for a zoning change on the lot before he legally owned it.
Tutino bought the lot in July 1971.
The St Leonard planning committee approved a zoning change for the lot.
Tutino sold the lot for a profit of $67,000.
Tutino stated the profit was entirely his, and he didn't sell the lot on behalf of a group.
Tutino denied receiving a $3,000 commission on the sale of the land.
Tutino admitted he loaned Lino Saputo $50,000 three months after the sale of the lot. He said he was receiving interest on his loan.

Lino Saputo
Lino Saputo testified that he backed Tutino when he applied for a $100,000 loan before he purchased the lot.
Saputo said he asked Tutino for a piece of the profit on the land sale, but Tutino turned him down.

Giuseppe Borsellino

Borsellino testified that he advised Tutino on his land transaction but had no involvement with the finances.

He said he did not know the content of the seized Saputo documents.

Borsellino admitted he regularly attended Saputo family meetings but did not recall being present at meetings listed in the document involving the land deals.

Saputo Documents as interpreted by the Crown

A handwritten document from Saputo's briefcase showed that a profit of $61,000 resulted from Tutino's property sale.

Seven people would share equally in the profit after four received their commissions.

The document indicated that Tutino received a $3,000 commission.

The Lino Saputo lot

Saputo testified he pressured St Leonard for a zone change for the lot before he owned it.

He applied in early February 1970.

He applied again in March 1970.

He purchased the property in April 1970.

He appeared before the St Leonard city council in the spring of 1970.

St Leonard approved the zoning change.

The Giuseppe Borsellino lot

Borsellino admitted that he got a zoning change and made a profit on the property's sale.

Four St Leonard councillors denied making any money on the zoning changes for the four properties.

At one point in the hearing, Inquiry Chairman Pierre Bolduc warned Tutino and Giuseppe Borsellino to stop giving evasive answers.

> September 12, 1972
> Justice Jean St Germaine ruled that the MacLean's Magazine evidence failed to establish that Vic Cotroni headed the Montreal Mafia or that he was a leader of the criminal operations of the organization. However, the justice only awarded Cotroni $2 in damages because his reputation was already in the dumpster. Cotroni had launched a $1.25 million dollar lawsuit against

MacLean's because they called him the head of the Montreal Mafia in a 1963 edition.

THE VIOLI RIZZUTO FEUD HEATS UP

September 22, 1972
Dom Arcuri picked up Bonanno Capos Nicolino Alfano and Nick Buttafuoco at Dorval airport. They had come to Montreal to arbitrate a dispute between Calabrian Paulo Violi and Sicilian Nicolo Rizzuto. Police watched as they met Violi, who welcomed them warmly, later they sat down with Nicolo Rizzuto.

Late 1972
Nicolo Rizzuto moved to Venezuela after learning Paolo Violi put a hit out on him. Other information suggests that the Bonanno leaders in New York refused to sanction a hit on Rizzuto.

December 1972
A fire at Luigi Greco's Gino's Pizzeria severely injured the Mafia leader. He and others were cleaning the floor with a flammable liquid when something ignited it. Greco lingered in the hospital before dying.

January 8, 1973
Judge Gilles Belanger dismissed extortion charges against Vincent "Jimmy" Soccio. Judge Belanger had dropped the charges against Frank Cotroni early in the preliminary hearing. Restaurant owner Dyonysos Chionis accused the two of attempting to extort a 50% ownership in his St Hyacinth business.

February 1, 1973
A jury found Joe DiMaulo, Joe Tozzi, and Julio Ciamarro not guilty in their second trial for the Casa Loma murders of March 12, 1971. The girlfriend of victim Rioux had changed her story so much that she was no longer credible.

The Crime Inquiry

All the bad guys wanted to avoid testifying before the Police Commission Inquiry because of the bad publicity plus the real possibility you could end up behind bars on a contempt charge. For simplicity reasons I will use the label "Crime Inquiry" to designate the hearings although that is not the proper name.

February 7, 1973
Vic Cotroni made his first appearance before the Crime Inquiry.

February 27, 1973
Vincent "Jimmy" Soccio testified before the Crime Inquiry. He said that Vic Cotroni contributed to a fund to beat Mayor Drapeau in 1956.

February 28, 1973
Meat dealer and financier William Obront testified before the Crime Inquiry.

May 1, 1973
Tony Mucci fired three shots at Le Devoir reporter Jean-Pierre Charboneau who was hit once in the arm. Charboneau didn't know his assailant.

June 6, 1973
Before the Crime Inquiry, gambling junket operator Albert Herman testified that he used to give 50% of his profits to Luigi Greco. When Greco died in December 1972, Herman stopped making the payments, and no one else tried to muscle in. The junkets went to the Hilton Hotel/Casino in Las Vegas.

YOUNG FRENCH CANADIAN DRUG DEALERS RESIST

July 10, 1973
French gangsters killed Cotroni men Salvatore Sergi and Mario Cambrone in a drug dispute.

July 11, 1973
Police taped Paolo Violi and Vic Cotroni plotting revenge for the Sergi and Cambrone hits.

September 1973
Someone shot Karol Brosseau in the ear in a dispute in a pool room. A few years later the Crime Commission lawyers questioned him about it and tapes that implicated him.

September 2, 1973
Moreno Gallo killed drug dealer Angelo Facchino with five shots in Facchino's car. Police arrested Gallo and Tony Vanelli after a short chase.

September 14, 1973
Cotroni Associate Antonio DiGenova was killed by French gangsters avenging the death of Angelo Facchino on September 2.

October 9, 1973
A US federal grand jury indicted Canadians Frank Cotroni, Guido Orsini, Frank Dasti, and others for a cocaine conspiracy.

ELECTING A NEW BONANNO BOSS

October 20, 1973
Gambino Soldier John DeMatteo visited Violi. He passed along an invitation from Rastelli for Violi to come to NY as the Bonannos tried to pick a new Boss.

November 6, 1973
Underboss Phi Rastelli phoned Violi and invited him to NY and said to bring Frank Cotroni.

November 7, 1973
Vic Cotroni nixed the idea of Frank Cotroni traveling to NY City due to his drug indictment.

November 8, 1973
RCMP officers arrested Frank Cotroni as he was enjoying a meal at Moishe Steak House. The Americans wanted him on a drug indictment.
Officials locked Cotroni up at the Parthenais Detention Center.

November 11, 1973
Paolo Violi flew to New York City while Joe DiMaulo and Rene Desjardins drove down. They were to meet with Underboss Phil Rastelli, who was campaigning to become the new Boss.

THE DONALD COTE AFFAIR

November 11, 1973
Two gangsters invaded the Donald Cote home and murdered Mrs. Cote, her five-year-old son, and a male friend. Donald Cote was upstairs and avoided death. Cote traveled in criminal circles, so the police assumed the killings were due to some dispute.

November 14, 1973
The following account is from the information provided by Joseph Rodriquez, a participant in the events.

Eddie Chiquette and Robert de Courcy attended the funeral of the Cote family. They hoped to avoid the suspicion that they were involved in the murders. Cote associates "arrested" the two at the funeral home and took them to Cote's jewelry store.

Once there, Cote called to say they had the right men. Greco Jr took de Courcy in a back room and killed him with a silenced gun with one shot to the head. Ray Rodriquez Sr walked Chiquette to the back room and shot him in the stomach to make him suffer. The other men also shot Chiquette. The coroner later said he had six shots in him. Joe Rodriquez, Ray Sr, Ray Jr, Greco Jr. and some Henry guy came to help clean up. Rodriquez later identified a picture of Dominic Sicari as being there as well as a man named Marcel.

November 27, 1973
Vic Cotroni appeared before the Crime Inquiry. A Quebec Provincial Police officer testified that Cotroni was the leader of the Montreal Underworld and that four separate criminal organizations reported to him.

November 29, 1973
Workers injured in the pizza fire that killed Luigi Greco sued his estate.

December 7, 1973
Judge Andre Bourdon accepted guilty pleas from Paolo Violi and William Obront, through their lawyers, on tax matters. He fined each man $200.

December 11, 1973
Justice Ruston Lamb ordered the extradition of Frank Cotroni to the United States. Lamb had conducted a hearing on the matter.

December 17, 1973
Frank Cotroni filed a request for a review of his extradition order. The petition asked the Appeal Court to set bail or have Immigration Canada set bail.

January 25, 1974
Frank Cotroni lost his extradition appeal in the Quebec Court of Appeals.

February 1974
Tony Mucci and another man tried to extort Joe Petrozza, owner of a pizzeria called the Tricolor. Petrozza complained to the police.

February 25, 1974
Paolo Violi traveled to NY City to meet the new Boss Phil Rastelli and his administration.

March 7, 1974
Tony Vanelli pled guilty to manslaughter in the September 2, 1973 murder of Angelo Faccino. A judge later sentenced him to seven years. At some point, Moreno Gallo, the shooter, received a life sentence. Their Bosses, Paolo Violo and Vic Cotroni, ordered them to plead guilty to avoid further investigation into the matter since they were behind it.

March 19, 1974
Violi met with Nick Rizzuto and told him who the new Bonanno leaders were. Violi explained to Rizzuto that he had sent Soldier Romeo Bucci to cast the Montreal crews' vote in New York City.

March 27, 1974
Before the Crime Commission, Jimmy Soccio testified that Vic Cotroni contributed to a 1956 fund to defeat Mayor Drapeau.

March 28, 1974
On a legal bug, police heard Vic Cotroni, Paolo Violi, and Armand Courville discussing Jimmy Soccio's testimony about Cotroni at the Crime Commission the previous day. Cotroni strongly rebuked the embarrassed mobster.

April 11, 1974
Justice James Hugesson rejected Frank Cotroni's habeas corpus writ that would have freed the gangster.

April 28, 1974
The Supreme Court agreed to hear Frank Cotroni's extradition appeal.

April 30, 1974
Montreal Police listened in on a meeting between Vic Cotroni, Paolo Violi, and Hamilton gangster John Papalia in Violi's Reggio Bar on Jean-Talon Street. A rough outline of the matter follows:

A shady stock dealer named Stanley Bader boasted to his partner Sheldon Swartz about ripping off some Montreal people for a great deal of money in a stock scam. Swartz then told his friend John Papalia who resided in Hamilton but was a Soldier in the Buffalo Mafia Family.

Papalia and Swartz decided to scam Bader by telling him the Montreal people he conned were using Vic Cotroni's money. Swartz then told Bader this fake story, which freaked Bader out. Papalia later confirmed the tale. The frightened Bader borrowed $200,000 and passed it to Swartz to give to Papalia, who was supposed to return it to the cheated Vic Cotroni.

About a year later, Bader became suspicious of Swartz and started asking questions in Montreal if someone had scammed Cotroni. Word of these inquiries got back to Cotroni, who ordered Papalia to Montreal for the April 30, 1974 meeting.

Papalia danced around fudging his story by saying he didn't know the men used Cotroni's name, and he wasn't involved until Swartz gave him some money. Violi said they heard the scam was for $300,000, and he and Cotroni wanted half. Papalia sputtered and said he only got $40,000. Vic then told the sweating Papalia that they would kill him if they found out differently. This conversation led to Cotroni, Papalia, Violi, and Stanley Swartz's arrest on November 6, 1975.

April 1974
At a hearing of the Crime Commission, reporter Jean-Paul Charboneau recognized the man who wounded him back in 1973. He identified Tony Mucci to the police.

May 15, 1974
Before the Crime Commission, Vic Cotroni testified that he was a simple businessman president of Reggio Foods. He stated the Jimmy Soccio lied when he testified that Cotroni had contributed to a 1956 fund to unseat Mayor Jean Drapeau.

May 23, 1974
At the Crime Inquiry, Vic Cotroni denied he suggested he might break a competitor's legs. When questioned on a taped meeting with Jimmy Soccio and others, Cotroni denied telling Soccio what to say when he testified.

May 30, 1974
Jimmy Soccio testified that he must have misunderstood the question when he said, on March 27, 1974, that Vic Cotroni contributed to a 1956 fund to defeat Mayor Jean Drapeau.

June 10, 1974
Judge Rheal Brunet of the Crime Inquiry ordered Jimmy Soccio to jail for six months for his evasive and misleading answers to questions.

June 13, 1974
Judge Rheal Brunet of the Crime Inquiry ordered Jimmy Soccio to jail for a year for refusing to testify.

July 3, 1974
Guido Orsini, a Frank Cotroni Associate, pled guilty to a narcotics conspiracy. Later a judge sentenced him to two concurrent 22-year terms.

July 4, 1974
The Crime Inquiry charged Vic Cotroni for contempt. They had him jailed immediately.

July 5, 1974
Justice Albert Mayrand granted Vic Cotroni his release on $25,000 bail. He had to surrender his passport and agree to stay within Quebec.

July 11, 1974
A judge sentenced Vic Cotroni to one year for contempt before the Crime Inquiry. Judge Rheal Brunet of the Inquiry said Cotroni's testimony was "voluntarily incomprehensible, disjointed, cloudy and equivalent to a veiled refusal to testify.

August 22, 1974
Prosecutors arraigned Tony Mucci for wounding reporter Jean-Pierre Charbonneau back on May 1, 1973.

September 14, 1974
The Quebec Court of Appeals refused to hear Vic Cotroni's appeal of his contempt sentence before the Crime Inquiry. Officials took Cotroni to jail but permitted him a two day pass during the Christmas holidays.

October 1, 1974
A judge sentenced Tony Mucci to eight years for wounding reporter Jean-Paul Charbonneau, two four year sentences for shooting another man in a brawl, and six years for a jewelry robbery. All the sentences were consecutive. That was a lot of time behind bars.

October 23, 1974
The Supreme Court upheld Frank Cotroni's transfer to the US by rejecting his lawyer's argument that Canada's extradition treaty with the US didn't cover a cocaine conspiracy. Immigration Canada extradited Cotroni the same day.

October 31, 1974
New York Judge Jacob Mishler rejected Frank Cotroni's bid for bail. The judge said he wanted to be sure Cotroni appeared for his trial in November.

December 5, 1974
Police taped Paulo Violi talking with Enzo Porco. They discussed a firebombing and various other crimes, which the Crime Inquiry would quiz Porco on later.

December 16, 1974
The Supreme Court upheld a Superior Court ruling that rejected Vic Cotroni's one-year contempt sentence from the Crime Inquiry.

January 9, 1975
Paolo Violi sent his advisor, Petro Sciara to New York to ask Boss Phil Rastelli to appoint him Acting Capo of the Montreal crew since Cotroni is in prison on a contempt sentence.

January 1975
A police bug overheard Paolo Violi complain to Joe DiMaulo that the Cotroni blood family should have picked up Frank Cotroni's legal costs instead of holding a fundraising dinner.

January 11, 1975
In New York, a federal jury found Frank Cotroni and Frank Dasti guilty of a cocaine conspiracy and trafficking in cocaine. Judge Mishler had earlier permitted Canadian wiretaps of the duo, although he said if the good guys made the tapes in the US, they would not be admissible.

Exposure of the Cotroni cocaine conspiracy resulted from complaints from wives and girlfriends about a gambling operation were their partners lost a lot of money. Cotroni ran the card game in Frank Dasti's Victoria Sporting Club, which caused the complaints.

The police began to monitor the personal phone lines of Frank Cotroni, Guido Orsini, Santo Mendola, and a barbershop. They came across the drug-dealing conspiracy. These tapes were crucial for the prosecution in the New York trial.

January 18, 1975
In a secretly taped conversation by the Montreal Police, Paolo Violi told Joe DiMaulo that he was now the Acting Capo of the Montreal crew.

February 1975
The Supreme Court ordered Vic Cotroni's release on bail until a court heard Cotroni's appeal of his contempt sentence from the Crime Inquiry.

March 5, 1975
In Vic Cotroni's Reggio Foods plant, a police bug heard Paolo Violi telling Vic Cotroni and Joe DiMaulo that the group should start a fund to help lawyers' costs. He said everyone was embarrassed when someone organized a dinner to raise funds for Frank Cotroni's defense. The tapes made it clear that Violi had assumed the leading role because of Vic Cotroni's health and legal problems.

March 24, 1975
Judge Jacob Mishler sentenced both Frank Cotroni and Frank Dasti to two 15 year sentences plus a fine of $20,000. The terms were to run concurrently.

May 16, 1975
Through a lawyer, Frank Cotroni offered the Secret Service $750,000 in counterfeit money. This move was a scam attempted by Cotroni in the hopes of decreasing his time behind bars.

May 20, 1975
Frank Cotroni told the Secret Service where to find $100,000 in counterfeit money and the plates that made them. It was a scam for Cotroni paid $100,000 for the bills and plates then hid them.

July 1975
Montreal revoked Vic Cotroni's license to operate the Reggio Foods meatpacking plant.

August 1975
Vic Cotroni filed a libel suit against two QPF officers who testified before the Crime Inquiry that Cotroni was the head of crime in Montreal. Cotroni asked for $10,000 in damages and $7,500 in costs. Later, in the civil proceedings discovery phase, Cotroni admitted he met Meyer Lansky in Mexico in April 1970.

October 1975
Somehow Montreal's William Obront received his American Citizenship, although he hadn't lived in the US for five years.

November 6, 1975
The RCMP arrested Paolo Violi, Vic Cotroni, John Papalia, and Sheldon Swartz for swindling Toronto stockbroker Stanley Bader. Montreal Police had overheard Violi, Cotroni, and Papalia discussing the matter back on April 30, 1974, in Violi's Reggio Bar.

November 11, 1975
A jury convicted Paolo Violi of a stock fraud involving Buffalo Gas and Oil between September 1, 1971, and March 31, 1972. The judge sentenced him to one year and a $25,000 fine but released Violi on $25,000 bail while he appealed.

November 18, 1975
At the Crime Inquiry, brothers Lino and Quinto Simaglia testified how Paolo Violi extorted them for $4,000 a year to "protect" their food packing firm. Violi returned later and demanded a $1,000 payment at Christmas.

Mauro Marchettine testified that, after ignoring advice to close his business, Francesco Violi beat him for opening a pool room too close to that of Paolo Violi. Marchettine was able to get out of his lease and left.

November 24, 1975
Montreal Police issued a warrant for the arrest of Paolo Violo for conspiracy to do bodily harm to Pasquale Tulio in 1972.

November 25, 1975
Before the Crime Inquiry, Tony Mucci said Jean-Paul Charbonneau's wounding was spontaneous, and Frank Cotroni

did not order it. He did admit that Paolo Violi sent him to extort pizzeria owner Joe Petrozza in February of 1974.

November 26, 1975
A correctional officer testified before the Crime Inquiry that he passed a message from Paolo Violi to Moreno Gallo and Tony Vanelli. One of them was to plead guilty to the murder of Angelo Facchino on September 2, 1973. Gallo followed orders in March of 1974 and got a life sentence. The judge gave Vanelli seven years after he pled guilty to manslaughter.

November 29, 1975
Police arrested Paolo Violi in Toronto based on an assault warrant from Montreal Police. When Violi deplaned in Montreal, officials served him with a subpoena to appear before the Crime Inquiry.

December 1, 1975
Police charged Paolo Violi for conspiracy to assault and assault of Pasquale Tullio on June 3, 1972. Judge D Reilly Watson presided over the arraignment.

December 2, 1975
Judge Jean Dutil of the Crime Inquiry sent Paolo Violi to jail for a year for his contempt before the Inquiry.

December 3, 1975
Judge Maurice Rosseau denied bail for Paolo Violi in Pasquale Tullio's assault case.

December 4, 1975
A judge released Paolo Violo on $50,000 bail on his extortion case.

December 11, 1975
During Violi's preliminary hearing, Judge Emile Trottier dismissed an assault charge against Violi for the Tullio attack since there was no evidence. He said Violi might have to go on trial for conspiracy to commit assault. Tullio testified that he and pool hall owner Michael Cutone argued over about $30. Later two men, Jimmy DeSantis and Enzo Porco, allegedly beat him.

December 23, 1975

Justice Paul Casey agreed to bail for Paolo Violi from his one-year contempt sentence before the Crime Inquiry. The Justice said it was appropriate for lawyers were fighting the constitutionality of the Inquiry before the Supreme Court.

Justice Charles Phelan allowed $10,000 bail for Violi on his Tullio conspiracy to assault case. He also freed fellow accused Jimmy DeSantis pending a decision on DeSantis's habeas corpus writ.

February 14, 1976

A shooter killed Violi advisor Pietro Sciara after he left the Riviera movie theatre with his wife. The building later becomes a strip club run by Moreno Gallo.

March 10, 1976

Someone killed Sebastiano Messino in his bar on Tillemont Street. Speculation was that this was revenge for the Sciara hit.

1976

The police charged William Obront with: fraud, forgery, conspiracy to commit forgery, and use of false documents. These counts had to do with the bankruptcy of Obie's Meats in 1975.

April 1, 1976

The Supreme Court ruled the Crime Inquiry could continue.

May 3, 1976

William Obront fled the US for Costa Rica after he heard there was a warrant for his arrest.

May 20, 1976

At the cost of $35,000, the RCMP flew Obront from Costa Rica to Montreal.

May 21, 1976

Judge Roger Craig presided over William Obront's arraignment on fraud charges. The judge remanded him to jail until they could arrange a bail hearing.

May 27, 1976
Judge Dutil of the Crime Inquiry sentenced Obront to a year in jail for contempt. Vic Cotroni claimed he was too ill to testify.

August 3, 1976
Paolo Violi was in court.

November 23, 1976
A jury found William Obront guilty of fraud in the bankruptcy of Obie's Meats.

December 3, 1976
Judge Andre Durauleau sentenced Obront to four four-year terms to run concurrently, plus a fine of $75,000.

December 16, 1976
A jury acquitted Donald Cote of the murders of de Courcy and Chiquette. The duo had slaughtered Cote's wife and child. They didn't believe the confession statement of Joseph Rodriquez, who claimed to have taken part in the murders of the two gangsters. His report said Rodriquez went back to the funeral home where Cote hugged him and offered money after the revenge killings.

January 2, 1977
Immigration Canada officials served William Obront with deportation papers while he was in prison.

1977
The Quebec Court of Appeals reduced Obront's fraud sentence to two years and slashed the fine to $10,000 due to his lack of previous convictions.

February 3, 1977
Frank Cotroni's New York lawyer sent a letter to US Attorney Thomas Puccio declaring that Cotroni's aid to the Secret Service back in May of 1975 was not a hoax. The lawyer felt that Cotroni deserved a reduction in his cocaine conspiracy sentence. Puccio felt the Cotroni effort was a scam and did not aid Cotroni. Puccio put the letter in his files and forgot about it. A few years later, someone found the document, which led to big trouble for Frank Cotroni in March of 1979.

PAOLO VIOLI'S END NEARS

February 8, 1977
A hitman murdered Francesco Violi by shotgun in his restaurant supply company, Violi Importing and Distributing. This hit was part of the Sicilian faction's move to unseat Paolo Violi as Capo.

March 9, 1977
The Crime Inquiry Judge sentenced Obront to one year for contempt. This date was the last day of public hearings for the Crime Inquiry.

November 30, 1977
The Supreme Court overturned Vic Cotroni's one-year sentence for contempt before the Crime Inquiry.

December 27, 1977
Montreal police began surveillance of three men and their red van after citizen complaints. They entered the vehicle and found a Zardini double-barreled shotgun and a short M-1 carbine. They left the weapons in the truck. They identified the three men as Domenico Manno, brother-in-law of Nicolo Rizzuto, Agostino Cuntrera, and Giovanni Di Mora. All three men were Sicilians and firmly in the camp of Nicolo Rizzuto.

December 29, 1978
Police saw Domenico Manno and Giovanni DiMora carried white plastic bags into Violi's former bar. That night the cops checked the suspect van and found the guns gone. They assumed the bags contained the shotgun and M-1 carbine they found in the truck earlier.

1978
A Judge sentenced Donald Cote to eight years for a conviction involving stolen Canadian Savings Bonds belonging to an American insurance company. Later the Quebec Court of Appeals ordered a new trial.

A Judge sentenced William Obront to 20 months for an extensive tax fraud.

PAOLO VIOLI IS KILLED

January 22, 1978
A shooter killed Paolo Violi with two blasts from a shotgun to the head in the Jean-Talon bar. Police found the Zardino two-barrel shotgun in a nearby snowbank. It didn't take the law long to figure out who their top three suspects were. Unluckily for the police, they had stopped their surveillance of the three men that very day to give the officers rest after a month-long vigil.

January 27, 1978
The Violi family held visitation at the Rene Theriault Funeral Home at 1120 Jean-Talon Street East, followed by a service at Notre Dame Della Difesa Church on Henri Julien Avenue. A large crowd, hordes of media, and many undercover police officers were in attendance. The law took a lot of pictures from an upper floor of a school. At the gravesite, a Violi soldier became angered at the media and swung his shovel without hitting anyone. It made a great picture, however.

CHAPTER SEVENTEEN

Montreal Timeline Part Three

THE RIZZUTO HAND EMERGES

February 8, 1978
After a week-long hearing, Coroner Maurice Laniel held Domenico Manno, Giovanni Di Mora, Agostino Cuntrera, and Vincenzo Randisi criminally responsible for Paolo Violi's death.

One of the hearing highlights was when an officer showed Domenico Manno the Zardini shotgun used in the murder. Manno denied ever seeing the weapon before. Police officers testified about their one-month surveillance of the three suspects and their discovery of the two weapons in the rented van. A police ballistic expert testified that the pellets in Violi match pellets fired from the discovered shotgun.
Lanier sentenced DiMora and Cuntrera to a year in prison for refusing to testify before the hearing.

September 15, 1978

After extensive negotiations between the Crown and the defense lawyers, three defendants pled guilty to conspiracy to murder Violi. Justice Claire-Barrette-Jonas accepted their pleas. She also freed Vincenzo Randisi and annulled the warrant of Paolo Renda. The police had been searching for Renda with no success. He was a son-in-law of Nicolo Rizzuto and an influential member of his entourage for decades to come.

September 23, 1978

Justice Claire Barrette-Joncas sentenced Giovanni DiMora and Domenico Manno to seven years for their conspiracy to murder plea. She gave Agostino Cuntrera a five-year term. DiMora and Manno spent eight months in prison waiting for justice, while Cuntrera put in four months in the slammer. Interestingly the justice stated she considered that the three immigrants had led hard-working and respectable lives. Cuntrera and Manno would continue their criminal ways for many decades.

1979

The Quebec Court of Appeals threw out William Obront's contempt sentence from the Crime Inquiry.

FRANK COTRONI THE RAT?

March 23, 1979

A wiretap of Genovese Associate William Masselli explained how he met Bonanno Capo Anthony "Sonny Red" Indelicato and talked about Frank Cotroni. Indelicato showed Masselli the lawyer's letter that made it appear that Cotroni had co-operated with the Secret Service. Unknown to Indelicato, this letter was part of a stupid attempt by Cotroni to con the good guys to get a reduction in his cocaine conspiracy sentence. Bonanno Boss Carmine Galante had ordered Indelicato to whack Cotroni.

March 28, 1979

A Masselli wiretap caught the gangster explaining to another man how he tried to talk Indelicato out of having Frank Cotroni whacked. It appears that he succeeded.

March 29, 1979

The FBI visited Frank Cotroni in Lewisburg prison and told him he was the target of a hit. They explained that Bonanno Capo Anthony "Sonny Red" Indelicato was to have the murder carried out after his Boss learned of Cotroni's interaction with the Secret Service about counterfeit bills and plates. Cotroni's con attempt to reduce his sentence had come back to bite him. Indelicato was one of the three Capos gunned down in May of 1981.

April 21, 1979

A Montreal Gazette article said that Frank Cotroni had called off a proposed charity dinner in his honor. Cotroni felt that the publicity the affair created wouldn't be worth doing it.

April 25, 1979

Prison officials released Frank Cotroni from Lewisburg Prison, and US Immigration agents immediately flew him to Montreal on an Eastern Airlines flight.

January 28, 1980

Police arrested Donald Cote and his future wife, Marie Louise Nolan, for conspiracy to traffic cocaine and possession of a pound of cocaine found in a parked car in a garage with Nolan present.

July 28, 1980

Assailants on a motorcycle tried to kill Rocco Violi as he drove his car. Police speculated this was an attempt to prevent Rocco from avenging his brother Paolo.

October 11, 1980

Nicolo Rizzuto's father-in-law, Antonio Manno, died in Montreal, where he had resided for years. At one time, Manno was the Boss of the Mafia Family in Cattolica Eraclea.

October 17, 1980

A sniper killed Rocco Violi as he sat in his home with his family. It appeared that this hit would prevent revenge against the men who conspired to kill Paolo, but memories are long, and more than twenty years later, revenge happened by someone.

THE DRUG DEALING ESCALATES

November 16, 1980
Montreal Bonanno Soldiers Vito Rizzuto and Joe LoPresti attended the wedding reception of prominent Sicilian Mafia Boss Salvatore Bono in New York. Many other Bonanno members were present, including Gerlando Sciascia, the Montreal Capo, even though he resided in New York.

February 25, 1981
A judge found Donald Cote and Marie Louis Nolan not guilty of their drug charges. He ruled that police testimony was contradictory.

1982
Vito Rizzuto, his father Nick Rizzuto, and his uncle Paolo Renda moved to new luxurious homes on Antoine Berthelet. Also living there was Joe LoPresti. Gerlando Sciascia owned a lot but never built a house.

September 24, 1982
Financial wizard Michael Pozza met with Joe LoPresti, Gerlando Sciascia, and Vito Rizzuto in Vito's home.

September 28, 1982
Frank Cotroni close Associate, Real Simard, killed Pozza in front of his home on Cotroni's orders. He was angry because Pozza was leaning more towards Rizzuto's Sicilian crew than his own.

June 15, 1983
Someone killed Frank Cotroni's brother-in-law, Michael Desormiers, in his home. Cotroni and Desormier's sister were separated, and the murder had nothing to do with the tension between the Calabrian Cotroni and the Sicilian Rizzutos.

FRANK COTRONI AND DRUGS AGAIN!

July 1983
A US grand jury indicted Frank Cotroni for a drug conspiracy in Connecticut.

July 21, 1983
US authorities arrested William Obront for drug dealing. He now lived in Florida.

August 30, 1983
Police arrested Frank Cotroni on a Connecticut indictment charging him with conspiracy to traffic heroin and possessing heroin to traffic. Not long afterward, a judge released him on $185,000 bail.

September 1983
Authorities paroled Moreno Gallo from his murder sentence. Gallo had pled guilty to the killing of rival gangster Angelo Facchino on orders from Paolo Violi.

February 23, 1984
Superior Court Justice Charles Phelan ruled there was sufficient evidence to extradite Frank Cotroni to the US. He remanded Cotroni to jail until a bail hearing.

April 3, 1984
Superior Court Justice Kenneth McKay upheld Frank Cotroni's extradition order. He did this by denying Cotroni's habeas corpus writ.

April 9, 1984
A Justice granted Frank Cotroni an extradition delay so he could appeal.

April 27, 1984
In the Quebec Court of Appeals, Justice Marc Beauregard listened to Frank Cotroni's lawyer plea for bail for Cotroni.

April 1984
An appeal court agreed to hear Frank Cotroni's appeals against extradition.

May 3, 1984
Justice Marc Beauregard of the Quebec Court of Appeals turned down Frank Cotroni's request for bail. He said Cotroni was a threat to society.

June 7, 1984
A Florida jury convicted William Obront of drug dealing.

July 27, 1984
A judge sentenced William Obront to 20 years and fined him $20,000.

VIC COTRONI DIES

September 16, 1984
Vic Cotroni died at his home of natural causes. Authorities gave his brother Frank permission to attend the funeral but only with an escort. He declined the offer.

March 1985
A jury convicted RCMP narcotics officer Paul Sauve and gangster Gerald Hiscock for drug trafficking. The two men then began a lengthy appeal process.

January 3, 1986
A three-judge panel of the Quebec Court of Appeals approved bail for Frank Cotroni. He had to pay $100,000 in cash plus $83,000 in a property.

1986
The leaked Bernier Report on Boxing said Frank Cotroni was the kingpin.

March 17, 1987
US authorities indicted William Obront for dealing in counterfeit Quaaludes.

June 24, 1987
William Obront pled innocent to a conspiracy to illegally transfer $3 million-plus from the Bahamas to the US.

November 30, 1987
The RCMP charged Vito Rizzuto and others with a conspiracy to smuggle hashish into Canada. They had seized the Charlotte Louise ship, which had transported the drug to a small island near Newfoundland.

FRANK COTRONI AND MANSLAUGHTER

December 8, 1987
Frank Cotroni, Frank Cotroni Jr, Dan Arena, and Frank Raso pled guilty to a reduced charge of manslaughter in the 1981 killing of Joe Montegano. Prosecutor Guy Dupre told the court that Frank Cotroni had ordered the hit after learning Montegano had talked to the police. When Cotroni Associate Real Simard became a government witness, he confessed to this murder and named the others involved.

Judge Andre Chaloux sentenced Frank Cotroni to eight years and gave Dan Arena seven. He would deal with Frank Cotroni Jr and Frank Raso at a later date.

February 12, 1988
Venezuelan National Police arrested Nicolo Rizzuto and some other Canadians on cocaine charges. They locked Rizzuto up without bail.

September 5, 1989
A judge arraigned Vito Rizzuto, Rene Desjardins, Michel Routhier, and Gerard Hiscock on conspiracy to traffic in drugs charges. This event was related to the 1987 seizure of hashish on a small

island near Newfoundland. They used the ship, Charlotte Louise, to transfer the drugs.

December 18, 1989
A jury acquitted Vito Rizzuto of conspiracy to smuggle 32 tons of Lebanese hash into Canada aboard the Jeanne d'Arc. A key element in his acquittal was the refusal of the boat skipper to testify against Cotroni. For Norman Dupuis' story to be told properly, I'd need at least half a chapter.

February 7, 1990
A New York jury found Bonanno Soldier Joe LoPresti, Bonanno Capo Gerlando Sciascia, and Gambino Soldier Eddie Lino not guilty of drug charges. It had been a lengthy process with Sciascia fleeing to Canada then spending two years fighting extradition after the RCMP arrested him.

A mistrial followed before the final trial and conviction. Later, turncoat Gambino Underboss Sammy "The Bull" Gravano revealed that he bribed a juror with $10,000, which aided in the not guilty verdict.

VITO RIZZUTO DODGES A BULLET

November 8, 1990
Justice Leo Barry dismissed hashish smuggling charges against Vito Rizzuto due to illegal bugging by RCMP officers. This case involved the Charlotte Louise ship. When freed, Rizzuto said, "One word can mean so much, especially if that word is acquitted."

July 21, 1991
Frank Cotroni Jr married the daughter of Joe DiMaulo. Prison officials permitted his father, Frank Cotroni, to attend the ceremony with an escort.

February 26, 1991
Frank Cotroni consented to his extradition to Connecticut to face heroin trafficking charges. The agreement was that he would

appear in court there on February 28 and return to Canada within 72 hours. He would serve any sentence in Canada.

February 28, 1991
Frank Cotroni pled guilty to the illegal use of interstate communication in a heroin deal. The Judge gave him a six-year sentence that Cotroni would serve in Canada.

THE RIZZUTOS CLEAN HOUSE

April 29, 1992
Railroad workers discovered the body of Joe LoPresti along a section of tracks. This murder was a startling event since LoPresti was part of the inner circle of the Rizzuto clan. When Bonanno Underboss Sal Vitale became a government witness, he told the FBI that Bonanno Capo, Gerlando Sciascia asked permission to kill LoPresti. Street talk suggested that Rizzuto and Sciascia had become concerned about LoPresti's cocaine use. The LoPrestis lived just down the street from Vito Rizzuto, so it must have been quite awkward in that neighborhood for a while. LoPresti's son was not happy, of course, and would take action in the future.

April 1993
Prison officials released Frank Cotroni on parole from his Connecticut conviction.

May 27, 1993
Nicolo Rizzuto returned to Montreal after completing his drug sentence in Venezuela. The police arrested him in February 1988, and a jury found him not guilty at his first trial. The prosecutors appealed and won, which meant they tried Nicolo again. This time the jury convicted him for possession of cocaine. Rizzuto served a total of five years in prison in Venezuela before flying back to Montreal.

August 25, 1993
The RCMP arrested Raynald Desjardins and 16 others for a drug conspiracy. The group had purchased 700 kg of cocaine in Venezuela and shipped it by boat somewhere off Newfoundland.

They transferred the drugs to the Fortune Endeavor, but this vessel broke down and required a Coast Guard tow. Fearing discovery, the smugglers dumped the huge pipes containing the cocaine overboard on August 1. Unbeknownst to them, the RCMP had already infiltrated their organization and knew what had happened.

Desjardins was the big catch as he was a significant gangster very closely associated with Vito Rizzuto. He would be a player in the criminal milieu for years to come.

BIKER WAR BEGINS

The Nomad Chapter of Quebec's Hells Angels decided to attempt to dominate the drug trade in Montreal in areas not controlled by the Mafia. Leader Maurice "Mom" Boucher helped form a "puppet" club called the Rockers. Most of these men sought to become full patch Hell Angels so they were willing to do just about anything. They would carry the brunt of the action against their rivals.

The Rivals of the Hells Angels were three loosely connected groups who desired independence and didn't want to be subjected to having to buy Hells Angels drugs arbitrarily priced. The Pelletier Clan, the Rock Machine, and the Dark Circle fought violently against the Hells. Over the next eight years approximately 162 people died including a number of innocents. This war made any Mafia conflict in North America pale in comparison.

March 11, 1994
A grand jury in southern Florida indicted Domenico Manno and others on heroin, cocaine, and counterfeit money charges.

BIG MONEY WASH

August 30, 1994
The RCMP concluded a highly successful sting operation by arresting about 57 men for money laundering and various other criminal activities.

They had opened a currency exchange in Montreal, which lured in high-priced lawyer Joseph Lagana who had Vito Rizzuto as a client. The operation began back on September 29, 1990, and laundered upwards of $95 million from many customers. One notable client was Vincenzo "Jimmy" DiMaulo, brother of major player Joe DiMaulo. Vincenzo pled guilty to laundering over $10 million through the RCMP's phony company.

The main target, Vito Rizzuto, avoided all exposure and was never charged in this case.

October 24, 1994
Judge Jean-Pierre Bonin sentenced Raynald Desjardins to 15 years and a $150,000 fine after Desjardins pled guilty to drug charges.

July 12, 1995
Police arrested Domenico Manno in Montreal for US officials in southern Florida who wanted Manno to face drug charges there.

1996
A judge sentenced Emanuele Ragusa to 12 years for a drug conspiracy.

FRANK COTRONI AND DRUGS AGAIN!!

April 18, 1996
Officials arraigned a large group of men in court on charges involving two conspiracies. Among the group connected to cocaine trafficking were Frank Cotroni, his son Frank, and their Associates Tony Volpato and Daniel Arena. In the hashish group was Luigi Vella, a son-in-law of Emanuele Ragusa.

April 4, 1997
Before Judge Bonin, Frank Cotroni and his son Frank pled guilty to conspiracy to traffic in cocaine. The judge sentenced Frank Cotroni to seven years and ordered that he serve half that time before applying for parole. Frank Cotroni Jr received a term of eight years. Frank Cotroni was in jail since his arrest a year ago.

June 19, 1997
The Supreme Court of Canada ended a long fight by Domenico Manno to avoid being extradited to Florida to face drug charges. They refused to hear his appeal.

May 1998
Parole officials moved Emanuele Ragusa to a halfway house.

June 20, 1998
Nicole Rizzuto returned to Montreal from Venezuela.

1998
Domenico Manno pled guilty to dealing in heroin, cocaine, and counterfeit money in the Southern District of Florida. The judge sentenced him to 240 months and a forfeiture of $250,000 with no right to appeal.

August 23, 1998
Hitman Gerald Gallant and another man killed Paul Cotroni in his driveway. This killing was a drug dispute and had nothing to do with the tension between the Rizzuto group's Sicilian and Calabrian wings. Gallant admitted to the hit years later when he rolled over.

THE RIZZUTOS BEGIN EDGING AWAY FROM THE BONANNOS

March 18, 1999
Boss Joe Massino decided that Capo Gerlando Sciascia had to die. The reasons behind the killing ranged from Massino not liking Sciascia's criticism of a Massino friend or that Massino feared Sciascia's growing power. Whatever the reason, Massino ordered Underboss Sal Vitale to take care of it.

Vitale put Bronx Capo Patrick DeFilippo in charge of killing Sciascia and provided a silenced gun to do the job. DeFilippo conned Sciascia to attend a meeting, and they drove in a vehicle driven by Johnny Joe Spirito. DeFilippo, sitting in the passenger seat, suddenly turned around and filled Sciascia full of lead. Then they dumped the body in the street to be found later. They hoped Sciascia's friends would think it was a drug deal gone wrong.

Hoping to mask his involvement Massino had Vitale talk around pretending they were trying to figure out what happened. Then Massino ordered a bunch of Capos to attend Sciascia's wake. They weren't fooling Sciascia's Canadian friends like Vito Rizzuto. He turned down a Massino request to replace Sciascia as the Capo in charge of the Canadian crew, plus he stopped the annual tribute coming down from Montreal to Massino.

The Sciascia killing was a watershed invent in the relationship between the Rizzuto organization and New York's Bonanno Family. The Rizzutos, already independent, would act even more so, for they didn't need the label of being a Bonanno crew any longer. They could stand on their own as an independent organization.

July 13, 2001
Police arrested veteran gangster Christian Deschenes and Denis-Rolland Girouard as they drove to the Rizzuto HQ, the Consenza Club on Jary Street. Deschenes planned to kidnap Rizzuto heavyweight Francesco Arcadi and Frank Martorano because they owed him $800,000 for a deal long ago. Unfortunately for Deschenes, Girouard was an informer, so the police arrested the duo before reaching the club. They wouldn't be the last group making a hostile visit there.

August 2001
Vito Rizzuto and Revenue Canada made a deal on monies allegedly owed by Rizzuto on his Penway stock transactions. Originally Revenue Canada demanded $1.5 million and a fine of $127, 690. Street talk suggested that Rizzuto settled for far less.

2002
Parole officials revoked Raynald Desjardins' parole after they spotted him shaking hands with Frank Cotroni Jr.

March 2002
US prison officials released William Obront from his drug sentence.

May 2002
Montreal police arrested Vito Rizzuto for drunk driving and refusing to take a breathalyzer test.

July 22, 2002
Rizzuto pled not guilty to impaired driving in municipal court.

BIKER WAR ENDS

Late 2002
The biker war between the Hells Angels and the Rock Machine petered out with arrests, peace deals, deaths, and the realization by all involved that nobody was safe. It had been eight years of violence, murders, and terror.

December 8, 2002
Vito Rizzuto was in court on his impaired driving charge.

January 2003
While on vacation in the Dominican Republic, Vito Rizzuto told Francisco Arcadi about his participation in the famous 1981 Three Capos Hit, including firing a gun. Dominican police recorded his conversation, but the quality of the tape was inferior. On that trip were: Paulo Renda, Domenico Chimineti, Giuseppe Triassi, Vincent Spagnolo, and Joe DiMaulo.

June 2003
Montreal police planted bugs in the Consenza Social Club, the headquarters of the Rizzuto group.

2004
Prison officials release Raynald Desjardins from his parole violation sentence.

January 19, 2004
Veteran gangster Paolo Gervasi died in a shooting while sitting in his vehicle. Someone had murdered his son earlier, and Gervasi

was determined to discover who. This revenge-seeking may have been the reason behind his murder.

VITO RIZZUTO IN TROUBLE

January 20, 2004
Canadian police officers arrested Vito Rizzuto at the request of American law officials. They announced a 20 count indictment that devastated the Bonanno Family's leadership and included Vito Rizzuto for the Three Capo Hit. Emanuele Ragusa and Domenico Manno probably couldn't believe their luck at not being included.

April 8, 2004
Justice Jean-Guy Boilard authorized Vito Rizzuto's extradition.

June 2, 2004
Prison officials released Raynald Desjardins.

July 30, 2004
Bonanno Boss Joe Massino became a government witness shortly after being convicted and receiving a life sentence.

August 6, 2004
Justice Francois Doyon of Quebec's Court of Appeals denied bail for Rizzuto.

2004
Prison officials released Emanuele Ragusa after he completed 2/3 of his 12-year sentence handed down in 1996. Ragusa was lucky that the Americans never requested his extradition to New York to face charges in the Three Capos hit from back in May 1981. They did not have enough evidence for turncoat Underboss Sal Vitale only saw him for a short period. Also, the FBI never got incriminating pictures of him in the area as they did with Vito Rizzuto.

December 8, 2004
Canada's Federal Justice Minister Irwin Cotler ordered Vito Rizzuto's extradition.

February 2, 2005
Montreal area gangster Sergio Piccirelli and Domenico D'Agostino traveled to Toronto to confer with Calabrian Boss Franco Mattoso. Piccirelli later met with Giuseppe and Domenico Violi in Hamilton. They are the sons of Paolo Violi, murdered in 1978.

2005
A series of kidnappings, killings, and beatings erupted in Montreal during this period. There were various reasons for these events, but the most crucial factor was that Vito Rizzuto was in prison and unable to arbitrate the endless squabbles among the bad guys.

March 10, 2005
Rizzuto enforcer Mike Lapolla died after being shot in the Moomba night club. Lapolla's friends gunned down his shooter, Theirry Beaubrun, as he fled the club. This event had all the hallmarks of a "macho" conflict rather than a serious mob attack.

LOSS OF CONTROL IN THE STREETS

April 2005
Someone kidnapped entrepreneur Tony Magi, a Rizzuto Associate, on Saint-Jacques Street in LaSalle. Magi later claimed to the police that he escaped. Few believed that story and suspected Magi's friends paid a ransom.

May 1, 2005
Someone kidnapped Leonardo D'Angelo due to a drug debt. They released him later, and we have to assume someone came up with the money.

May 11, 2005
Veteran Calabrian mobster Moreno Gallo was secretly filmed bringing tribute money to the Consenza Social Club. Nicolo Rizzuto was present in the backroom, and he took a cut of Gallo's money.

May 25, 2005
Someone kidnapped Frank Martorano from a barbershop on Jean-Talon, but they released him later. Again we assume someone paid his debt.

June 23, 2005
The US 11th District Court of Appeals affirmed a District Court ruling that Domenico Manno had to pay his $250,000 forfeiture. Manno argued that his lawyer recommended he take the 1998 plea deal based on faulty advice. The lawyer believed that authorities could transfer Manno to a prison in Canada where his time behind bars would be much shorter due to more lenient Canadian rules. Furthermore, Manno could ignore the $250,000 forfeiture. When Mann learned that the transfer didn't apply to him, he appealed and lost at both levels.

THE D'AMICOS ARE ANGRY

October 31, 2005
Sergio Piccirelli and friends kidnapped Nick Varacalli from his home.

November 29, 2005
A Superior Court Justice had refused to hear Vito Rizzuto's lawyers' arguments that the statute of limitations had passed on his extradition. They appealed to a three-Judge panel of Quebec's Court of Appeals, but they backed the Superior Court Judge's ruling

December 1, 2005
Veteran gangster Luca D'Amico delivered a letter to Nicolo Rizzuto at the Consenza asking him to arbitrate a dispute between the D'Amico's and Rizzuto power Francesco Arcadi.

December 8, 2005
The Piccirilli group released Nick Varacalli, who refused to co-operate with the police. This move may have been a goodwill gesture by the D'Amico's hoping Nicolo Rizzuto would intervene in their dispute with Arcadi.

December 23, 2005
A group of D'Amicos entered the Consenza in a show of force then left in a cavalcade of vehicles. Among them was Sergio Piccirilli. This event was an intimidation tactic since Nicolo Rizzuto did not agree to arbitrate their complaints.

December 31, 2005
Police arrested Nicolo Rizzuto for drunk driving after he got into an accident.

February 16, 2006
The police warned Sergio Piccirilli that he was the subject of a hit. Later that night, he ordered some guns from a native contact. The next day the police intercepted the native connection and confiscated the weapons.

March 1, 2006
Police taped Sergio Piccirilli telling the D'Amicos that he was armed and ready to attack the Rizzutos.

March 16, 2006
The Supreme Court refused to hear an appeal of the Quebec Court of Appeal's decision not to listen to arguments about the statute of limitations in the Vito Rizzuto case.

Raynald Desjardins is Angry

August 11, 2006
Three shooters gunned down veteran gangster Giovanni Bertolo in Riviere des Prairies. He had angered Francesco Arcadi by dealing drugs in his former area that Arcadi gave away when Bertolo went to prison. Bertolo was a close friend of Raynald Desjardins.

This killing would be another watershed event in the Rizzuto organization for Desjardins; a dangerous man would soon break away.

VITO RIZZUTO VISITS THE STATES-
-INVOLUNTARILY

August 17, 2006

The Supreme Court ended Vito Rizzuto's long and costly legal battle to avoid extradition. Officers flew him to New York the same day. He didn't look happy.

CHAPTER EIGHTEEN

Montreal Timeline Part Four

CHAOS IN THE STEETS

August 30, 2006
A shooter killed Domenico Marci sitting on the passenger side of a vehicle escorting Rizzuto leader Francesco Arcadi. The driver Mario Iannitto was slightly wounded. Everyone assumed the hitmen blew the job, for the real target must have been Arcadi.

September 4, 2006
Police filmed Rizzuto men Giuseppe Fetta and two others handling weapons inside a warehouse belonging to Rizzuto heavyweight Francisco Del Balso.

September 5, 2006
The Macri family held Domenico's funeral, with most of the significant Rizzuto organization players present.

September 12, 2006
The police raided Giuseppe Fetta's garage and seized some weapons and other materials. They hoped to prevent an escalation of violence.

PROJECT COLISEE

November 22, 2006
Police arrested many major mobsters as part of their Project Colisee investigation. Among those picked up were Nicolo Rizzuto, Paulo Renda, Francesco Arcadi, and Rocco Sollecito. Along with the imprisoned Vito Rizzuto, these men were Montreal's Bonanno Family crew's ruling panel. Their power was much more significant than a regular Bonanno crew, although few in New York understood this.

The court dropped drunk driving charges against Vito Rizzuto laid back in 2002.

November 24, 2006
Police arrested Nicolo Rizzuto on tax charges.

December 2006
Agents of Revenue Canada seized the Laval luxury home of Lorenzo Giordano, a second-level power in the Rizzuto organization.

2007
Police arrested Moreno Gallo for a parole violation. They had secretly filmed the gangster making regular visits to the Consenza Social Club, the Rizzuto headquarters.

March 9, 2007
Shooters killed Carmine Guarino at the Cafe Albano on Jarry Street.

VITO RIZZUTO TAKES A PLEA DEAL

May 4, 2007
In New York, Vito Rizzuto took a plea deal for conspiracy to murder in the Three Capos Hit in May of 1981. Judge Nicholas Garaufis sentenced Canada's top mobster to 10 years and a $250,000 fine. Rizzuto admitted that he was a member of a criminal organization.

May 8, 2007
Police arrested Rizzuto power, Lorenzo Giordano, in Toronto. He had been on the run since the November 2006 Project Colisee roundup of Rizzuto gangsters.

December 2007
Police believed someone tried to kill Tony Mucci as he left Francesco Arcadi's Cafe Maida.

May 25, 2008
At his final sentencing hearing, Vito Rizzuto tried to plead poverty. Judge Nicholas Garaufis was having none of it. He gave Rizzuto three months to pay his $250,000 fine.

2008
Salvatore Scoppa pled guilty to being a part of a group that abducted a man and held him for nearly two days before releasing him. The victim was an Associate of Rizzuto power Francesco Arcadi. The judge sentenced Scoppa to a year behind bars.

August 11, 2008
Someone shot and seriously wounded Tony Magi in his car at Cavendish and Monkland Ave in NDG.

RIZZUTO LEADERS MAKE A DEAL

September 18, 2008
Nicolo Rizzuto, Francesco Arcadi, Paolo Renda, Francesco Del Balso, and others took plea deals in Project Colisee.

October 16, 2008
A Judge sentenced Nicolo Rizzuto to four years but credited him with time served, so the court released Rizzuto the same day. The judge gave Arcadi 15 years, Renda six years, and Del Balso 15 years.

November 14, 2008
Prosecutors dropped drug charges against Sergio Piccirilli and others.

November 25, 2008
Charles Battista, Giuseppe Fetta, and Danny Canas all pled guilty to handling high powered weapons as they acted as bodyguards for Del Balso and Giordano.

December 4, 2008
Mario Marabella was abducted and not seen again. He was associated with the Rizzutos and especially Agustino Cuntrera.

December 21, 2008
Police believed two men in a van took shots at Tony Mucci.

2009
Raynald Desjardins was finally off parole.

January 16, 2009
Shooters killed Sam Fasulo at the corner of Henri Bourassa and Langelier. He was a Rizzuto Associate.

February 9, 2009
A judge sentenced Rizzuto power, Lorenzo Giordano, to 15 years but credited him with five years for time served awaiting trial. Thus he might be out in 5 years.

SAL MONTAGNA ARRIVES FROM THE STATES

April 2009
American Immigration officials deported Bonanno Acting Boss Sal Montagna to Canada. He had a minor criminal record, but it was enough to get him deported as an undesirable.

June 2009
Police arrested Francesco Catalano and others for the kidnapping of Nino De Bartolomeis, who owed them money. Only Sal Scoppa was convicted. He is the brother of Calabrian leader Andrea Scopo.

June 17, 2009
Immigration Canada's attempt to deport Moreno Gallo failed after a judge ruled the process was unfair.

August 21, 2009
A shooter killed close Rizzuto friend, Frederico Del Peschio, behind La Cantina restaurant. Del Peschio served time in a Venezuelan prison with Nick Rizzuto and remained his friend for five decades.

September 17, 2009
Members of Toronto's powerful Commisso clan flew to Montreal and met with Vittorio Mirarchi.

November 24, 2009
A shooter wounded Ennio Brunio four times, but he lived.

November 29, 2009
The Federal Court of Canada turned down Moreno Gallo's appeal of his deportation order.

A MAJOR BLOW!

December 28, 2009
A black gunman killed Nick Rizzuto Jr beside his parked Mercedes near FTM Construction at 5730 Upper Lachine in Montreal. Later, police concluded that street gang leader Ducarme Joseph drove the getaway car.

Nick Rizzuto Jr took over supervision of building projects his father and Tony Magi controlled in Montreal's old port through Magi's FTM Construction.

January 2, 2010
The Rizzuto family held a funeral for Nick Rizzuto Jr at the Madonna della Difesa church on Henri-Julien Street in Little Italy.

January 5, 2010
Someone firebombed the St Michel Cafe.

February 8, 2010
Revenue Canada charged Nicolo Rizzuto with income tax evasion.

February 10, 2010
Prison officials released Paulo Renda from his six year sentence

February 11, 2010
Nicolo Rizzuto pled guilty to income tax evasion. A judge ordered him to pay $628,000 in back taxes plus a $209,000 fine.

March 18, 2010
Street gang members attacked Ducharme Joseph in his store. They killed two men and wounded another, but Joseph escaped. Later, police arrested three men in the shooting, and a jury convicted them of first-degree murder (2014). None of them revealed who ordered the hit. Most people assumed the Rizzutos were seeking revenge for Nick Jr's death.

April 12, 2010
Immigration officials held a deportation hearing for Moreno Gallo after authorities released him from a minimum-security prison.

ANOTHER BLOW!

May 20, 2010
Rival gangster, pretending to be police officers, kidnapped Paulo Renda near his home. No one in the family ever saw Renda again. He was the son-in-law of Nicolo Rizzuto and a power in the Rizzuto organization.

May 27, 2010
Immigration Canada ordered Moreno Gallo's deportation.

YET ANOTHER BLOW!

June 29, 2010
A rifleman killed Agustino Cuntrera and his bodyguard Liborio Sciascia outside Cuntrera's business. He had recently agreed to direct the Rizzuto organization due to Nick Rizzuto Jr's killing and the decline in Nicolo Rizzuto's health.

September 29, 2010
A gunman shot and killed Ennio Bruni in Laval. He was near the Cafe Bellerose in a strip mall on Beerose Blvd.

October 5, 2010
Police arrested Rizzuto rival Giuseppe "Pony Tail" DeVito.

October 2010
Recently deported Bonanno Acting Boss Salvatore Montagna joined a loosely organized group that opposed the Rizzuto's control of Montreal. Leaders of the dissidents were veteran Calabrian gangster Joe DiMaulo, his brother-in-law Raynald Desjardins, Vittorio Mirachi, and Domenico Arcuri.

October 8, 2010
A judge released veteran mobster Tony Mucci on bail from his gun charge.

A HUGE BLOW!

November 10, 2010
A sniper, firing from the bushes behind Nicolo Rizzuto's home, killed the old gangster. Rizzuto was in the house near his wife and daughter when the shot penetrated a window, and part of the bullet tore into a significant neck artery. Street talk suggested that Sal Montagna had recently visited Rizzuto and asked him to step down as the Montreal crew leader. He refused.

November 16, 2010
The Rizzuto family held Nicolo's funeral at the Madonna della Difesa church on Henri-Julien Street in Little Italy. This location was the same church where Paolo Violi's family had his funeral after Rizzuto Associiates killed him in 1978.

January 6, 2011
Street gang members firebombed the funeral home owned by the Rizzutos.

January 2011
Members of the Giuseppe DeVito crew firebombed the Cafe Monte Cristo. In 2014 police arrested some of the DeVito crew for this offense.

January 31, 2011
Someone found the murdered body of Antonio Di Salvo. He was an Associate of the imprisoned Francesco Arcadi.

June 2011
Authorities arrested Rocco Sollecito for breaking his parole.

THE END NEARS FOR SAL MONTAGNA

August 30, 2011
Members of the Sal Montagna group approached Desjardins associate Calagero Milito to kill Raynald Desjardins. He promptly told Desjardins. This event was a clear indication that the alliance against the Rizzutos was falling apart.

September 2011
Police watched as Salvatore Montagna met with Antonio Pietrantonio and Joe Renda in a park.

September 16, 2011
A member of the Montagna group lured Raynald Desjardins to a meeting. As Desjardins sat in his vehicle, a gunman opened up with an AK-47 on him then fled across a park to a SeaDoo. Jonathan Mignacci, Desjardins bodyguard, chased the man firing at him

with his Glock semi-automatic. Then Mignacci tossed his weapon in the Riviere des Prairies where walkers found it the next spring when the water level was lower. Desjardins phoned Dom Arcuri telling him he knew he was behind the hit and that he wouldn't miss. Shortly afterward, the RCMP surveilled a meeting between Arcuri, Montagna, and Bertolo at a Tim Hortons.

October 24, 2011
A sniper killed Larry LoPresti as he stood on his apartment balcony. He was the son of the late Joe LoPresti, a long-time ally of the Rizzutos who fell out of favor, and they killed him. Larry LoPresti had lined up with the Montagna group against the Rizzutos.

November 8, 2011
Tony Magi pled guilty to the improper storage of a registered weapon. The Crown dropped four other firearms charges from his September 21, 2010 arrest.

November 15, 2011
Someone killed Tony Gesale.

November 24, 2011
After the September 2011 attempted hit on Raynald Desjardins, he and his men began plotting to kill Sal Montagna. Unbeknownst to them, the police were able to monitor their cell phones. Montagna made a desperate attempt to convince Desjardins that he had nothing to do with the attack. Desjardins played along but continued to plot his revenge.

Unbelievably Montagna agreed to a meeting and was picked up by Jock Simpson, one of Desjardins' men. They traveled to Simpson's home, where he shot Montagna. The latter fled across the yard and the nearby river only to die on the opposite bank. It wasn't long before the police knew everything.

December 2011
In Operation Abduction, police arrested some drug dealers, including brothers Marco and Massimo Campellone. The good guys claimed that brother Emanuele and Carmelo Pedula were

in charge of this group while their leader Giuseppe DeVito was in prison.

December 13, 2011
Someone tried to kill Anthony Pietrantonio, who had been working with the Montagna Desjardins alliance. He met with Montagna a few days before a gunman tried to kill Desjardins in September.

RAYNALD DESJARDINS GOES DOWN

December 20, 2011
Police arrested Raynald Desjardins for the Sal Montagna hit. Also detained at some point were other members of his group, including Vittorio Mirarchi, Felice Racaniello, Jack Simpson, and later Colagero Milioto and Peter Magistrale.

2012
A judge sentenced Rizzuto rival Giuseppe DeVito to 15 years in prison.

March 1, 2012
A gunman shot Giuseppe "Closure" Colapelle while he was sitting in his SUV. He had been bouncing back and forth between the Desjardins and Montagna groups. Colapelle was close to Giuseppe DeVito.

April 4, 2012
Giuseppe Renda (Not a relative of Paolo Renda) disappeared. He had aligned himself with Salvatore Montagna. Police had watched him meeting with Montagna a few days before the September 2011 failed ambush of Desjardins.

August 12, 2012
There was an arson attack on a Dom Arcuri building. He was a member of the ill-fated Sal Montagna group.

August 17, 2012
There was another arson attack on an Arcuri building at Mirabeau and Vauban in Anjou.

August 24, 2012
Arsonist attacked the first Dom Arcuri building at 7272 Maurice Duplessis Blvd in Riviere-des-Prairies for the second time.

THE CHARBONNEAU COMMISSION

September 2012
The provincial Charbonneau Commission inquiry into Quebec's construction industry began.

September 29, 2012
Someone wounded Tommy Pietrantonio in a club in Sainte-Marguerite- du- Lac- Maison. He is the son of Vincent Pietrantonio.

VITO RIZZUTO IS FREE----LOOK OUT!

October 5, 2012
The family of Vito Rizzuto's father-in-law held his funeral in Montreal. The same day prison officials in Colorado freed Vito Rizzuto, and American immigration agents flew him to Toronto. Rizzuto went underground there.

October 10, 2012
A gunman wounded Vincent Pietrantonio and killed his companion.

October 15, 2012
Prison officials released Rocco Sollecito.

RIZZUTO REVENGE?

November 4, 2012
A gunman killed Joe DiMaulo in his driveway. DiMaulo was a long time power in Montreal. The Calabrian DiMaulo was a member of the Cotroni/Violi group but aligned with the Rizzutos when

they took over. He was close to Vito Rizzuto and was a significant player in keeping the Calabrian and Sicilian factions at peace. However, when Vito Rizzuto went to prison, DiMaulo joined with his brother-in-law Raynald Desjardins to unseat the Rizzutos from power. This decision didn't work out well for the wealthy gangster.

December 12, 2012
After his release from Fort Dix prison in New Jersey, Immigration officials flew Domenic Manno to Montreal.

December 17, 2012
Someone wounded Giuseppe Feta.

December 28, 2012
A gunman killed Domenico Facchini, a member of Giuseppe DeVito's crew. This event may have been a revenge move by the Rizzuto side.

2013
An informant told the RCMP that Lorenzo Rizzuto (Son of Vito), Stefano Sollecito (Son of Rocco), Tonino Callocchio, and Vito Salvaggio were powerful Mafia leaders.

January 16, 2013
Vito Rizzuto flew to the Dominican Republic probably for revenge strategy meetings.

RIZZUTO REVENGE?

January 22, 2013
A gunman killed close Desjardins friend Gaetan Gosselin. In 2017 five members of a street gang pled guilty to conspiracy to murder Gosselin. None of them told who had hired the group to do the hit.

RIZZUTO REVENGE?

January 31, 2013
A shooter killed Vincenzo Scuderi, an ally of Desjardins, in St Leonard. In June of 2017, Oliver Gay pled guilty to this murder. He and fellow street gang members admitted to the January 22, 2013 slaying of Gaetan Gosselin.

March 27, 2013
Police charged Pietro Magistrale with first degree murder in the Sal Montagna hit.

September 2013
Daniel Pierre and Mohamed Quzi Ali went missing. They were members of Salvatore Scoppa's crew.

RIZZUTO REVENGE?

April 9, 2013
Giuseppe Carbone and the Scaduto brothers lured Juan"Johnny Bravo" Fernandez and his buddy Fernando Pimentel to a remote location near Palermo Sicily and killed them. The gangsters then dumped the bodies and burned them. Later, Carbone rolled over after being arrested and told the whole story of the hit.

The Italian police said the order for the murder came from Canada and that Fernandez and Carbone had been in frequent contact with a Montreal lawyer. The police had Fernandez's vehicle bugged for quite some time and learned about his mob connections. Strangely Fernandez claimed that Vito Rizzuto had inducted him into the Mafia, although he was Portuguese. No one took that boast seriously, but no one had the guts to call the powerful man on it.

Fernandez met Raynald Desjardins in prison and, through that connection, became close to Rizzuto. I won't outline Fernandez's Mafia career here but point out that he seemed to waver in where his loyalties should lie when things went south for the Rizzutos. Fudging his bet, Fernandez stalled at attending a Rizzuto meeting once the Americans released Rizzuto from prison. That was probably the last straw for Vito.

April 18, 2013
Someone murdered Harry Mytil in his car parked in his garage in Laval.

May 15, 2013
Police arrested four street gang members for the January 12, 2013 murder of close Desjardins associate Gaetan Gosselin. They locked up Edrick Antoine, Oliver Guay, Stanley Minuty, and Kevin Tate.

July 8, 2013
Fierce Rizzuto rival, Giuseppe DeVito, died in prison from cyanide poisoning. It was impossible to tell whether it was suicide or murder. When DeVito was on the run, his distraught wife killed their two daughters. That would be a devastating blow to anyone. DeVito's violent attempts to overthrow Rizzuto also failed.

RIZZUTO REVENGE?

July 12, 2013
A gunman killed Salvatore Calautti and James Tusek outside a stag party in Woodbridge, Ontario. The Rizzutos suspected Calautti was the sniper who killed Nicolo Rizzuto with a shot through Nicolo's rear window. This suspicion does not prove that Calautti fired the shot nor that the Rizzutos had him killed.

September 2013
Vito Rizzuto was in the Dominican Republic again with his wife.

RIZZUTO REVENGE?

November 10, 2013
A shooter killed long time Rizzuto Associate Moreno Gallo in Acapulco, Mexico. The Canadian government had finally succeeded in deporting Gallo to Italy after a long battle. Street talk said Gallo

tried to straddle the fence during the insurrection against the Rizzuto family. It is possible he even took an active role against the Rizzutos. In any case, he was dead, and the best guess is that Vito was behind his demise.

December 18, 2013
A gunman killed Roger Valiquette Jr, a close Associate of the late Joe DiMaulo.

VITO RIZZUTO DIES

December 23, 2013
Vito Rizzuto died in hospital from pneumonia, complicated by his lung cancer.

I give no credence to the conspiracy theory that someone poisoned the veteran mobster. A semi-fictional TV series about events in Montreal took the literary license and had the main character, poison Rizzuto. This decision means the poison myth will live on far longer than the truth.

December 31, 2013
The Rizzuto family held Vito's funeral at the Madonna della Difesa church in Little Italy. As usual, a large crowd of the curious, police and their cameras, and a media horde lined the street opposite the church.

February 1, 2014
A gunman wounded Tonino Callocchio, a building contractor who was against the Rizzutos. Earlier, an informant told the police that Callocchio was an important Mafia figure.

April 24, 2014
Someone killed Carmine Verducci in Toronto. He had aligned himself with the Sal Montagna anti-Rizzuto faction in Montreal. This fact does not mean the Rizzutos were behind his killing, but they may have been.

June 12, 2014
Police arrested various members of the anti-Rizzuto Bastone and DeVito crews.

RIZZUTO REVENGE?

August 1, 2014,
A gunman murdered Ducharme Joseph in the street. On March 18, 2010, a spectacular hit attempt against him killed two and wounded another, but Joseph fled. Police had long suspected that Joseph drove the hit car in the murder of Nick Rizzuto Jr. A reasonable guess would be that the Rizzuto clan hired street gang members to finish Joseph.

January 27, 2015
Judge Gilles Garneau convicted Desjardins bodyguard Jonathan Mignacca of five gun charges. He had chased after the man who ambushed Desjardins, then dropped his gun in the river where walkers found it the next spring when water levels were lower.

July 6, 2015
After negotiations, Raynald Desjardins pled guilty to murder conspiracy in the killing of Salvatore Montagna.

THE COPS LISTEN IN

August 2015
Secret police tapes made in the conference room of lawyer Loris Cavaliere overheard Lorenzo Rizzuto, Greg Woolley, and Stefano Sollecito discussing Salvatore Scoppa. Sollecito said he didn't trust Scoppa but Rizzuto nixed the idea of killing him.

September 2015
Police watched as Marco Campellone met with Steve Ovadia and Stefano Sollecito over a drug dispute. Ovadia was a member of Calabrian gang leader Andrea Scoppa's crew.

September 18, 2015
A gunman killed Marco Campellone outside his home. He was the brother of Massimo Campellone.

November 15, 2015
In Canada, a Bonanno Capo inducted Enzo Morena into the Family. Morena secretly taped the ceremony in a great coup for the good guys. The FBI had arrested him on drug charges in New York in August 2014, and he flipped.

November 19, 2015
Police arrested Hells Angel Mom Boucher, his daughter Andrea Mongeau, biker associate Gerald Wooley, Leonard Rizzuto, Stefano Sollecito, Hells Angel Salvatore Cazzette, Loris Cavaliere, and others in a big crackdown.

Police charged Boucher and his daughter with plotting to kill Raynald Desjardins while he was behind bars. Boucher was serving a life sentence at the time of the alleged plot.

Authorities said Wooley was a vital liaison between Montreal street gangs, the Mafia, and the Hells Angels.

December 2015
Prison officials released Rizzuto powerhouse, Lorenzo Giordano.

March 2, 2016
Allegedly members of the Andrea Scoppa crew killed Lorenzo Giordano in a parking lot.

March 4, 2016
A judge refused bail for Leonardo Rizzuto and Stefano Sollecito.

March 30, 2016
Before a judge Vittorio Mirachi, Jack Simpson, Calogero Milioto, Pietro Magistrale, Steve Fracas and Steve D'Addario pled guilty to conspiracy to kill Salvatore Montagna.

May 2, 2016
A judge sentenced Sergio Piccirillo to 15 years for a drug conviction. The judge credited him for time served waiting for trial, so Piccirillo had about nine years left behind bars. He was a member of the DeVito crew, which was opposed to the Rizzutos.

May 27, 2016
A gunman killed veteran Rizzuto mobster Rocco Sollecito while he sat in his SUV. Speculation was that the Andrea Scoppa crew was behind the hit. Sollecito was the father of Rizzuto power Stefano Sollecito.

June 15, 2016
A judge refused bail for Lorenzo Rizzuto but granted the same to Stefano Sollecito for medical reasons.

October 2016
Lawyer Gerardo Nicolo pled guilty to an obstruction of justice charge. He had tried to persuade an RCMP officer to leak information about Giuseppe DeVito and Nicolo DiMarco.

October 11, 2016
A jury convicted Pietro and Salvatore Scaduto for the April 9, 2013 murders of Juan Fernandez and Fernando Pimentel in Sicily. Participant and informer Giuseppe Carbone received sixteen years. There was no mention of who ordered the hit from Canada.

October 15, 2016
Someone killed Vincenzo Spagnola, a close friend of the late Vito Rizzuto.

December 19, 2016
A judge sentenced Raynald Desjardins to 14 years for his guilty plea to conspiracy to murder Salvatore Montagna. He will be free in six and a half years after receiving credit for the time he spent awaiting trial.

January 9, 2017
After their preliminary hearing, a judge ruled that there was enough evidence to take Leonardo Rizzuto and Stefano Sollecito to trial.

February 1, 2017
Police charged veteran Calabrian gangster Andrea Scoppa with trafficking in cocaine. He was a long-time close Associate of Vito Rizzuto in the 1990s. Police tapes showed he didn't like the new administration of Rizzuto's son Leonardo and Stefano Sollecito.

February 3, 2017
Lawyer Loris Cavaliere took a plea deal to charges he facilitated meetings of Rizzuto leaders. Judge Pierre Labelle sentenced him to 34 months behind bars. Lorenzo Rizzuto and his sister Bettina both worked in the Cavaliere law firm.

February 21, 2013
Rizzuto rival Salvatore Scopa survived a murder attempt as he was leaving a restaurant in Terrebonne. He was the brother of Andrea Scopa, a powerful Calabrian gangster. Later investigations alleged that veteran gangster Frederick Silva was the shooter.

April 25, 2017
Someone attempted to firebomb the Loreto Funeral Home owned by the Rizzutos.

April 2017
At a bail hearing for Andrea Scoppa, the prosecutor played a tape, made on September 15, 2016, on which Scoppa expressed concern about the recent police arrest of Steve Ovadia. He said he might have to flee the country. Scoppa was facing cocaine trafficking charges.

May 6, 2017
Marc Laflamme Berthelet and David Cormier invaded the home of Rizzuto loyalist Francesco Del Balso when his wife and kids were present. The police arrested the duo after a brief chase. Ironically the police arrested Del Balso for a parole violation. It is a reasonable guess that these men wouldn't have carried out this action if Lorenzo Rizzuto was on the street.

May 11, 2017
The prosecutor dropped charges against Scoppa crew member Steve Ovadia.

June 22, 2017

Five street gang members pled guilty to conspiracy in the murder of Desjardins loyalist Gaetan Gosselin. Oliver Gay, Edrick Antoine, Stanley Minuky, Kevin Tate, and Leonard Etienne were the defendants. Harry Mytil passed on the order to kill Gosselin from Toronto. Gay also pled guilty to conspiracy in the murder of Vincenzo Scuderi, a lieutenant to Rizzuto rival Giuseppe DeVito.

August 18, 2017

A judge refused bail for Francesco Del Balso, whom the police arrested when two men invaded his home.

October 12, 2017

Old William Obront, a famous Vic Cotroni financier, died in Florida.

RIZZUTO REVENGE?

October 2017

A brother of the imprisoned Raynald Desjardins disappeared.

RIZZUTO AND SOLLECITO DODGE A BULLET

February 19, 2018

Justice Eric Downs ruled that prosecutors could not use the evidence the police gathered by bugging Stefano Sollecito and Lorenzo Rizzuto's lawyers' conference room. He stated that the law did not put safeguards to protect other lawyers and clients using the space. With their wiretap evidence excluded, the prosecution told the Judge they had no other evidence. Judge Downs acquitted both men of gangsterism and cocaine trafficking. It was a shocking turn of events for everyone, and I'm sure to the Rizzuto rivals as well.

May 11, 2018
Calabrian Mafia leader Andrea Scoppa walked free after the prosecutor dropped drug charges against him. Police tapes of his conversations clearly showed he opposed the new Rizzuto administration.

June 28, 2018
Steve Ovadia, an Andrea Scoppa gang member, died after being shot in a parking lot in Laval.

October 26, 2018
Powerful gangster Greg Woolley pled guilty to drug trafficking. Police believed he was an important liaison man between street gangs, the Mafia, and the Hells Angels.

February 15, 2019
Judge Julie Riendeau acquitted Lorenzo Rizzuto of two gun charges and possession of five grams of cocaine. The police had confiscated these materials when they arrested Rizzuto at his home on September 21, 2010. The judge ruled that the police violated Rizzuto's rights; thus, the evidence gathered wasn't admissible. With no other evidence to present, the prosecution threw in the towel.

April 2019
Jonathan Mignacci gained his freedom after serving his weapon offenses conviction from the Raynald Desjardins hit attempt on September 16, 2011.

May 4, 2019
A gunman killed Salvatore Scoppa in the lobby of the Sheraton Hotel in Laval. Police suspected Scoppa was involved in the separate murders of Rocco Sollecito and Lorenzo Giardano, both Rizzuto powers.

October 16, 2019
Police arrested three men and a woman associated with Salvatore Scoppa. Police alleged they were involved in many crimes, including the deaths of Rocco Sollecito, Lorenzo Giordano, and brothers Giuseppe and Vincenzo Falduto. Arrested were Jonathan Massari, Dominico Scarfo, Guy Dione, and Marie-Josee Viau.

The police identified the late Salvatore Scopa and Jonathan Massari as the leaders in the four killings. They said they believed Salvatore Scopa died because of these actions.

October 21, 2019
Someone found the body of Andrea Scoppa in a parking lot in Pierrefonds.

As of February 2021 it appears that the Rizzuto/Sollecito organization remains near the top of Montreal's organized crime life. However, things can change quickly.

CHAPTER NINETEEN

Mafia Profile

JOSEPH "BAYONNE JOE" ZICARELLI

October 9, 1912-August 23, 1983

Zicarelli is one of the more interesting La Cosa Nostra members. Joe Bonanno inducted him in 1955 and placed him in Carmine Galante's mostly New Jersey crew. Like many Mafia Soldiers, Zicarelli had numerous brushes with the law as a young person, but it was not until the late 1950s that his actions were intriguing. Below is a list of some of his travels into the Caribbean area.

June 30, 1957
Zicarelli landed in NYC from the Dominican Republic.

January 12, 1958
Zicarelli arrived in NYC aboard a plane from the Dominican Republic.

February 21, 1958
Zicarelli flew from the Dominican Republic to Puerto Rico.

May 3, 1958
Montreal hoods broke into a bank in the small eastern Ontario town of Brockville. They rifled through deposit boxes and made off with an estimated 4-10 million dollars' worth of bonds and other valuables. Montreal Mafia power Giuseppe Cotroni then used his American contacts in an attempt to move the stolen bonds.

December 18, 1958
Zicarelli arrived in Puerto Rico from the Dominican Republic.

July 20, 1959
Zicarelli arrived in NYC from Zurich, Switzerland. Without any proof, I suspect that Zicarelli was part of the effort to move the stolen Brockville bonds. Some of them ended up in Switzerland, which made me suspicious this was the purpose of his travel there. Zicarelli was in Galante's crew, which dealt with the Montreal Mafia repeatedly. No one ever charged Zicarelli with involvement in the heist, so my speculation may very well be off base.

December 23, 1960
Zicarelli arrived in NYC from the Dominican Republic.
From the scant information available, it seems that Zicarelli was involved in illegal gun sales to Dominican Republic dictator Rafael Trujillo. Another possibility would be that Zicarelli had some exploratory interest in Dominican casinos just like other mobsters had in Cuba. He would keep his fingers in the pie even after dissidents assassinated the aging dictator in 1961.

BUGGING ZICARELLI

After the 1957 Apalachin event, it was clear to FBI Director J Edgar Hoover that his agency was way behind the Bureau of Narcotics in Mafia Intelligence. Within a few years, they began a massive illegal bugging operation to catch up. Zerilli would become a target.

1960

The FBI bugged Zicarelli's Manhattan apartment at the Park Royal Hotel. They also put a wiretap on a phone booth in his favorite bar. It wasn't long before they struck gold.

June 21, 1960

Zicarelli was not happy. The Bayonne, New Jersey city police had staked out his key gambling spots costing him a lot of money. The mobster felt a top police official was messing with him despite being on the payroll. In his anger, Zicarelli quickly contacted his Congressman, Cornelius "Neil" Gallagher.

Gallagher was a combat veteran of both World War Two and the Korean War. He rose through the House ranks, ultimately sitting on the House Committee for Foreign Affairs and the House Government Operations Committee. In the latter, Gallagher opposed increased government investigations of organized crime and said that the Mafia threat was vastly overblown.

Once Zicarelli connected with Gallagher, the agents heard the Congressman's promise to contact people in Bayonne to find out what was going on. On another occasion, Gallagher left the House floor after receiving a message that Zicarelli had called under an assumed name. It was clear to lawmen that Gallagher was corrupt, and Zicarelli controlled the powerful Congressman. It would take years for all this to become public, for the good guys could not use all the information in court due to the bugs' illegality.

ACTING CAPO

November 1960
Carmine Galante appointed Zicarelli his Acting Capo while Galante was facing heroin conspiracy charges.

June 25, 1962
After Carmine Galante's conviction on drug conspiracy charges, he demoted Zicarelli to Soldier.

ENTERPRISES

1962
After Trujillo's 1961 assassination, a former puppet president, Juan Betancourt, returned to the throne. In an odd coincidence, both Gallagher and Zicarelli's lawyer were at the inauguration. The American embassy was not happy, for they knew the lawyer's mob connection. For them, it was an embarrassment. It turned out that Zicarelli was interested in acquiring the Republics' failing airline, Companhia Dominicana de Aviation. By this time, the mob's Cuban goldmine had disappeared with the rise of Fidel Castro. Zicarelli probably figured there would be many tourists eager to go to an alternative playground, the Dominican Republic and its casinos. Whatever his reasons, the deal never took place.

October 13, 1962
Bayonne businessman Bernard "Barney" O'Brian disappeared after spending the evening watching boxing at his ice cream joint. The importance of this will become clear later in this chapter.

BONANNO WAR

August 1964
The FBI had planted a bug in the Kenilworth, NJ office of Boss Sam "The Plumber" Decavalcante. Zerilli would be a frequent visitor at the time internal fighting tore the Bonanno Family apart. It's from Zerilli's conversation that we learned a lot of the inside story. I will concentrate on his talk in the office. None of the following discussions became public knowledge until 1969.

September 21, 1964
After hearing of the escalating Bonanno Family dispute from others, Decavalcante invited Zicarelli to his office to discuss the matter. Sam informed his friend that the Commission had just deposed Bonanno and his administration. Zicarelli was stunned. He spent some time arguing Bonanno's position with Sam. To listeners, it was clear he was a Bonanno supporter.

1964
Feared mob Associate Harold "Kayo" Konigsberg began revealing some of his crimes, but none of the good guys paid too much attention. However, some of the bad guys secretly disinterred some bodies from a New Jersey burial pit.

BONANNO DEPOSED

February 5, 1964
Zicarelli arrived at Decavalcante's and learned that Bonanno Underboss John Morale had turned himself into the Commission backed faction. Sam related that Morale acknowledged Gaspar DiGregorio as Boss. He advised Zicarelli that it was acceptable to try to get the straggling members to join DiGregorio, but he mustn't promise they'd keep their positions.

In the same long conversation, Zicarelli complained about a problem one of his Associates was having with Lucchese men in Florida. Lucchese complained that Zicarelli was suddenly claiming interests in Florida. As always, the disputes were over money and who would get the lion's share.

Then Sam related to Bayonne Joe that he had lost a lot of money in a recent Las Vegas trip and wondered if Zicarelli could make him a loan.

February 8, 1964
Zicarelli brought Sam the $15,000 loan he needed but quickly asked if he could transfer to Decavalcante's Family. He complained that too many guys with legal problems were coming around him. Zicarelli feared the police would start believing he was involved in all kinds of other shenanigans when he wasn't.

Bayonne Joe told a vague story about completing an action right under the noses of someone. It certainly sounded as if he was bragging about a successful hit that the police never discovered. The men ended the day with Sam promising to bring up the matter of Joe's transfer with Bosses Carlo Gambino and Tommy Lucchese.

September 1964
The Commission deposed Joe Bonanno and blessed Capo Gaspar DiGregorio as his replacement.

June 9, 1965
Zicarelli and Decavalcante had a wide-ranging discussion of recent events in the Bonanno Family. Boss DiGregorio had split Zicarelli's large crew into two. He would now be under new Capo Mike Sabella. It also appeared that Zicarelli's long-held hopes of being able to transfer to the Decavalcante Family were dead. The next month the FBI ripped the bug out of Sam's office after President Johnson ordered an end to all the FBI's illegal bugging.

KAYO KONIGSBERG

February 1967
Bonanno Associate Harold "Kayo" Konigsberg rolled over and began telling the police everything about his sordid career. He took the law officers to the site of a burial pit. Although he claimed that the bodies of Barney O'Brian (see October 13, 1962) and Genovese Capo Anthony "Tony Bender" Strollo were in the pit, no corpses emerged after digging. However, the orthopedic shoes of O'Brian were there. The lawmen unearthed two other victims in nearby holes. The bad guys had moved the bodies after Konigsburg began talking back in 1964.

Konigsberg claimed that Gallagher had called Kayo to his home where the body of O'Brian rested in the basement. After Zicarelli told Konigsberg to help Gallagher, the gangster took the body and buried it in the NJ burial site. This tale seemed very questionable, and nothing came of it. Gallagher was embarrassed, however.

A STAR IS BORN

As mentioned earlier the FBI had secreted a bug in the Kenilworth plumbing offices of Sam "The Plumber" Decavalcante. The illegal bug was in place from August 1964 until July 1965. Some of the output from this bug involved Zicarelli.

March 21, 1968
After a grand jury indictment, Judge Anthony T Augelli issued bench warrants to arrest Decavalcante and two others. The indictment charged them with conspiring to violate federal statutes against extortion. Decavalcante Associates had robbed two gamblers in the American Motel in the Philadelphia area. They then insisted the gamblers make regular payments so the operation could continue to function. The judge released Decavalcante on a $50,000 bond.

April 1968
US Attorney David Statz Jr. admitted that the FBI bugged Decavalcante's office, but they did not use the tapes in the extortion case.

August 5, 1968
Life Magazine ran an article on the relationship between Zicarelli and Congressman Gallagher. They both were now national figures.

June 10, 1969
At the request of Decavalcante's defense team, the US Attorney filed 2,300 pages of transcripts of the FBI's illegal bugs. This Decavalcante request was a bluff, for he hoped the feds would drop the case rather than release the illegal bug information. He was wrong and soon regretted his choice, for the media went wild with the data. Zicarelli and Gallagher would be front-page news.

ENDLESS LEGAL COMPLICATIONS

Below I've summarized a seemingly endless list of Zicarelli's legal problems. In the hopes of making the information easier to follow, I've labeled the trials for everything related to them did not follow chronologically. The list indicates the tremendous stress both financially and mentally Zicarelli must have carried during this period. Some readers might prefer to skip this section.

August 20, 1969
(Case One)
Zicarelli appeared before the State Investigative Commission in the Trenton State House Annex. He refused to testify, and a judge

sentenced him to an indefinite term for contempt but released him on bail.

November 13, 1969
A statewide New Jersey grand jury indicted Zicarelli and two other men for conspiracy to commit kidnapping, aggravated assault, battery, and murder. Police arrested Zicarelli and Frank Mallamaci the same day. Judge Kingfield released them on $25,000 bail each.

November 15, 1969
Zicarelli told the press that, "There is no case." They described him as a small, thin, quiet man with grey hair.

November 27, 1969
In a brief to the New Jersey Supreme Court, Zicarelli's lawyer, Michael Querques, admitted that Zicarelli and another man were in the Mafia.

January 20, 1970
(Case One)
The New Jersey Supreme Court upheld Zicarelli's earlier contempt conviction for refusing to testify before the New Jersey State Investigations Committee.

January 28, 1970
(Case One)
Zicarelli began serving his contempt sentence in Yardville Prison.

February 5-25, 1970
(Case One)
Zicarelli was in the hospital for a gallbladder operation.

February 26, 1970
(Case One)
Zicarelli turned himself in again at Yardville.

May 6, 1970
A grand jury indicted Zicarelli and five others for obstruction of justice. The allegation was that they intervened in a Hudson County prosecution of three men for gambling.

May 20, 1970
(Case Two)
A grand jury indicted Zicarelli with bribing Hudson County Republican leader John Beir Theurer with $400 a month to appoint prosecutors who would protect Zicarelli's gambling interests. Zicarelli was still in Yardville when they served him with the warrant.

June 3, 1970
(Case Three)
A grand jury indicted Zicarelli and Detective Stanley Walczak of the Hudson County prosecutor's office for bribery.

June 8, 1970
(Case One)
The New Jersey Supreme Court upheld the ruling that refused bail to Zicarelli.

June 17, 1970
(Case Five)
A grand jury indicted Guttenberg mayor Herman Klein for conspiracy to take bribes to protect Zicarelli's gambling operations.

June 29, 1970
(Case Six)
Superior Court Judge Frank Kingfield moved Zicarelli's conspiracy trial from Jersey City to Trenton, citing concerns for a witness's safety.

July 1, 1970
(Case Seven)
A statewide grand jury indicted Zicarelli for bribing Hudson County Chief of Detectives Ray Louf for five years at $100 a month. Louf was to protect Zicarelli's gambling interests.

November 4, 1970
(Case Eight)
A grand jury indicted Zicarelli and others for conspiracy to bribe and bribing West New York Mayor John Armellino.

January 28, 1971
Zicarelli was in Mercer County Jail.

February 5, 1971
Correctional officers took Zicarelli to St Francis Hospital in Trenton.

February 7, 1971
Correctional officers took Zicarelli to St Mary's Hospital in Hoboken.

February 24, 1971
Zicarelli returned to Mercer County Jail from the hospital.

March 3, 1971
(Case One)
Officials sent Zicarelli back to Yardville to continue his contempt sentence.

April 3, 1971
(Case Eight)
At Mount Holly, a jury found Zicarelli and four others guilty of bribing West New York Mayor John Armellino. The mayor testified that the conspirators paid him $1,000 a week to protect Zicarelli's gambling interests.

April 23, 1971
(Case Eight)
At the Burlington County Courthouse, Judge J Gilbert Van Sciver sentenced Zicarelli to 12 to 15 years for his bribery conviction.

July 22, 1971
(Case Seven)
A jury convicted Zicarelli of paying Hudson County Detective Ray Louf to protect his gambling interests.

ZICARELLI APPEALS

March 17, 1972
(Cases Two and Three)
Deputy Attorney General Richard McGlynn dropped the indictments against Guttenberg mayor Herbert Klein and Hudson County prosecutor Detective Stanley Walczak in a Burlington County courtroom. A key prosecution witness had died. McGlynn also dropped three indictments against Zicarelli.

October 4, 1972
(Case Eight)
A three-judge federal panel heard Zicarelli's appeal of his bribery sentence.

January 24, 1973
(Case Eight)
The Appellate Division of Superior Court upheld Zicarelli's bribery conviction.

July 2, 1973
(Case Seven)
The Appellate Division of Superior Court threw out the convictions of Zicarelli and Detective Louf on the grounds of double jeopardy.

October 9, 1973
(Case Eight)
The United States Supreme Court refused to hear Zicarelli's appeal of his bribery conviction.

October 25, 1973
(Case Eight)
Zicarelli asked the NJ Governor to commute his sentence on medical grounds. It didn't work.

November 1975
(Case Eight)
A three-judge panel of the US 3rd Circuit Court of Appeals overturned Zicarelli's bribery conviction. They said the move of the trial from Hudson County to Mount Holly violated Zicarelli's

rights to have people from Hudson County on the jury. The State would appeal to the 3ʳᵈ Circuit Court of Appeals' full-body, and Zicarelli would remain in prison until then.

December 19, 1975
(Case Eight)
Judge Edward Martino denied Zicarelli's plea to terminate his bribery conviction. He also stated that he had no power to give Zicarelli three years' credit when he served a contempt conviction.

January 21, 1976
(Case Eight)
The nine-member US 3ʳᵈ Circuit Court of Appeals threw out the earlier ruling by a three-judge panel that the trial move violated Zicarelli's constitutional rights. Zicarelli would stay in prison.

July 30, 1976
(Case Eight)
Judge McGann refused to release Zicarelli from his bribery sentence due to ill health.

April 4, 1977
(Case Eight)
The Appellate Division of New Jersey's Superior Court upheld Judge McGann's ruling on July 30, 1976.

July 5, 1977
(Case Eight and Case One)
Authorities released Zicarelli on parole from his bribery conviction. He had done five years, but they immediately sent him back to Trenton to continue his indeterminate contempt sentence.

October 26, 1977
(Case One)
In Trenton, Judge George Schoch refused to release Zicarelli from prison on medical grounds.

December 1977
(Case One)
Authorities released Zicarelli from prison to take treatment at home for his various ailments.

May 31, 1978
(Case One)
Judge George Schoch permitted Zicarelli to remain at home on a medical release until October 1, 1978. He refused to quash Zicarelli's contempt sentence.

BLACKLISTED

November 24, 1981
The New Jersey Casino Commission entered Zicarelli into the book of excluded persons. My guess is the exclusion had zero effect on the very unhealthy mobster.

THE LAETRILE CANCER DRUG AND ZICARELLI

Laetrile was a supposed cancer drug manufactured in Canada by Bioenzymes International Ltd. and promoted by the McNaughton Foundation. During this period, the drug was illegal in both Canada and the United States. However, many people who had seemingly incurable cancer wanted access to the drug. This book is not the place to discuss the history of Laetrile but to summarize Zicarelli's involvement with its promotion.

April 1970
The Food and Drug Administration gave preliminary testing approval for the Laetrile drug. A few days later, they reversed their decision after the Hackensack Sunday Record ran an expose of Zicarelli's connection to the drug.

June 11, 1970
A grand jury indicted Zicarelli for failure to pay $960,000 in taxes. They also named controversial Montreal stock promotor Steven Schwartz as an unindicted co-conspirator. The accusations were that the two men were buying and selling securities and making investments using nominees. Zicarelli and Schwartz were attempting to hide their involvement in the transactions to avoid paying taxes.

July 18, 1970
A judge released Zicarelli on $25,000 bail on his income tax case.

Allegedly hiding behind other people's names, Zicarelli invested in Bioenzymes stock. His lawyer, Stephen Hoffman, made open investments.
They hoped that an extensive promotion of the drug in the United States might lead to the Food and Drug Administration approving its use. Meanwhile, Zicarelli moved some of his stock based on the income tax he allegedly avoided.

According to a 1970 interview given to Life Magazine in Montreal, Andrew McNaughton revealed that Zicarelli smuggled the drug into the United States for 150 patients in New Jersey. Also, McNaughton said that he believed both Hoffman and Zicarelli were shareholders in his company, probably under assumed names. Furthermore, McNaughton stated that Representative Gallagher was going to talk to various government agencies about the drug's merit. The hope was to get the drug legalized in the US. Nothing came of these efforts. Laetrile is still around, and its cancer-fighting qualities remain controversial.

March 10, 1973
Canada's National Post ran a feature story on the history of Laetrile. The headline read, "Ultimate Stock Swindle." It went on to say that even if the company were able to get on a Canadian or American stock exchange, most of the profits would go to Associates of Joseph "Bayonne Joe" Zicarelli, a mob figure residing in Trenton State Prison.

It is impossible to know how much money Zicarelli made with his Laetrile involvement, but the episode gives us another glimpse into the many ways he attempted to make money.

THE FAT LADY SINGS

August 23, 1983
Zicarelli passed away in Dade County, Florida, at the age of 70. It had been quite a ride.
What a Life!

CHAPTER TWENTY

Mafia Profile Two

THE CHILLIS AND ANTHONY SPERO

This chapter summarizes a period in the Mafia lives of the Chilli family and the chaotic years of Consigliere and sometimes Acting Boss Anthony Spero. Neither lived like the Brady Bunch.

The Chillis

Gerard Chilli and his older brother Joseph Jr. were long time Bonanno members operating in New York and Florida. Gerard had a son, whom I will call Joey to avoid confusion. Joseph Jr. also had a son I will refer to as Joseph 3rd. Both the younger Chilli's were Mafiosi. At one time or another, Gerard and Joseph Jr were Capos.

> November 7, 1968
> DA Eugene Gold called Gerard and Joseph Jr before a grand jury investigating violence in the Bonanno Family. They refused to testify, were granted immunity but still wouldn't testify.

March 1969

A judge ordered both Chillis to testify, but they refused. He then cited them for contempt and gave them a second chance. They still said no. The judge then sentenced each of them to 30 days in civil jail and a $250 fine.

December 4, 1969

The Court of Appeals of New York State rejected Gerard and Joseph Jr's appeals to throw out their contempt sentences.

June 16, 1977

Prosecutor John F Keena announced a perjury indictment against Gerard Chilli. An assistant deputy warden had revealed that Gerard told him his brother Joseph Jr had paid a prison captain for a transfer. When called before a grand jury, Gerard denied making that statement.

1981

Bonanno Soldier Benjamin "Lefty," Ruggiero told undercover FBI Agent Joe Pistone (Donnie Brasco) that one Chilli brother was sending his Capo Dominick "Big Trin" Trinchera $1,000 a week while the other tossed in $3,500 every seven days. There is no way of knowing whether this was an exaggeration.

May 8, 1981 (Approximate date)

Soldier Frank Lino had survived the massacre of the three Capos on May 1. The leaders told Lino he would become Acting Capo if he could bring in the dead men's crews. Lino took Joseph Chilli Jr to Joey Massino's home, for Chilli had been in the late Dominick "Big Trin" Trinchera's group. Chilli Jr would have to express his loyalty to the Bonanno administration.

January 15, 1984

The police found Gerard's son Joey and Thomas Sbano dead in a rented Lincoln's front seat. The car was sitting on the second floor of a parking garage at 299 Pearl Street. The location suggested that they had planned a rendezvous of some kind, but it went wrong. Joey was a made man, so he wasn't some innocent victim. Sbano was the step-son of legendary Bonanno Soldier Lefty Ruggiero, conned by FBI undercover agent Joe Pistone (Donnie Brasco.)

January 23, 1984
A shooter filled Anthony O'Conner with five slugs in Dottie's Bar in Manhattan, but the guy lived. His partner, Anthony Bonventura, was already in hiding. The authorities believed the shooting was retaliation by Joseph Chilli Jr for the murder of his nephew, Joey Chilli.

September 1984
Informer John Napoli paid Joseph Chilli 3rd $7,000 for about six ounces of coke.

1987
Prison officials released Gerry Chilli from his sentence for passing fraudulent checks.

February 5, 1988
Someone shot Alfred Scarpa, son-in-law of Gerard Scarpa, while he was in the Holiday Bar at 116 Madison Avenue.

April 1988
The US Senate Permanent Subcommittee on Investigations listed Gerard Chilli, Joseph Jr Chilli, and Joseph Chilli 3rd as members of the Bonanno Family.

June 1988
The feds arrested Joseph Chilli 3rd for selling coke to informant John Napoli.

April 5, 1989
The feds came knocking. They arrested Gerard Chilli in his Hollywood, Florida apartment to face racketeering charges of murder conspiracy, a credit card scam, and loansharking. The murder conspiracy count was related to the Chillis' efforts to avenge the killing of Joey Chilli. The feds also charged Gerard's brother Joseph Jr and his son Joseph 3rd for the same murder conspiracy charge for targeting Anthony O'Conner Jr and Anthony Bonventura.

May 19, 1989
New Jersey banned Joseph 3rd from all their casinos due to his criminal record.

November 1989
Joseph Chilli 3rd pled guilty in Manhattan's Supreme Court and accepted a five year to life sentence for selling cocaine to an undercover agent. Supreme Court Justice Juanita Bing-Newton agreed to make the sentence concurrent with any federal sentence he might receive.

December 1989
Joseph Chilli Jr and his son Joseph 3rd pled guilty to a RICO count after the feds dropped a boatload of other charges.

June 22, 1990
Gerard Chilli's daughter, Margaret Scarpa, had pled guilty to briefly harboring fugitive Gus Farace after he killed DEA undercover agent Everet Hatcher. At her sentencing, she told Judge Joseph McLaughlin that she did it because she was afraid that Farace might harm her children. McLaughlin then gave her 27 months in the slammer.

July 2, 1990
Federal Judge Robert Patterson sentenced Joseph Chilli Jr and his son Joseph 3rd to 15 years each for their December 1989 guilty plea to a RICO count. He fined Chilli Jr $250,000 and Joseph 3rd $150,000.

February 4, 1992
In Brooklyn, a judge in the US District Court rejected Joseph Chilli Jr's appeal to reduce his sentence.

February 18, 1993
The FBI arrested Capo Gerry Chilli for running a criminal enterprise in south Florida.

1995
The feds indicted Gerard Chilli for credit card fraud. He launched several appeals to no avail.

1995
Gerard, Joseph, and Joseph 3rd all pled guilty to various charges, including attempted manslaughter in the Anthony O'Conner shooting on January 23, 1984. The judge sentenced Gerard to nine years.

April 1998

Gerard Chilli pled guilty to a credit card conspiracy case while behind bars. He arranged for confederates to get counterfeit cards out of Staten Island, and he received 50% of the profits from the scam.

June 26, 1998

Judge William Ferguson sentenced Gerard Chilli to two years for the credit card scam and a restitution order of about $49,000.

December 2002

Prison officials released Gerard Chilli from his 1995 manslaughter conspiracy sentence.

2003

Joseph Chilli 3rd pled guilty to drug dealing while he was still in prison for his 1989 conviction.

February 3, 2005

Broward County Sherriff's Office officials arrested a pile of men, including Capo Gerard Chilli. He faced RICO and RICO conspiracy charges. Among the predicate acts were bookmaking, dealing in stolen property, violations of financial and drug laws. They accused Chilli of controlling gambling machines in JJ's Slot in Hollywood and Bikini Bob's Slots in Fort Lauderdale. The court set Gerard Chilli's bond at $5 million.

April 19, 2005

Judge Stanton Kaplan lowered Gerard Chilli's bond to $2.5 million. He stayed in prison.

July 1, 2005

Prison officials released Joseph Chilli Jr from his 1995 manslaughter conspiracy sentence.

2006

The good guys locked Gerard Chilli up for his Broward County, Florida violations.

June 12, 2008
Joseph John Jr Chilli died. He was born on July 7, 1933, to Joseph and Margaret Chilli (nee Sacco.) Carmine Galante inducted Joseph Jr into the Bonanno Family in the back of a bar on June 14, 1977. Others made that day included future Boss Joey Massino and future Consigliere Anthony Spero.

September 19, 2008
Officials arraigned Gerard Chilli in New York on loansharking charges.

August 27, 2009
Judge Nicholas Garaufis sentenced Joseph Chilli 3rd to four more years of supervision for a parole violation. Chilli had been in jail for two months previous to this ruling.

December 20, 2012
Gerry Chilli told his federal probation agent that he would travel to New York. Not surprisingly, the good guys were hiding in the shadows when Chilli arrived in the Big Apple. Over the next week or so, they saw him meeting with Bonanno members Anthony Rabito, Acting Boss Tom DiFore, and other hoods. Chilli would pay the price for these meetings.

May 2013
Judge Sterling Johnson sentenced Gerard Chilli to 18 months for a parole violation. He had pled guilty in April. Officials observed him in the company of other mobsters in New York in December 2012.

2013
A judge sentenced Joseph Chilli 3rd to two more years for a parole violation.

August 28, 2015
Officials released Joseph Chilli 3rd after he completed 26 years on state and federal charges. He returned to the New York home of his aging and ill mother, Rose.

September 10, 2016
Gerard Chilli died in Florida of throat cancer. He was born in New York on July 26, 1934.

April 17, 2019
NYPD detectives arrested Joseph 3rd at his home for parole violations.

June 14, 2019
Officials released Joseph Chilli 3rd from prison.

ANTHONY SPERO

September 18, 1929-October 6, 2008

Spero had a lengthy criminal career, but I will focus on the era when he became part of the Bonanno Family administration. During this period, the Bath Avenue Crew, a bunch of violent mob wannabees, brought Spero lots of money and a pile of headaches.

1984
Boss Phil Rastelli appointed Spero as his new Consigliere replacing the ill Steve Cannone. Technically the membership was polled by the Capos, who then passed on the votes to the Boss. In this case, I am unaware of such a process.

1987
Boss Phil Rastelli appointed Spero as Acting Boss replacing Salvatore "Sally Fruits" Ferrugia. Jailed Underboss Joe Massino told Salvatore Vitale, "Whatever you and Anthony Spero want to do is fine with me." Massino wasn't just a nice guy; he wanted to avoid any impediment to prison release.

1988
Nick Tuzzio stole a car. Charles Calco borrowed the vehicle and killed a man in a hit and run accident. When the cops found the car, Nick Tuzzio's fingerprints were in it, so they arrested him. Consigliere Anthony Spero allegedly worked out a deal where Nick would keep his mouth shut, and the Calco family would cover his legal expenses. Not everyone was happy. Nick went off to prison.

Hot-headed Louis Tuzzio killed Charles Calco by hanging him in the Calco family basement. When prison officials released Nick

Tuzzio, his brother Louis told him what he had done. The Calco revenge would have to wait a few years.

January 30, 1990

As explained earlier, Louis Tuzzio had angered Gambino Boss John Gotti by severely wounding a Gambino Associate during the Gus Farace hit. The Bonannos wanted good relations with Gotti, so they decided to kill Tuzzio. Spero et al. conned the young man into thinking they would induct him into the Bonanno Family. Despite his misgivings, Tuzzio got dressed up and went off to his death. Soldier Robert Lino shot Tuzzio in the head as he sat behind the wheel of his car. Later Lino apologized to Tuzzio's brother Nick saying it wasn't personal but only business.

1991

From prison, Underboss Joe Massino ordered Salvatore Vitale to tell Consigliere Spero to call an election to get Massino voted in as the new Bonanno Boss. Spero did that. Joe Massino appointed Consigliere Anthony Spero as Acting Boss for Massino remained behind bars.

September 25, 1991

Shooters killed low-level thief Vincent Bickelman in Brooklyn. He had made the deadly mistake of breaking into the home of a Spero daughter and stealing some things. Capo Joe Benanti and other Bonannos scoured the neighborhood and soon learned that Bickelman was the culprit. When Spero ordered a hit, ambitious Associate Paul Gulino stepped up to the plate. Informers gave the details of this murder about ten years later in court testimony.

1992

Some of the Bath Avenue street gang, robbed the Chase Bank in the Staten Island Mall and got away with a reported $400,000. Joey Calandra and Tommy Reynolds did the heavy lifting with Chris Paciello driving the getaway car.

October 18, 1992

Bonanno Associates Joey Calco and Tommy Reynolds killed drug dealer Neil Mastro and his uncle. The problem was that Mastro was a Lucchese Family Associate. Consigliere Anthony Spero had to step in to try and calm the waters.

February 19, 1993
Innocent housewife Judith Shemtov died in an attempted robbery of her Richmond Valley home. Bonanno Associates James Calandra and Tommy Reynolds were at the door when Mrs. Shemtov opened it. Reynolds fired his .45 semi-automatic, killing the lady instantly. The two mutts fled in a car driven by Chris Paciello.

May 10, 1993
A judge sentenced Bonanno Associate James Calandra to six years for the Staten Island Mall bank robbery in 1992.

July 25, 1993
Bath Avenue Crew leader Paul Gulino got carried away in 1993. He was infuriated with Spero's lack of support when Gulino got into a violent dispute with a street gang associated with another Family. He was also pushing Spero to induct him into the Bonanno Family. In a death wish move, Gulino pushed Spero in the face in front of witnesses. Realizing his mistake, Gulino compounded his problem by planning to kill Spero and Capo Joe Benanti. His buddy, Joey Calco, ratted out Gulino to Benanti. After consulting with Spero, Benanti came back to Calco with orders to kill Gulino. Calco and Tommy Reynolds visited Gulino at his parent's home, where Calco shot him twice in the head and left the body there. These details emerged when Calco testified in the Spero trial in 2001.

1995
Spero began a two-year sentence for being involved with illegal joker poker gambling machines.

January 18, 1995
Bonanno Associate Joey Calco killed suspected informer Jack Crerin with six shots to the head. The murder took place at the corner of 16th Avenue and 78th Street in Brooklyn. These details emerged when Calco rolled over in 2000.

January 1997
Prison officials released Spero after he completed his extortion sentence involving Joker Poker machines.

May 1999

The feds indicted Anthony Spero for conspiring to murder Associate Paul Gulino in 1993. Spero and others faced counts of racketeering and drug dealing. Included in that group were Capo Joe Benanti and Soldier Fabritzio De Francisci. Spero pled not guilty, and US Magistrate Judge Joan Azrack bound him over for a detention hearing the following week. At that point, they released Spero on a massive $13.5 million bond.

October 15, 1999

US Attorney Loretta Lynch announced a federal indictment that charged Anthony Spero, Joe Benanti, and Soldier Fabritzio De Francisci for conspiracy to murder Vincent Bickelman in 1991. Associates James Calandra and Thomas Reynolds faced attempted robbery and felony murder charges involving the 1993 death of Judith Shemtov.

May 2000

Bonanno Associate Joey Calco began talking to the feds. He had a lot to tell about the Bath Avenue Crew, Consigliere Anthony Spero, and Capo Joe Benanti.

September 11, 2000

Before Judge Edward Karman, Capo Joe Benanti, Soldier Fabritzio DeFrancisci, and Associate Thomas Reynolds pled guilty to various charges but not all applied to each man. There were six murders, five attempted murders, and five conspiracy to murder counts, conspiracy to distribute cocaine and marijuana, and some bank heists. Reynolds admitted he accidentally killed Judith Shemtov in a botched robbery.

February 2001

Boss Joe Massino demoted Anthony Spero to Soldier and promoted Anthony Graziano to Consigliere. Massino thought Spero was too occupied with his legal problems to do the job.

March 5, 2001

The Spero trial began before Judge Ed Korman. Spero was still free on $3.5 million bail. Noted lawyer Gerald Shargel defended Spero. The prosecutor was Chris Blank.

March 7, 2001
Actor Dan Grimaldi, who played Patsy Parisi in the Sopranos TV series, attended the trial. He was supporting his sister, who was the girlfriend of Spero.

Some Spero Trial Testimony

Louis Tuzzio's mother, Antoinette, testified that her son indicated by gestures that he would either be killed or inducted into the Bonanno Family at the meeting he was going to. He ended up dead.

Nick Tuzzio, Louis' brother, said that Louis worried they might kill him at a Bonanno induction ceremony but got dressed up and went anyway.

Bath Avenue Crew member Michael Yammine testified about Paul Gulino's "mushing" Anthony Spero. He said "mushing" was pushing someone in the face. He also confirmed that Gulino was planning to kill Anthony Spero.

Joey Calco testified that Paul "Paulie Brass" Gulino volunteered to kill Vince Bickelman after Spero ordered the hit. He also gave the details behind the Gulino murder.

Former Lucchese Acting Boss Al D'Arco testified about Spero and his place in the Bonanno Family. Carmine Sessa, a former Consigliere from the Colombo Family, did the same. Both men were in the Witness Protection Program.

April 5, 2001
A federal jury found Spero guilty of murder, loansharking, and gambling. The three murders were Louis Tuzzio (1990), Vincent Bickelman (1991), and Paul Gulino (1993.) Judge Edward Korman ruled there would be no bail.

April 2002
Judge Ed Korman sentenced Spero to life, a fine of $250,000 and $7,000 restitution for the Louis Tuzzio funeral. Spero took the verdict calmly.

April 23, 2002
Capo Joe Benanti was sentenced to 50 years after he pled guilty to various charges in September 2000, including the Vince Bickelman and Paul Gulino hits.

2003
Judge Edward Korman permitted former Bonanno Associate Tommy Reynolds to withdraw his guilty plea for killing four men.

March 18, 2004
Capo Robert Lino pled guilty to the Louis Tuzzio killing and another hit. Lino fired the gun that killed Tuzzio. A judge later sentenced him to 27 years.

2004
In a plea deal, Tommy Reynolds admitted to killing Judith Shemtov and received a 42-year sentence. It was an improvement on his original life term.

2004
After testifying in the Spero trial and admitting to killing two men, former Bonanno Associate Joey Calco faced sentencing before Judge Korman. Calco said, "If you give me another chance, Judge, I won't let the court down, and I won't let you down, your honor. With that, Judge Korman sentence him to nine years. The Judge credited him with the six years he had been in prison awaiting trial, which left him three years to go. Later events would show that Calco's promise was an empty one.

August 28, 2008
Officials transferred Spero from a federal prison in Coleman, Florida, to the Federal Medical Center at the Butner Federal Correction Complex in NC.

October 2, 2008
The mistress of Spero's former partner in the lucrative Big Apple Car Service launched a civil racketeering suit against Spero's daughter Diane Clement. The allegation was that Clement purchased 74% of Big Apple from Murray Kufield in 1996 after threatening him. The deal required Clement to pay Kufield $1,200 a month until 2013. When Kufield died in June of 2008 while doing time for a drug conviction, the payments stopped. The mistress wanted the agreement to continue to completion. Diane Clement dismissed the merits of the suit. I do not know what eventually happened.

October 6, 2008
Spero died in the Federal Medical Center in NC.

2008
An 18-year-old employee of Joey Calco's Florida pizza joint accused him of sexual harassment. Calco was using his Witness Protection name of Joey Merlino.

January 23, 2009
When two customers of his Goomba Pizzeria joint in Palm Coast, Florida, complained about their calzones, Joey Merlino got hostile, pulled a gun from a shelf, and then jumped over the counter to fight with the two men. Fortunately, he dropped the weapon behind the counter. It was all caught on tape. The police charged Joey Merlino with aggravated assault.

February 6, 2009
After an area newspaper dug into Joey Merlino's background and discovered he was probably Joey Calco, a circuit court judge issued a warrant for Merlino's arrest and used Joey Calco's name. The cops arrested Calco on two charges of possession of a weapon by a felon. Eventually, Calco received a 13-year sentence for assault and possession of a gun.

Spero made a lot of money with the Bath Avenue Crew, but in the end, their wildness and lack of loyalty to each other doomed the former Bonanno Consigliere.

Appendix A

The Bonanno Administration History

Bonanno
19??-1910

<u>Boss</u>
Paolo Orlando
19??-1910

<u>Underboss</u>
Unknown

<u>Consigliere</u>
Unknown

Bonanno
1910-1912

<u>Boss</u>
Sebastiano Di Gaetano
1910-1912

<u>Underboss</u>
Unknown

Bonanno
1912 -1930

<u>Boss</u>
Nicola "Cola" Shiro
1912 -1930
Retired

<u>Underboss</u>
Unknown

<u>Consigliere</u>
Unknown

Bonanno
1930-1931

<u>Boss</u>
Salvatore Maranzano
1930-1931
killed September 10, 1931

<u>Underboss</u>
Angelo Caruso
1930-1931

<u>Consigliere</u>
Unknown

Bonanno
1931-1964
Estimated size 260

<u>Boss</u>
Joseph Bonanno
1931-September 1964
Deposed by the Commission

<u>Underboss</u>
John Bonventre
1931-1953
Retired

Frank Garofalo
1953-1956
Retired

Carmine "Lilo" Galante
1956-1963
Jailed

John "Johnny Burns" Morale
1963-1964
Deposed

<u>Consigliere</u>
Frank Italiano
1931-1932

Phillipe Rapa
1932-1939

John Tartamella
1940-1964
Retired due to ill health

Salvatore "Bill" Bonanno
1964-1964
Deposed

Bonanno
1964-1966

<u>Boss</u>
Gaspar DiGregorio
1964-1966
Resigned in May 1966 due to ill health and pressure

<u>Underboss</u>
Peter Alfano
1964-1966

Consigliere
Angelo Caruso
1964-1966

Bonanno
1966-1970

Boss
Paul Sciacca
1966-1970
Retired

Underboss
Peter Croatia
1966-1967
Demoted? Stepped Down?

Frank Mari
1967-1969
Last seen alive on September 18, 1969

Phil Rastelli
1969-1970

Consigliere
Mike Adamo
1966-1969
Last seen alive on September 18, 1969

Sereno Tartamella
1969-1970

Bonanno
1970-1973

Boss
Natale Evola
1970-1973
Died August 28, 1973

Underboss
Phil Rastelli
1970-1973

Consigliere
Vito DeFilippo
1970-1973

Bonanno
1973-1991
Estimated 100 members and 375 associates by NY Commission
of Investigations

Boss
Phil Rastelli
1973-1991
Died June 24, 1991, of liver cancer

Acting Boss
Carmine Galante
1975-1979
Murdered July 12/79
Galante was never an official Boss or Acting Boss. He just assumed
the role.

Sal Catalano
1979-1981
Stepped down

Salvatore Ferrugia
1981-1987
Was Underboss at this time.

Anthony Spero
1987-1991
Was Consigliere at this time.

Underboss
Nick Marangello
1975-1979
Demoted after Galante hit

Salvatore Ferrugia
1979-1987

Joey Massino
1987-1991

Consigliere
Steve Cannone
1973-1984
Stepped down due to ill health

Anthony Spero
1984-1991

Bonanno
1991-2004
Estimated 130 members
Time Magazine estimate in 2004 was 121 members

Boss
Joey Massino
1991-2004
Turned informer

Acting Boss
Anthony Spero
Consigliere at this time
1991-1992

Anthony Urso
Acting Consigliere at this time
2003-Jan 2004
Arrested

Vincent Basciano
Capo at this time
2003-Nov 2004
Arrested Nov 19/04

Underboss
?????
1991-2003

Sal Vitale
2003
Informer

Acting Underboss
Louie Attanasio

Richard Cantarella
2002
Informer 2002

Joe Cammarano
2003-2004
Arrested Jan 2004

Consigliere
Anthony Spero
1991-2001
Jailed 1995-1997
Convicted 2001
Demoted

Acting Consigliere

James Tartaglione
1995-1997
Indicted January 29, 1998, for loan sharking

Anthony Graziano
2001-2002
Indicted Mar 19/02
Guilty plea Dec 23/02

Anthony Urso
2003-2004

Bonanno

Boss
Vincent Basciano
2005
Incarcerated since November 19, 2004

Acting Boss
Mickey Mancuso
2005

Salvatore "Sal the Ironworker" Montagna
2006-2009
Deported to Canada 2009

Ruling Panel
2010
Joseph "Sammy" Sammartino,
Vincent (Vinny TV) Badalamenti

Acting Boss
2011-2012
Vincent (Vinny TV) Badalamenti
Arrested Jan 27/12

Committee
2012-2013
Anthony Rabito
Vincent Asaro
Thomas DiFiore

Acting Underboss
Mickey Mancuso

Acting Underboss
Nicky Santora
Arrested Jan 27/12

Consigliere
Anthony Graziano
Consigliere
Arrested
2004-2006
Demoted 2011

Acting Consigliere
Anthony Rabito
2006-20011

Bonanno
2013-present

Boss
Mickey Mancuso
June 2013-

Acting Boss
2015-2019
Joe Cammarano Jr
March 22, 2015
Demoted March 2019

John Palazzolo
2019-

Underboss
Thomas DiFiore
June 2013

Perhaps
Vito Badamo
January 2014

Acting Underboss
Joe Cammarano Jr
2016-March 2019

Consigliere
John Zancocchio
? 2019
Demoted March 2019

Appendix B

Changing the Guard

Some of the La Cosa Nostra Bosses were lucky enough to die in their beds. Others retired for various reasons. Many were booted out of office by way of the gun. The incomplete list below presents the names and fates of many Bosses. We may know when the guy died or was killed but not necessarily when his Family voted him into office. So please take the days and months with caution, but the years are correct.

A reminder that the Al Capone organization did not become a La Cosa Nostra Family until the spring of 1931 after Boss of Bosses Joe Masseria's death. In Chicago, the new Boss of Bosses, Salvatore Maranzano, formally recognized Capone as the Boss of the Chicago Family. Before that, men like D'Andrea, Lombardo, and Joseph Aiello led the Chicago LCN Family. This Family disappeared after Capone's coronation by Maranzano.

188?
New Orleans Family
Joseph Macheca – Tony Matranga

1910
Bonanno Family
Paolo Orlando retires – Sebastiano Di Gaetano
(I am uncertain of these facts)

1912
Bonanno Family
Sebastiano Di Gaetano retired – Nicola Shiro
(I am uncertain about Di Gaetano being Boss)

1917
Cleveland Family
Dr. Joe Romano retired – Joe Lonardo

September 24, 1919
Pittsburgh Family
Gregorio Conti killed – Stefano Monastero

February 6, 1921
Milwaukee Family
Vito Guardalabene died – Peter Guardalabene

May 12, 1921
Chicago Family
Anthony D'Andrea killed – Mike Merlo

1922
New Orleans Family
Tony Matranga retired – Corrado Giacona

May 22, 1922
Los Angeles Family
Vito Digiorgio killed – Joe Ardizzone

July 9, 1922
Buffalo Family
Joe DiCarlo died – Stefano Magaddino

1924
Milwaukee Family
Peter Guardalabene died – Joe Amato

November 8, 1924
Chicago Family
Mike Merlo died – Tony Lombardo

1927
Philadelphia Family
Salvatore Sabella retired – John Avena

March 28, 1927
Milwaukee Family
Joseph Amato died – Joseph Vallone

October 13, 1927
Cleveland Family
Joe Lonardo killed – Sam Todaro

September 7, 1928
Chicago Family
Tony Lombardo killed – Joe Aiello

October 10, 1928
Gambino Family
Salvatore D'Aquila killed – Al Mineo

June 11, 1929
Cleveland Family
Sam Todaro killed – Joseph Porello

August 6, 1929
Pittsburgh Family
Steve Monastero killed – Joseph Siragusa

February 14, 1930
Detroit Family
Sam Catalonette died – Gaspar Milazzo

February 20, 1930
Dallas Family
Carlo Piranio died – Joseph Piranio

February 26, 1930
Lucchese Family
Tommy Reina killed – Joe Pinzola

May 31, 1930
Detroit Family
Gaspar Milazzo killed – Cesare LaMare

1930
Bonanno Family
Nicola Shiro stepped down – Salvatore Maranzano

July 5, 1930
Cleveland Family
Joe Porello killed – Frank Milano

September 5, 1930
Lucchese Family
Joe Pinzola killed – Tom Gagliano

1931
New England Family
Gaspar Messina retired – Phil Buccola

February 6, 1931
Detroit Family
Cesare LaMare killed – Joe Zerilli

September 13, 1931
Pittsburgh Family
Joe Siragusa killed – John Bazzone

October 15, 1931
Los Angeles Family
Joe Ardizzone disappears – Jack Dragna

October 23, 1931
Chicago Family
Joe Aiello killed – Family defunct – Capone organization became
the only La Cosa Nostra Family in Chicago

November 5, 1931
Gambino Family
Al Mineo killed – Frank Scalise

April 15, 1931
Genovese Family
Joe Masseria killed – Lucky Luciano

September 10, 1931
Bonanno Family
Salvatore Maranzano killed – Joe Bonanno

September 13, 1931
Pittsburgh Family
Joe Siragusa killed – John Bazzano

October 15, 1931
Los Angeles Family
Joe Ardizzone disappeared – Jack Dragna

1932
Kansas City Family
Paolo Di Giovanni died – James Lazia

August 8, 1932 (approximate)
Pittsburgh Family
John Bazzano killed – Vince Capizzi

February 18, 1933
Denver Family
Joe Roma killed – James Colletti

1933
Bufalino Family
Santo Volpe died – John Sciandra

July 10, 1934
Kansas City Family
John Lazia killed – Charles Carrollo

August 17, 1936
Philadelphia Family
John Avena killed – Joe Bruno

1937
Pittsburgh Family
Vince Capizzi resigned – Frank Amato

February 22, 1937
Newark Family
Gaspar D'Amico wounded, stepped down – Family disbanded
by the Commission.

June 14, 1937
San Francisco Family
Frank Lanza died – Tony Lima

1939
Kansas City Family
Charles Carrollo jailed – Charles Binaggio

1940
Bufalino Family
John Sciandra died – Joseph Barbara

194?
Tampa Family
Steve Italiano died? – James Lumia

1942
Cleveland Family
Frank Milano retired – Al Polizzi

March 19, 1943
Chicago Family
Frank Nitti suicide – Paul DeLucia briefly – Tony Accardo

July 25, 1944
New Orleans Family
Corrado Giacona died – Frank Todaro

November 29, 1944
New Orleans Family
Frank Todaro died – Sam Carollo

1945
Cleveland Family
Al Polizzi retired – John Scalish

1946
Philadelphia Family
Joe Bruno retired – Joe Ida

April 30, 1947
New Orleans Family
Sam Carollo deported – Carlos Marcello

1949
Milwaukee Family
Joseph Vallone retired – Sam Ferrara

April 6, 1950
Kansas City Family
Charles Binaggio killed – Anthony Gizzo

June 5, 1950
Tampa Family
James Lumia killed – Santos Trafficante Sr.

February 16, 1951
Lucchese Family
Tom Gagliano died – Tom Lucchese

April 1951
Gambino Family
Vincent Mangano disappeared – Albert Anastasia

December 1952
Milwaukee Family
Sam Ferrara forced retirement – John Alioto

April 1, 1953
Kansas City Family
Anthony Gizzo died – Nick Civella

April 27, 1953
San Francisco Family
Tony Lima jailed, forced retirement – Mike Abati

1954
New England Family
Phil Buccola retired – Ray Patriarca Sr.

August 11, 1954
Tampa Family
Santos Trafficante Sr. died – Santos Trafficante Jr.

1956
Pittsburgh Family
Frank Amato resigned – John LaRocca
The Commission made LaRocca serve a three year probation
period before final approval.

February 23, 1956
Los Angeles Family
Jack Dragna died – Frank Desimone

October 27, 1956
Dallas Family
Joseph Piranio suicide – Joe Civello

May 14, 1957
Decavalcante Family
Phil Amari retired - Nick Delmore

October 25, 1957
Gambino Family
Albert Anastasia killed – Carlo Gambino

May 22, 1958
Rockford Family
Tony Musso died - Jasper Calo - Joe Zammuto.

January 1959
Philadelphia Family
Joe Ida retired - Angelo Bruno

June 17, 1959
Bufalino Family
Joseph Barbara dies – Russell Bufalino

September 10, 1959
San Jose Family
Onofrio Sciortino died - Joseph Cerrito

June 17, 1959
Bufalino Family
Joe Barbara died – Russell Bufalino

1960
St Louis Family
Anthony Lopiparo died – John Vitale

1961
San Francisco Family
Michael Abate deported – James Lanza

1961
St Louis Family
John Vitale – retired – Anthony Giordano

December 27, 1961
Milwaukee Family
John Alioto retired – Frank Balistrieri

June 6, 1962
Colombo Family
Joe Profaci died – Joe Magliocco – deposed by the Commission
– Joe Colombo

February 2, 1964
Decavalcante Family
Nick Delmore died – Sam Decavalcante

September 1964
Bonanno Family
Joe Bonanno deposed by the Commission – Gaspar DiGregorio

1966
Bonanno Family
Gaspar DiGregorio retired – Paul Sciacca

July 3, 1967
Lucchese Family
Tommy Lucchese died – Carmine Tramunti

August 4, 1967
Los Angeles Family
Frank Desimone died – Nick Licata

1969
Denver Family
James Colletti retired – Joe Spinuzzi

January 17, 1970
Dallas Family
Joe Civello died – Family defunct

1970
Bonanno Family
Paul Sciacca retired – Natale Evola

1971
Colombo Family
Joe Colombo incapacitate by gunfire – Acting Boss Vinnie Aloi

June 6, 1972
Rochester Family
Frank Valenti forced retirement – Sam Russotti

1973
Rockford Family
Joe Zammuto moved to Consigliere – Frank Buscemi

August 28, 1973
Bonanno Family
Natale Evola died – Phil Rastelli

1974
San Francisco Family
James Lanza died – Tony Lima

July 19, 1974
Buffalo Family
Stefano Magaddino died – Sam Pieri

August 22, 1974
Springfield Illinois Family
Frank Zito died

October 19, 1974
Los Angeles Family
Nick Licata died – Dominick Brooklier

September 6, 1975
Colorado Family
Joseph Spinuzzi died – Gene Smaldone

October 15, 1975
Gambino Family
Carlo Gambino died – Paul Castellano

May 26, 1976
Cleveland Family
John Scalish died – James Licavoli

October 30, 1976
Detroit Family
Joseph Zerilli died – Jack Tocco

October 15, 1978
Lucchese Family
Carmine Tramunti died – Tony Corallo

March 21, 1980
Philadelphia Family
Angelo Bruno killed – Phil Testa

August 31, 1980
St Louis Family
Anthony Giardano died – Mike Trupiano

March 15, 1981
Philadelphia Family
Phil Testa killed – Nicky Scarfo

March 12, 1983
Kansas City Family
Nick Civella died – Carl Civella

July 11, 1984
New England Family
Raymond Patriarca died – Raymond Patriarca Jr.

July 18, 1984
Los Angeles Family
Dominick Brooklier died – Peter Milano

December 3, 1984
Pittsburgh Family
John LaRocca died – Michael Genovese

November 23, 1985
Cleveland Family
James Licavoli died – John Tronolone

December 16, 1985
Gambino Family
Paul Castellano killed – John Gotti

November 24, 1985
Cleveland Family
James Licavoli died – John Tronolone

January 13, 1987
Lucchese Family
Tony Corallo retired – Vic Amuso

March 17, 1987
Tampa Family
Santos Trafficante Jr. died – Vince LoScalzo

December 7, 1987
Rockford Family
Frank Buscemi died – Charles Vince?

1990
New England Family
Ray Patriarca Jr. retired – Nicky Bianco

1990 (approximately)
Bufalino Family
Russell Bufalino stepped down – Acting Boss

June 24, 1991
Bonanno Family
Phil Rastelli died – Joey Massino

March 1992
Denver Family
Gene Smaldone died – Family defunct

1993
New Orleans Family
Carlos Marcello died – Anthony Corallo

February 1993
Milwaukee Family
Frank Balistrieri died – Peter Balistrieri

October 1, 1994
Kansas City Family
Carl Civella died – Anthony Civella

1991
New England Family
Nicky Bianco jailed – Frank Salemme

1995
New England Family
Frank Salemme jailed – Luigi Manocchio

1997
Milwaukee Family
Peter Balistrieri died – Joe Caminiti

October 22, 1997
St Louis Family
Mike Trupiano died – Anthony Parino

2004
Bonanno Family
Joey Massino became an informer – Acting Bosses

February 14, 2006
Kansas City Family
Anthony Civella died – Joe Sciortino

2007
New Orleans Family
Anthony Corallo died – Family defunct

2008 (approximately)
Bufalino Family
William D'Elia becomes an informer – Family defunct.

2009
New England Family
Luigi Manocchio retired – Anthony DiNunzio

2013
Detroit Family
Jack Tocco died – Jack Giacalone

June 2013
Bonanno Family
Ruling Panel—Mikey Mancuso

January 2014
Milwaukee Family
Joe Caminiti died – ?

November 3, 2014
St Louis Family
Anthony Parino died – Family defunct

Appendix C

Joe Bonanno and Lino Saputo

December 8, 1978
Utica Cheese Ltd, 99.8% owned by Lino Saputo, applied for a New York State license to operate a cheese manufacturing business in Oriskany, New York. After two official conferences, the Department of Agriculture and Markets' lower-level officials kicked the decision upstairs.

May 22, 1980
The State Commissioner of Agriculture and Markets authorized a Hearing Officer, retired Judge Charles Breitel, to conduct administrative hearings on the application and make a recommendation.

There were ten days of hearings from May 23, 1980, to July 2, 1980. The transcript was over 2,000 pages, and there were 80 exhibits. I've summarized Judge Breitel's report below.

Judge Breitel wrote that the main issue was whether the Agricultural Department had established, by the preponderance of the evidence, that Saputo had sufficient connections with Joe Bonanno to disqualify him because of character from obtaining the license.

Because Lino Saputo had denied any connection with Bonanno other than a brief encounter in 1964, if a relationship did exist, Saputo had made false or misleading material statements in support of his application and had failed to furnish reports or information required by the Commissioner.

Breitel stated that he recommended that the Department deny the license application. He said the preponderance of the evidence established that Joe Bonanno had a significant economic and transactional involvement over a substantial period of years with several Canadian cheese companies owned by the Saputo family members by Lino Saputo in particular.

1963

Giovanni Di Bella, a good friend of Giuseppe Saputo, visited the Saputos in Montreal and suggested they upgrade their plant. Lino Saputo traveled to Wisconsin to examine Di Bella's cheese operation and returned to Montreal, convinced that modernization was the way for Saputo to go. When DiBella returned to Montreal in 1964, the friends agreed that he would buy a share in the Saputo business.

May 24, 1964

DiBella returned to Montreal with Joe Bonanno, whom he introduced as his business associate. At the meeting were Giuseppe Saputo, Lino Saputo, Joseph Borsellino, Giovanni DiBella, and Joe Bonanno. Borsellino had recently married Lino Saputo's sister. DiBella wanted the Saputos to sell his potential shares to Bonanno instead. In return for $8,000, Bonanno would receive 20% of the Saputo companies.

A letter of intent addressed to Joseph Bonanno, typewritten on G Saputo & Sons stationery, dated May 20, 1964, and signed by Giuseppe Saputo, expressed a willingness to sell to Bonanno 20% of three companies, G Saputo & Sons, Cremerie Cosenza, and Cremerie Stella.

1980

Lino Saputo said there was no agreement to sell interests in Cremerie Stella and Cremerie Cosenza, which he stated he owned alone, not his father.

Lino stated that on May 25 or 26, 1964 he discovered that Bonanno was a prominent organized crime figure from the Montreal Matin newspaper. From that time onwards, Lino Saputo said no Saputo company had anything to do with Bonanno, and the transaction from May 24, was never completed.

The Agricultural Department disagreed, wrote Breitel. They contended that Bonanno had a hidden interest in the Saputo cheese businesses from May 24, 1964, until late 1977, if not until now (1980.) The Department presented evidence to establish that Bonanno had a continuing economic connection with the Saputo companies.

The Department produced an application made by Bonanno and addressed to the Canadian Department of Citizenship and Immigration for admission to Canada, dated May 25, 1964. The application listed G Saputo & Sons as the name of a person in Canada willing to assist. Bonanno characterized G Saputo & Sons as a "friend" and "partner." Attached to the application was the May 24, 1964 letter of intent.

Because Bonanno may have fudged his relationship with the Saputos on the application and the possibility that Lino Saputo may already have canceled the potential deal, the Hearing Officer refused to use this information as a finding of fact as the Department of Agriculture wished.

Breitel wrote that additional evidence of Bonanno's connection with the Saputos came from minutes of a purported meeting of Cremerie Stella Inc's shareholders on May 27, 1964. The minutes listed the only shareholders as Emanuele "Lino" Saputo, Joseph Bonanno, and Elena Borsellino (Lino's sister.) Lino Saputo signed the minutes.

Lino Saputo admitted that he learned Bonanno bought the shares in Cremerie Stella from a non-member of the Saputo family. He then tried to close the company, but technical difficulties prevented him from doing so legally. But the company wasn't doing any business anyway by the end of 1965.

Judge Breitel ruled that it was a fact that Lino Saputo, the majority shareholder in Cremerie Stella, participated in the election of Bonanno as an officer and director of the corporation. The Hearing Officer admitted that because the minutes' date was so close to the time, Lino Saputo learned of Bonanno's unsavory background, he would not use these facts on their own but with other evidence.

He said more substantial evidence of the connection between Bonanno and the Saputos came from papers discovered in Lino's briefcase during the police raid on the Saputo plant on May 18, 1972. The police found accounting sheets relating to the Saputo cheese enterprises providing for the division of moneys for 1969 and 1970.

In Lino's handwriting, these accounting sheets provided percentages and dollar amounts for members of the Saputo family, who Lino said were the only owners. But also included were a share, usually 15%, and dollar amounts for "Mr. JB." Lino Saputo denied that Mr. JB referred to Joe Bonanno but asserted it referred to his brother-in-law Joseph Borsellino.

Judge Breitel described this explanation as "implausible," for on the same accounting sheet, there was an entry for Joseph Borsellino. In addition, there was an entry on one sheet of a payment already made to "Joe Borsellino per (for) JB." Judge Breitel ruled that based on the evidence, it was a fact that Lino's handwritten notes showed Bonanno received or was entitled to receive payments from Saputo Cheese Company at least until 1970.

Breitel then addressed the information gathered by the Arizona Narcotics Strike Force when they operated a trash cover on Bonanno's home in Tucson from 1975 to 1979. The judge concluded that the many notes referencing "Lino" referred to Lino Saputo. Telephone numbers belonging to Saputo, his companies and his brother-in-law, contributed to his conclusion. He stated that the Lino references were of various types, some personal with Bonanno desiring to convey greetings to Lino. Another set of notes indicated a plan to bring Saputo, his wife, and child to Long Beach, California. The judge pointed out that these possible contacts contradicted Saputo's claim to have never communicated with Bonanno after May 1964.

Other notes revealed telephone contacts between the Saputo Company and Bonanno, especially with Saputo's brother-in-law Joseph Borsellino. FBI surveillance of Bonanno indicated that when a note arranged a time for a Montreal phone call to come in, Bonanno was at that phone. The RCMP conducted surveillance at the Montreal end to confirm the contact.

Judge Breitel wrote that failure to disclose contacts with an organized crime figure despite the Department of Agriculture's request to do so would be grounds to deny the license.

Breitel went on to say that some of the references to Lino in Bonanno's notes were full of economic involvement. The trash sheets suggested alternative dispositions of shares in Saputo Holding Company, including "JB" as a significant shareholder. One alternative proposed trading some of "JB" s shares in Cremerie Stella for shares in Saputo Holding. Since only Bonanno, not Joe Borsellino, held shares in Cremerie Stella, the identity of JB in these papers in Bonanno's trash is beyond reasonable dispute.

Also in Bonanno's trash was a page of figures in Lino Saputo's handwriting. It listed distributions of money for the years 1966 and 1967.

Included were entries of $2,400 "given to JB" for four months of 1966 and $7,200 for all of 1967. Also included was a list of distributes by percentage, including a "Mr. JB" and a "Mr.?". Saputo, at a hearing, made no effort to explain the presence or the contents of this page, in his handwriting, in Bonanno's garbage.

Breitel concluded that it was an indisputable fact that the contents of Bonanno's trash papers established repeated contacts and familiarity by Bonanno with Lino Saputo and the Saputo companies and their affairs in the years following 1964 well into the late 1970s.

The judge stated that the Department of Agriculture sought to establish, using Bonanno trash papers in combination with bookkeeping records, bank records, and other documents, that the Saputo companies made a $51,000 payment to Bonanno. The alleged plan went like this.

B&T Cheese Company distributed products from a Montreal firm called Produits Caillette owned by Saputo. B&T always paid their bills by check.

Suddenly on December 7, 1977, B&T's bank, National Central Bank in Pennsylvania, arranged to have $50,000 in cash sent to them. On December 9, 1977, Peter Terroso, part-owner of B&T, withdrew $51,000 in cash. A later explanation for this transaction, by the Saputo side, was that Montreal's Produits Caillette demanded cash because B&T were late paying their bill.

A later examination of the books of Produits Caillette showed someone paid B&T's bill in Canadian funds. The Agriculture Department argued that the $51,000 in Canadian currency plus the exchange difference covered the $51,000 withdrawn by Peter Terroso. In other words, it was a scam. The Department believed Terroso's $51,000 made its way to Bonanno.

Some Bonanno notes included instructions for someone to drive to JFK Airport and then take a taxi to Bonanno's niece's home. Presumably to drop off the $51,000. A cash disbursement journal maintained at B&T Cheese showed a petty cash payment to a B&T employee, most likely Liborio Borsellino, for a December 10, 1977 trip to JFK airport. The notes from Tucson and the disbursement journal from Pennsylvania confirmed the theory that the $51,000 wasn't going to Montreal but to Bonanno in Tucson.

Bonanno's sister-in-law then flew the money to Tucson. Because of Bonanno's notes, the FBI knew who she was and when she was traveling. They tracked her the entire time, including when Bonanno and his wife met her at the Tucson airport. Shortly after her arrival, the Narcotics Strike Force agents found a money wrapper in Bonanno's trash. A bank employee back in Pennsylvania identified it as coming from the cash sent to the bank used by B&T Cheese Company. The wrapper even included the December 7, 1977 date when head office sent the $50,000 to B&T's bank in Pennsylvania.

The judge pointed out that Saputo didn't produce any witness to confirm that the payment made to B&T's creditor in Montreal came from B&T rather than another source. He found the transaction records at B&T's creditor unique, and it did not follow their standard practices.

Judge Breitel concluded that it was a fact that the $51,000 in US currency, supposedly paid by B&T to Produits Caillette, with the knowledge and collusion of Produits Caillette and its principals, was instead shipped to Bonanno in Tucson. Lino Saputo was a principal at Produits Caillette.

Breitel wrote that the testimony by an FBI Agent connected Bonanno and Saputo more closely. The FBI learned that Lino Saputo and his wife met with Bonanno late in January of 1970 or early February of 1970. Further investigation showed that a Lino Saputo and his wife boarded a plane leaving Tucson for Los Angeles on February 1, 1970. The contact number provided to the airline was that of a hotel that had an "L. Saparo" registered from January 30 to February 1, 1970. The home address listed by the guest was the California address of a close Bonanno associate. Yet Lino Saputo testified that he did not recall ever having been in Tucson or even in Arizona.

Judge Breitel decided it was a fact that, contrary to his assertions, Lino Saputo and his wife met with Bonanno in Tucson in early 1970.

Lino Saputo made a second visit to Grande Cheese in Wisconsin long after Mr. DiBella told him Bonanno was associated with the firm. He also knew of Bonanno's involvement in organized crime, yet Saputo went to Wisconsin anyway. When investigators asked Saputo why the visit to Wisconsin despite all he knew, Saputo explained that he learned Bonanno was no longer involved with Grande Cheese. Judge Breitel found this answer unconvincing since Saputo testified he didn't learn that Bonanno had no part in Grande Cheese until he reached Wisconsin and an owner in Grande Cheese told him.

Judge Breitel wrote that he found it mystifying why Lino Saputo incorporated Saputo Holding Company just before Bonanno's May 24, 1964 visit. He said G Saputo and Sons was a small family business with few outside employees, making all its product by hand. He said the need for a holding company other than to facilitate outside involvement was not apparent.

Several instances of Lino Saputo's memory lapses and ignorance were implausible, according to Judge Breitel. His purported lack of knowledge or memory of critical elements of the 1964 conversations among his father, John DiBella and Bonanno is astounding when the importance of these conversations to Lino Saputo and the family business wrote the judge.

Judge Breitel described Saputo's inability to explain the method used to value the Saputo business for purposes of sale in 1964 strained credulity. He felt the same of Saputo's failure to interpret and correlate the financial items in his briefcase seized in 1972, also strained credulity.

The judge was puzzled by Lino Saputo's explanation on entries in his briefcase for Reggio Foods. The papers indicated a division of Reggio Food money along much the same lines as Saputo Cheese money. Saputo denied that he or any of his family had any ownership interest in Reggio Food, admitted that Reggio Food was owned in part by men reputed to be involved in organized crime, and contented that Reggio was nothing more than a supplier. The judge wondered why money from a supplier should be divided among shareholders in Saputo Cheese. It was never adequately clarified, Judge Breitel wrote.

Judge Breitel criticized Lino Saputo for failing to produce his father, Giuseppe Saputo, his brother-in-law Joe Borsellino, Yvonne Scattolin, a brother-in-law associated with Produits Caillette, and the owners of B&T Cheese. He said they might have been able to clarify or explain away the troubling inconsistencies in Lino Saputo's testimony or the grave inferences to be drawn from the briefcase papers, the Bonanno trash, or the unusual B&T transactions.

The judge found as fact that Lino Saputo's version of the material discussed was not acceptable. Moreover, his versions' implausibility on such issues weakened the value of his testimony on other aspects of the case.

Several character witnesses for Saputo impressed Judge Breitel, but he said they were not familiar with the evidence in the case. It did not overcome the balance of the evidence establishing the Saputo hidden connection with Bonanno.

Judge Breitel concluded his report by recommending that the Agriculture Department deny Utica Cheese's application for a dealer's license. He wrote, "The continuing connection between Lino Saputo and the companies with which he is associated and Joseph Bonanno, including payments made to Bonanno, make Lino Saputo unfit for reasons of character, and therefore his corporation, to hold a milk dealer's license. For the same reasons, issuing a license would not be in the public's interest. Moreover, because Lino Saputo had attempted to conceal from the Department his and his companies' involvement with Bonanno, he has failed to furnish all the material information required by the Commissioner and has made material statements that are false, misleading, and deceitful."

On August 1, 1980, J Roger Barber, Commissioner of the Agriculture and Markets Department turned down Utica Cheese' application for a dairy license.

The Appellate Division of New York's Supreme Court ruled, on May 21, 1981, that the Commissioner was justified in refusing a dairy license for Utica Cheese.

Lino Saputo has consistently denied any connection to Joe Bonanno since the May 24, 1964 meeting.

Appendix D

The State of New Jersey Commission of Investigation 1989 Report

BONANNO/RASTELLI/VITALE FAMILY

The Bonanno/Rastelli/Vitale family of La Cosa Nostra consists of approximately 195 members and 500 associates, situated from coast to coast, primarily in New York, Arizona, Florida, New Jersey, Pennsylvania and California. The group's patriarch, 85-year-old Joseph "Joe Bananas" Bonanno, is retired and living in Tucson, Arizona. Bonanno was forced into exile by other LCN bosses because he attempted to expand his sphere of influence in the late 1960's and early 1970's, not only within New York City but also in other areas that were already the territories of other bosses.

The current family boss is Salvatore Vitale of Dix Hills in Suffolk County, New York. His elevation came as a direct result of the lengthy incarcerations of other high level family members, including boss Philip "Rusty" Rastelli, of Brooklyn. Vitale is the owner of a Long Island catering business, where he meets almost daily with other significant family members.

The group's criminal enterprises include narcotics trafficking, pornography, labor racketeering, hijacking and other forms of receiving stolen property, casino fraud, tax fraud, credit card fraud and forgery, gambling, loansharking, extortion and money laundering. Although the family is active in most of the traditional LCN criminal activities, it is noted primarily for its involvement in the importation and sale of narcotics, mostly heroin. Extensive undercover investigations have revealed that the group has close ties to the Sicilian Mafia in its heroin trafficking. Boss and family founder Joseph Bonanno, a native of Sicily, was at one time recognized as the predominant figure in this illicit market, despite the fact that narcotics distribution purportedly was contrary to original LCN principles. The strong bond between the Sicilian Mafia and the Bonanno group over the past two decades has resulted in billions of dollars' worth of heroin being imported into the United States, and criminal liaisons that extend beyond Italy and the United States into Canada and South America.

The Bonanno family's continued involvement in narcotics trafficking was demonstrated during the investigation of the 1989 murder of DEA undercover agent Everett Hatcher. At the time of his assassination, Hatcher had been investigating the multi-kilo cocaine distribution network of Bonanno associate Constabile "Gus" Farace. Immediately after Hatcher's murder, a nationwide manhunt for Farace began, along with 24-hour-a-day police surveillances and harassment of Bonanno family members, especially those believed to be involved in the drug business. The family reportedly became uncomfortable with the unrelenting pressure and decided the best way to end it was to give up Farace. Shortly thereafter, a murder contract was placed on the life of Farace, who was lured to a Brooklyn street corner and shot to death on November 17, 1989. The man suspected of killing Farace was himself found murdered just two months later, in January, 1990.

The family also controls gambling and loan-sharking at the famous Fulton Fish Market in lower Manhattan through caporegime Joseph Chilli Jr. of Staten Island. Chilli had been acting boss of the family (along with Anthony Spero of Brooklyn) for two years before the elevation to boss of Salvatore Vitale. Chilli owns at least four fish companies in the market, which is the largest wholesale fish market in the nation and is the principal source of seafood for the metropolitan area and much of the northeastern United States.

Family associate Anthony Amico Jr. of Florida is currently under federal investigation by postal authorities for his involvement in potentially fraudulent, high pressure, multi-million dollar telemarketing sales schemes that originate in Florida and Georgia but have a nationwide impact.

In New Jersey, the Bonanno family has elevated some of its younger members to positions of authority. Following the death in 1983 of caporegime Joseph "Bayonne Joe" Zicarelli, Gabriel Infanti of Bloomfield became the predominant family member in northern New Jersey. Infanti, who had controlled a gambling network in New York, was well respected in New Jersey, as evidenced by his meeting on December 16, 1985, with John Riggi, boss of the DeCavalcante family. Interestingly, this was the same day that Gambino boss Paul Castellano was murdered in New York City. Infanti himself was declared missing nearly two years later, on December 22, 1987. He is presumed to be dead. It is believed that Infanti has been replaced by caporegime James Tartaglione of Queens, who has been observed meeting with Bonanno family boss Salvatore Vitale almost daily.

Another New Jersey resident who has been gaining influence in the family is Louis J. Attanasio Jr. of Holmdel, a caporegime. Attanasio ran a gambling operation out of a club he owns in Brooklyn. However, he was recently incarcerated for five years for bribing a state trooper and for income tax evasion. When he is released from prison, probably in November, 1990, it is believev d that Attanasio will regain his position of authority within the Bonanno family or with the Genovese/Gigante group, with which he also does business.

To fill the void left by several deaths and incarcerations of members in the group, Salvatore Ferrugia of West Orange has come out of retirement and been assigned the status of caporegime. Ferrugia, who is now 75 years old, was at one time family underboss but had been demoted to caporegime by Rastelli. Ferrugia is best known for his close ties to the Sicilian Mafia and the smuggling of illegal aliens from Sicily to the United States.

As previously mentioned, the strength of this organization lies in its long and prosperous involvement in the trafficking of narcotics, supported by its affiliation with the Sicilian Mafia. In addition the group is operating legitimate pizza parlors, cafes and restaurants, from which it can conduct illegal transactions and conceal illegal aliens. The family has also been involved in criminal activity in Atlantic City, such as illegal junkets, credit schemes and other frauds.

Appendix E

The FBI's Bonanno Leadership in 1968

On August 8 and August 20, 1968, NY T-121 advised
that to his knowledge the entire BONANNO "family" is still
expelled from LCN, until they resolve the problem of what to
do with JOE BONANNO, as he is not acceptable to the "Commission".

In light of the foregoing, the following is considered
to be the leadership of the SCIACCA "family". In the absence
of concrete information linking them with BONANNO, all the
listed "Capodecinas" are considered to be loyal to SCIACCA.

PAUL SCIACCA	"Boss"
FRANK MARI	"Underboss"
PETER CROCIATA	"Consiglieri" (former "Underboss")
GASPARE DI GREGORIO	former "Boss" and advisor

"Capodecinas"

MICHAEL ADAMO	
NICK ALFANO	(OO:Newark)
JOSEPH DI FILIPPI	N.J.
GIOVANNI FIORDILINO	(Italy)
PATSY GIGANTE	(Acting)
JOHN JOSEPH MORALE	
ARMANDO POLLASTRINO	
PHILLIP RASTELLI	
DOMINICK SABELLA	

- 31 -

Appendix F

The FBI's List of Bonanno Family Members in 1963

They didn't know all the members at this time.

BONANNO FAMILY

Set forth below are individuals specifically named by sources as members of the JOSEPH BONANNO "family" or "avrugad" within the framework of "Causa Nostra".

Name	Alias	FBI Identification #
ARGENNI, GEORGE		
ARMINANTE, LOUIS	Gee-gee	
* ARMONE, JOSEPH	Piney	
ARMONE, STEVE (dead)		320 533
BONANNO, JOSEPH	Joe Banannas	2534540
BONDEFEO, MICHAEL	Mike Bond	
BONGIORNO, FRANK	Frankie Brown	225 874
BUSSO, JOHN	Johnny Connecticut	2449560
CARLINO, JOSEPH	Joe Woppi	
CARUSO, ANGELO		
CESTARO, VINCENT	Gigalee	
CICCONE, WILLIE		
CONSOLO, MICHAEL		285 487

*ARMONE has also been named in the GAMBINO "family".

-90-

Name	Alias	FBI Identification #
CONTALDC, THOMAS	Crazy Tommy	477 828
CUSAMANO, JAMES	Jimmy Yago	174 494
D'ANGELO, THOMAS	Smitty	484 621
DE BERNADO, CHARLES	Charley Fish	
DE STEFANO, ALBERT		
DI LORENZO, ANTHONY		
DI LORENZO, MATTEO	Matty	
DI MAGGIO, ANTHONY		
DULCE, RALPH		
EVOLA, NATALE	Joe Diamond	449 296
FILIPONI, GEORGE		
GAGLIODOTTO, CHARLES	Schalutz	590 366
GALANTE, CARMINE	Lilo	119 495
GAROFALO, FRANK		
GIARRUSO, SAM	Little Sammy	
GIGANTE, PASQUALE		323 231
GIGLIO, SALVATORE		1 967 931
GRANELLO, JOHN	Johnny Burns (TN not verified)	
GRIPPO, DOMINICK		
GUIGA, LOUIS		

-91-

Name	Alias	FBI Identification #
LANZA, HARRY		
LEONE, ANTHONY		
LE PORE, JAMES	Jimmy Marino (dead)	
LISI, ANTHONY	Tony	771 146
LONGOBARDO, JACK		
MARCIANO, FRANK	Frankie Hot Dogs	
MARI, FRANK	Frankie T.	
MARONE, DOMINICK		
MARTELLO, NICHOLAS		54716
MARULLI, ANTONIO		3 800 125
MAZARINE, JOSEPH	Dorsey	400 1933
NOTARO, JOSEPH		452 993A
PARISI, ANTHONY		983076A
PETRONE, JOHN	John Bennett	
PRESENZANO, ANTHONY	Little Moe	187717
RIZZO, GEORGE	Georgie Lefty	
RUSSO, CARMINE	Big Carmine	
SABELLA, MIKE		4989684
SOBELLA, GUS		

-92-

Name	Alias	FBI Identification #
SPADARO, JOE		
TARTAGLIA, EUGENE		588 015
TARTAGLIA, PHILIP	Philly Brush	285 793A
TRAMAGLINO, EUGENE	Genoa Joe	588 015
TRAMAGLINO, JULIO		
TRAMAGLINO, VICTOR		263075
VALENTE, COSTANZO		
VALVO, BENNY		
VALVO, MATTIE		
ZAPARANA, NICK		
ZICARELLI, JOSEPH	Bayonne Joe	

-93-